STUDIES IN THE FRENCH EIGHTEENTH CENTURY

PRESENTED TO

JOHN LOUGH

BY COLLEAGUES, PUPILS
AND FRIENDS

EDITED BY

D.J. MOSSOP
G.E. RODMELL
D.B. WILSON

UNIVERSITY OF DURHAM

Published by

THE UNIVERSITY OF DURHAM

Old Shire Hall
Old Elvet
Durham

*   *   *   *

University of Durham 1978

ISBN 0 900926 28 7

*   *   *   *

The initial letters and other decorations in this book are taken from the
early editions of the *Encyclopédie* in Durham University Library and the
Chapter Library. Durham' They are not reproduced to scale.
Designed by D.B.W. and printed by the University of Durham Printing Unit.

CONTENTS

BIOGRAPHICAL NOTE

Born in Newcastle upon Tyne in February 1913, educated at the Royal Grammar School, Newcastle and at St. John's College, Cambridge, John Lough spent three years in Cambridge and Paris working for his Ph.D., which he was awarded in 1937. In the same year he was appointed as an Assistant in the University of Aberdeen, becoming a lecturer in 1945 and moving back to Cambridge in 1946. In 1952 he returned to the North East and since then has been Professor of French in Durham. His contributions to scholarship and to the academic world in general have been recognised by the honours which have been bestowed upon him. He is Hon. Doct., Clermont-Ferrand, Hon. D. Litt., Newcastle upon Tyne, Officer de l'Ordre National du Mérite, Fellow of the British Academy.

Yet these honours give only a partial picture of John Lough as his friends and colleagues know him. With his retirement the French department and indeed the whole University of Durham will sustain an irreplaceable loss. His years at the Royal Grammar School, Newcastle and the University of Cambridge helped to form a sceptical yet sympathetic and humanist turn of mind which stood him in good stead during his service in Aberdeen and his years as a teacher in the University of Cambridge just after the war. Lough came to Durham in 1952. Although it had been originally founded way back in 1832, these were still the early years of the University as it exists nowadays, and in universities up and down the country the 1950's were the period during which the foundations of French studies as we now know them were laid.

To the post-war expansion both of French studies and of the University of Durham, John Lough's contributions were immense. On the Durham front it remains easier to ask him a question than to consult the University Calendar, much of which he had helped to create, especially during his term as a highly respected and efficient Dean of the Faculty of Arts. Serving on Senate for a period of 25 years almost without remission, devoting much of his time to acting as a curator of the university library when the curators were a small and relatively powerful body and before university libraries were to see themselves threatened by progress, a member of innumerable other university committees, he refused to be overwhelmed by his duties. Indeed he continues to be sceptical of the advice of those of his colleagues who would make administration the principal aim of university life. Scholarship has always been his first priority and recently the breadth and variety of his interests have been focussed on Diderot's *Encyclopédie,* a field which appears to have been chosen in conformity with the definition of *encyclopédie*: 'embrassant le cercle entier des connaissances'. Through this and other work John Lough can well be said to have become a dominant influence in French scholarship in this country and indeed in Europe.

Even so, it has seemed appropriate to choose as the frontispiece to this collection of essays a photograph of him as he is most warmly remembered — a photograph taken surreptitiously by one of his pupils — as a teacher, lecturing to undergraduates and, as he has often said, teaching them that two and two make four. This is perhaps the side of his activities which may be said to have been the most genuinely influential and this influence has always extended, albeit in a different way, as much to his colleagues as to his students. An outstanding head of department in a period when, in many universities, fashion seems to be trying to make the role disappear, he has always been remarkable for tolerance, for sympathy and for getting his own way — a way which, with a regularity depressing to many, has so often turned out to be the right one.

One trusts that the recipient of this tribute, inadequate but well-deserved, will live for many years to be amused by its necessarily 'obituary' flavour.

D.B.W.

PUBLICATIONS BY
JOHN LOUGH

'Helvétius and D'Holbach', *Modern Language Review,* 33 (1938), 360–384.

'Barnave and the French Revolution', *Modern Quarterly,* 2 (1939), 68–78 .

'Essai de bibliographie critique des publications du Baron d'Holbach', *Revue d'Histoire Littéraire de la France,* 46 (1939), 215–234, 47 (1947), 314–318.

'D'Argenson and Socialist Thought in Eighteenth-Century France', *Modern Language Review,* 37 (1942), 455–465.

'Some Eighteenth-Century French Books in Aberdeen University Library', *Aberdeen University Review,* 29 (1942), 201–206.

'The *Encyclopédie* in Eighteenth-Century Scotland' *Modern Language Review,* 38 (1943), 38–40.

'The Relations of the Aberdeen Philosophical Society (1758–73) with France', *Aberdeen University Review,* 30 (1943), 144–150.

'The *Esprit des Lois* in a Scottish University in the Eighteenth Century', *Comparative Literature Studies,* 13 (1944), 13–16.

(with M. Lough) 'Aberdeen Circulating Libraries in the Eighteenth Century', *Aberdeen University Review,* 31 (1945), 17–23.

'The Earnings of Playwrights in Seventeenth-Century France', *Modern Language Review,* 42 (1947), 321–336.

'The Size of the Theatre Public in Seventeenth-Century Paris', *French Studies,* 1 (1947), 143–148.

'D'Allainval's *École des Bourgeois*', *French Studies,* 3 (1949), 39–52.

'Condorcet et Richard Price', *Revue de Littérature Comparée,* 24 (1950), 87–93.

'Comment travaillait le grand Corneille', *Revue d'Histoire du Théâtre,* 2 (1950), 454–455.

'Locke's List of Books banned in France in 1679', *French Studies,* 5 (1951), 217–222.

'Le rayonnement de l'Encyclopédie en Grande-Bretagne', *Cahiers de l'Association Internationale des Études Françaises,* 2 (1952), 67–75.

'The *Encyclopédie* in Eighteenth-Century England', *French Studies,* 6 (1952), 289–307.

(ed.) *Locke's Travels in France, 1675–1679, As related in his Journals, Correspondence and other papers* (London: Cambridge University Press, 1953), lxvi + 309.

(ed.) Diderot, *Selected Philosophical Writings* (London: Cambridge University Press, 1953), viii + 223.

'Locke's Reading during his Stay in France', *The Library,* Fifth series, 8 (1953), 229–258.

An Introduction to Seventeenth Century France (London: Longmans, 1954), xxiii + 296.

(ed.) *The 'Encyclopédie' of Diderot and D'Alembert. Selected Articles* (London: Cambridge University Press, 1954), xv + 226.

'The Paris Theatre Audience in the early Seventeenth Century', *Durham University Journal,* 46 (1954), 49–62.

'French Actors in Paris from 1612 to 1614', *French Studies*, 9 (1955), 218–225.

'Mme de Staël et Earl Grey: une lettre inédite', *Revue de Littérature Comparée*, 30 (1956), 389–390.

Paris Theatre Audiences in the Seventeenth and Eighteenth Centuries (London: Oxford University Press, University of Durham Publications, 1957), xi + 293.

'Les Représentations théâtrales à la cour depuis Henri IV', *Cahiers de l'Association Internationale des Études Françaises*, 9 (1957), 161–171.

'*L'Ouverture des Jours Gras*', *French Studies*, 11 (1957), 260–264.

'Le Baron d'Holbach. Quelques documents inédits ou peu connus', *Revue d'Histoire Littéraire de la France*, 57 (1957), 524–543.

'A Paris Theatre in the Eighteenth Century', *University of Toronto Quarterly*, 1958, 291–304.

An Introduction to Eighteenth Century France (London: Longmans, 1960), xv + 349.

'Louis, Chevalier de Jaucourt (1704–1780). A Biographical Sketch', in *Essays presented to C.M. Girdlestone* (Newcastle upon Tyne, 1960), 195–217.

'The France of Louis XIV', in *The New Cambridge Modern History*, Vol. V (London, 1961), 222–247.

'Louis, Chevalier de Jaucourt. Some further notes', *French Studies*, 15 (1961), 350–357.

'The *Encyclopédie* and the Remonstrances of the Paris Parlement', *Modern Language Review*, 56 (1961), 393–395.

'Letters from France 1788–1789', *Durham University Journal*, 54 (1961), 1–12.

'The *Encyclopédie*: two unsolved problems', *French Studies*, 17 (1963), 121–135.

'Mme Geoffrin and the *Encyclopédie*', *Modern Language Review*, 58 (1963), 219–222.

'Luneau de Boisjermain v. the Publishers of the *Encyclopédie*', *Studies on Voltaire and the Eighteenth Century*, 23 (1963), 115–177.

'The Contemporary Influence of the *Encyclopédie*', *Studies on Voltaire and the Eighteenth Century*, 26 (1963), 1071–1083.

'Sets of the *Encyclopédie*', *Durham Philobiblon*, 2 (1964), 63.

'The Problem of the Unsigned Articles in the *Encyclopédie*', *Studies on Voltaire and the Eighteenth Century*, 32 (1965), 327–390.

'New Light on the *Encyclopédie*', *History Today*, 15 (1965), 169–175.

'The *Encyclopédie* in Voltaire's Correspondence', in *The Age of Enlightenment. Studies presented to Theodore Besterman* (Edinburgh, 1967), 51–65.

Essays on the 'Encyclopédie' of Diderot and D'Alembert, (London: Oxford University Press, University of Durham Publications, 1968), xiv + 552.

'The earliest refutation of Rousseau's *Contrat Social*', *French Studies*, 23 (1969), 23–33.

'The *Philosophes* and the Idea of Progress', in *Eighteenth Century French Studies. Literature and the Arts* (Newcastle upon Tyne, 1969), 41–53.

'Le Breton, Mills et Sellius', *Dix-Huitième Siècle*, 1 (1969), 267–287.

'French Universities from Napoleon to Danny le Rouge', *Durham University Journal*, 62 (1969), 17–24.

'Drama and Society', in *The New Cambridge Modern History*, Vol. IV (London, 1970), 239–259.

The *'Encyclopédie' in Eighteenth-Century England and Other Studies* (Newcastle upon Tyne: Oriel Press, 1970), viii + 256.

The 'Encyclopédie' (London, Longman: 1971), xii + 430.

The Contributors to the 'Encyclopédie' (London: Grant & Cutler, 1973), viii + 120.

'Molière's Audience', *Durham University Journal,* 66 (1974), 257–265.

'Who were the *Philosophes?* ', in *Studies in Eighteenth-Century French Literature presented to Robert Niklaus* (Exeter, 1975), 139–150.

'*Locke's Travels in France* — Additions and Corrections', *The Locke Newsletter,* 7 (1976), 113–119.

(ed. with J. Proust) Diderot, *Oeuvres complètes,* Vols. 5–8, *Encyclopédie* (Paris: Hermann, 1976). Vol. V, 551; Vol. VI, 553; Vol. VII, 715; Vol. VIII, 567.

(with M. Lough) *An Introduction to Nineteenth Century France* (London: Longman, 1977), ix + 337.

PENNY PLAIN, TWOPENCE COLOURED: LONGCHAMP'S MEMOIRS OF VOLTAIRE

W.H. Barber

ARLY in January 1746[1], S.–G. Longchamp was taken into service as a footman by Madame du Châtelet, who was already employing his sister as a maid. He attached himself to Voltaire shortly afterwards, initially as a valet and later as a secretary. Voltaire left him behind in Paris to look after his affairs when he went to Potsdam in 1750, and their association ended a few months later when it was made plain to Longchamp that he was not to be invited to join his master at the Prussian court. Subsequently, contact between them seems to have been restricted, as far as the evidence goes, to an exchange of letters in 1752[2], and apparently a brief encounter when Voltaire returned to Paris in 1778[3].

After Voltaire's death, Longchamp established contact with Panckoucke and others involved in the project which

1. According to Longchamp himself: Besterman suggests (Best. D3462 note 6) that the secretary of whose negligence Voltaire complains in a letter to Frederick of 22 September 1746, must have been Longchamp, and that the circumstances imply that he must have been working for Voltaire in late 1744 or early 1745. The suggestion however rests solely on Voltaire's description of the culprit as "un secrétaire que malheureusement madame du Chastelet m'avoit donnée elle même". The cap fits Longchamp, but he may well have had a predecessor.
2. See Best. D4854, Longchamp to Voltaire, 30 March 1752.
3. Longchamp et Wagnière, *Mémoires sur Voltaire*, Paris, A. André, 1826, ii. 359–60.

became the Kehl edition[4], offering them unknown Voltaire texts of somewhat mysterious provenance — notably the *Traité de métaphysique*, of which more later; and it consequently became possible for Decroix, the working editor of the Kehl project, to acquire from Longchamp, in 1786 or earlier, the autograph manuscript of the latter's memoirs. A version of this text finally appeared in print, edited by Decroix and Beuchot, in 1826 in the two-volume collection entitled *Mémoires sur Voltaire et sur ses Ouvrages, par Longchamp et Wagnière ses secrétaires, suivis de divers écrits inédits* (Paris, Aimé André). This edition contains an editorial warning that what is offered to the reader is not precisely what Longchamp wrote:

> Pour offrir aujourd'hui cet ouvrage aux lecteurs, il a été indispensable d'en corriger le style, et, par la transposition de divers articles, d'en former un ensemble plus régulier et plus chronologique. On n'a d'ailleurs point touché aux faits, ni aux idées, ni aux réflexions de l'auteur, et l'on a même assez souvent conservé ses expressions, lorsqu'elles n'ont été que simples et sans obscurité. (ii. 107—8)

The warning has been duly noted by some, at least, of those critics who have had occasion to use Longchamp's *Mémoires*[5], and his unreliability as a historical source has been widely recognised, though this has not, in practice, hindered the general acceptance of a number of picturesque and potentially significant anecdotes about Voltaire which depend entirely upon Longchamp's testimony. An examination of the manuscript material on the subject which is available puts the whole matter, however, in a rather different light.

The Bibliothèque Nationale possesses two manuscript versions of the *Mémoires*. One, in the Beuchot papers (n.a.fr.

4. Decroix to Ruault (an associate of Beaumarchais), 20 May 1781, Bibliothèque Nationale, MS n.a.fr. 13139, f.216^V. See also Decroix's 'Avertissement de l'éditeur' in Longchamp et Wagnière, *Mémoires*, ii. 109—10.
5. Ascoli quotes from the passage cited above in the opening paragraph of his introduction to *Zadig* (Paris 1962, I, iii)

25138), is a fair copy in the hand of Decroix, which gives a text differing in only minor respects from the published edition. This would appear to be the document referred to in Decroix's letter to Beuchot of 17 May 1825, the year before publication. The letter is rather more informative concerning editorial methods than the passage from the printed editorial note quoted above:

> Je vous addresse par la voie ordinaire les Mémoires de Longchamp. J'aurais voulu voir auparavant et à loisir, les notes qui sont chez Mr André[6], mais vu l'urgence, je ne peux différer davantage cet envoi. Je crois au fond que je n'aurais eu que bien peu de chose, et peut-être rien à changer ou corriger. (...) La manière dont Longchamp les avait arrangées pour en former des *Mémoires*, sans ordre, sans divisions précises, jointes aux défauts de l'écrivain, aurait presque étouffé l'intérêt que peut offrir le fond. C'eut été un livre inlisable; nous avons tâché de le rendre supportable. (B.N. MS. n.a.fr. 25135 f. 143^v)

The second manuscript at the Bibliothéque Nationale (n.a.fr. 13006) came into the library's possession by purchase some thirty years ago. It consists of 104 folios of octavo size, in Longchamp's hand, with extensive corrections and additions in the hand of Decroix. Decroix's changes on Longchamp's original produce a text which is still some way removed from that of the fair copy sent to Beuchot, described above. We thus have three manuscript states of Longchamp's text (which can be designated A, B and C), preceding the printed version (D), which differs little from C. The transformations of Longchamp's original thus effected by Decroix, in two major revisions, go in

---

6.   Aimé André, 'libraire-éditeur' was of course the publisher. It appears from an earlier letter from Decroix to Beuchot (3 October 1820; B.N. n.a.fr. 21535 f.68) that some material thought by Decroix to be written by Longchamp, but already used by the latter in his memoirs , was in Beuchot's hands at that date, but it is not clear whether Decroix ever saw these documents: if he did not, it could be these that constitute the 'notes' in André's possession. In another passage from the letter here quoted, Decroix expresses the wish that these 'notes' may be sent to him, so that, once the printed edition has appeared, they can be suppressed!

fact far beyond the stylistic improvements, and the chronological rearrangement to which Decroix admitted in print and in his letter to Beuchot. It seems to be true that he has suppressed no substantial information given by Longchamp — though a fair amount of trivial detail, of human interest to the modern reader, is eliminated as being incompatible with the dignity of the personages concerned[7]. On the other hand Decroix has silently added, apparently on nobody's authority but his own, a considerable number of factual statements of some importance for students of Voltaire. What is clearly required for the use of Voltaire scholars is an edition of Longchamp's original text, blemishes included, and this I hope in due course to produce. The purpose of this article is the more modest one of investigating the relationship between certain familiar passages in the printed version of Longchamp's memoirs which have been used as evidence by scholars, and what Longchamp actually wrote.

Our first case concerns the earliest *contes*. Longchamp accompanied his master into hiding at Sceaux after Voltaire's unfortunate indiscretion at the 'jeu de la Reine' at Fontainebleau, actually in the autumn of 1747 although Longchamp situates it in 1746. The description of their clandestine and predominantly nocturnal existence in the château of Madame du Maine is given in some detail, and has

---

7.   Longchamp's description of one of his first encounters with Mme du Châtelet provides some examples. He was anxious, one morning, to report to his employer on a task he had been given the previous day, but had to wait until she awoke and summoned her maid, and him, to her room. Longchamp puts things plainly, if inadequately, in A: 'Comme le lendemain j'attendois son réveil pour lui rendre compte de ce qu'elle m'avoit chargé, elle vint à sonner, et j'entrai chez elle en même temps que sa femme de chambre. Ayant tiré ses Rideaux, elle se leva.' (f. 5r). Decroix turns this in D into: 'Le lendemain, lorsque j'attendais son réveil pour lui rendre compte de la besogne dont elle m'avait chargé, le bruit de la sonnette se fit entendre. J'entrai chez elle en même temps que sa femme-de-chambre; elle fit tirer ses rideaux et se leva' (ii. 119). Ladies do not draw back their own bed curtains, and even the fact that they have to ring the bell themselves is better concealed by an impersonal reflexive verb!

attracted attention because of the references to *Zadig* and other *contes* which it includes. After describing Voltaire's arrival at Sceaux and the 'secret' accommodation which had been prepared for him, the printed text of D continues:

> C'est du fond de cette retraite qu'il descendait toutes les nuits chez madame la duchesse *du Maine*, après qu'elle s'était mise au lit et que tous ses gens etaient retirés. Un seul valet-de-pied, qui était dans la confidence, dressait alors une petite table dans la ruelle du lit, et apportait à souper à M. *de Voltaire*. La princesse prenait grand plaisir à le voir et à causer avec lui. Il l'amusait par l'enjoûment de sa conversation, et elle l'instruisait en lui contant beaucoup d'anciennes anecdotes de la cour qu'il ignorait. Quelquefois après le repas il lisait un conte ou un petit roman qu'il avait écrit exprès dans la journée pour la divertir. C'est ainsi que furent composés *Babouc, Memnon, Scarmentado, Micromégas*, *Zadig*, dont il faisait chaque jour quelques chapitres. (ii. 140)

A few pages further on, Longchamp tells us, in D, that Voltaire 'me faisait mettre au net les contes dont il voulait régaler tous les soirs madame *du Maine*' (ii. 144–5). And when, two months later, news was brought by Madame du Châtelet that Voltaire could safely emerge from hiding, his tales as well as his company, according to D, figured among the pleasures of the duchess's court:

> Parmi tant de plaisirs variés que l'on goûtait alors à Sceaux, il faut compter la lecture de plusieurs nouveautés en vers et en prose, qui se faisaient dans le salon lorsque la compagnie s'y rassemblait avant le dîné. Madame *du Maine* avait témoigné à M. *de Voltaire* son désir de le voir communiquer aux personnes qui composaient alors sa petite cour, ces contes et romans qui l'avaient tant amusée lorsqu'il venait tous les soirs prendre son repas dans la ruelle de son lit, et que personne n'aurait soupçonnés d'être sortis de la même plume qui avait écrit la *Henriade, Œdipe, Brutus, Zaire, Mahomet*, etc. (ii. 151–2).

So great was the enthusiasm for these tales, indeed, that Voltaire was obliged, we are told (ii. 152–3), to promise to have them published in Paris and send the company advance copies.

This episode has been received with some scepticism, notably by Ascoli [8], on the grounds that the original version of *Zadig* (entitled *Memnon*) was already in print by the autumn of 1747 and so could scarcely have been written during Voltaire's weeks in hiding at Sceaux, while in 1746, the year given by Longchamp, Voltaire's visit to the duchesse de Maine was in no way secret. Van den Heuvel [9] is prepared to allow more weight to Longchamp's account, in view of its circumstantial detail, and suggests that Voltaire's private readings to his hostess of passages of the first *Memnon* may have taken place during his earlier visit; he also attaches importance to Longchamp's statement that the duchess and her friends encouraged Voltaire to publish his tales.

What Longchamp himself committed to paper on these matters is a good deal less colourful, and provides less material for literary speculation:

> M. de Voltaire ne descendoit chez m.^{de} la Duchesse que lorsque tout le monde êtoit retiré; mangeoit un poulet dans sa ruelle, et êtoit servi par un des valets de pieds de m. ^e la dûchesse qui êtoit dans la confidence. M. de Voltaire ne remontoit à son appartement qu'un peu avant le jour. Lassé de cette vie oisive M. de *Voltaire* fit faire une provision de Bougies et de Lumiere et se mit à travailler pendant le jour. Il fit plusieurs petits contes ou romans tels que Zadig, Babouc et autres; et il m'occupoit à les mettre au net. (f. 21^{r-v})

Not only, moreover, is there no statement that the *contes* were read to, let alone written for, Mme du Maine; there is no mention of any disclosure of the tales to the guests at Sceaux after Voltaire had emerged from hiding, and no suggestion that his decision to publish any of them was in response to their encouragement. In the printed version, Article VII begins:

> Rentré dans ses foyers après trois mois d'absence, M. de *Voltaire*, ne voulant point manquer à la parole qu'il avait donnée à Sceaux résolut de faire imprimer quelques-uns des opuscules qu'on lui avait demandés. Il fit choix d'abord de *Zadig*, l'un des

8.   Voltaire, *Zadig*, édition critique, 2nd edition, Paris, 1962, I.iii.
9.   *Voltaire dans ses contes*, Paris, 1967, pp. 140-2.

plus marquans; son dessein était de n'en pas laisser jouir le
public avant que madame la duchesse *du Maine* et sa société n'en
eussent eu les prémices, et qu'il n'en eût aussi distribué des
exemplaires à tous ses amis; ce qui n'était pas sans difficulté, même
en faisant imprimer l'ouvrage pour son compte. (ii. 154)

And there follows the celebrated anecdote concerning the
division of the manuscript of *Zadig* between Prault and another
printer, Machuel. Longchamp actually wrote, more baldly, to
introduce the episode:

> Pendant son séjour à Sceaux M. de Voltaire avoit composés
> plusieurs petits Contes ou Romans comme Memnon, Zadig,
> Babouc et autres. Voulant les faire imprimer, il fit venir chez lui
> un imprimeur, lui fit voir le Roman de Zadig, et lui demanda ce
> qu'il lui feroit payer 1200 exemplaires qu'il vouloit faire tirer de
> ce petit ouvrage. (f.25^r)

It would appear, then, that Longchamp's authentic testimony concerning Voltaire's literary activities during his weeks in
hiding at Sceaux is limited to the assertion that he wrote certain
of the *contes* then, including *Zadig;* some of the difficulties
arising from Longchamp's mistake in situating this episode in
1746 rather than 1747 evaporate, however, if in fact there is no
question of a reading of *Zadig* to Mme du Maine as a newly-
written tale (when by 1747 it was already in print in its *Memnon*
version): Voltaire may well have been then working on the
revision of *Memnon,* and would naturally have begun soon
afterwards to think of arranging for its publication. The rest,
it seems, is legend.

A second example concerns an episode which has been
quoted, for example by René Pomeau[10], as casting some light
on Voltaire's scientific enthusiasm and his sense of religious awe
before the wonders of the cosmos. On a frosty winter's night
during a journey to Cirey, Mme du Châtelet's coach broke an
axle, and she and Voltaire were obliged to wait by the road-
side while the postillion rode to the nearest village for help. The
scene is described in D as follows:

10. *La Religion de Voltaire,* 2nd edition, Paris, 1969, pp. 216-8.

> En attendant son retour, M. *de Voltaire* et madame *du Châtelet* s'étaient assis à côté l'un de l'autre sur les coussins du carrosse, qu'on avait retirés et posés sur le chemin couvert de neige: là, presque transis de froid malgré leurs fourrures, ils admiraient la beauté du ciel; il est vrai qu'il était parfaitement serein, les étoiles brillaient du plus vif éclat, l'horizon était à découvert; aucune maison, aucun arbre n'en dérobait la moindre partie à leurs yeux. On sait que l'astronomie a toujours été une des études favorites de nos deux philosophes. Ravis du magnifique spectacle deployé au-dessus et autour d'eux, ils dissertaient, en grelottant, sur la nature et le cours des astres, sur la destination de tant de globes immenses répandus dans l'espace. Il ne leur manquait que des téléscopes pour étre parfaitement heureux. Leur esprit égaré dans la profondeur des cieux, ils ne s'apercevaient plus de leur triste position sur la terre, ou plutôt sur la neige et au milieu des glaçons. Leur contemplation et leurs entretiens scientifiques ne furent interrompus que par le retour du postillon....
> (ii. 168)

There are touches of lyrical eloquence here which one feels might come more naturally to a man of letters who had had the chance of reading Bernardin de Saint-Pierre than they would to a footman turned secretary of a generation earlier; but Longchamp's manuscript shows that Decroix here has gone some way beyond mere embellishment. The text of A reads:

> ... on detacha un postillon a cheval pour aller chercher du secours dans un village qui êtoit à une demye lieue. En attendant son retour, on avoit tiré les coussins du carosse qu' on avoit mis sur la neige, où M. ^{e} du *Châtelet* et M. de *Voltaire* s'etoient assis à coté l'un de l'autre, considerant les etoiles et mourant de froid. Le postillon revint avec quatre hommes...
> (f. 31^r)

On to Longchamp's eminently practical-minded account of a road accident and the discomforts and delays it caused, Decroix has grafted a passage apparently originating in his own creative imagination, to add cosmic significance to an otherwise banal mishap.

Our third example concerns an episode on which the testimony of Longchamp's printed memoirs has been given some weight in discussions of the development of Voltaire's thought. We owe the survival of the *Traité de métaphysique* to Longchamp, who offered the manuscript of this hitherto unknown work to the Kehl editors in 1780[11]. In view of the suspicions entertained by Voltaire, probably with good reason, that Longchamp was addicted to making clandestine copies of his manuscripts, this posthumous disclosure might have seemed incriminating; but the printed memoirs offer a plausible and respectable, if somewhat dramatic, explanation of how the *Traité* came into Longchamp's possession. The text of D describes how, after Mme du Châtelet's death at Lunéville in 1749, her husband insisted on examining the contents of a packet of papers which she had expressly ordered to be destroyed unopened on her death; little liking the letters which first met his eye, he ordered the whole to be burnt, and Longchamp was given the task of supervising the incineration in the fireplace. The text continues:

> L'opération tirait en longueur, parce que ces papiers, qui étaient serrés et entassés, et entremêlés de plusieurs cahiers brochés, brûlaient difficilement. J'étais las de me baisser; pour vaquer plus commodément à ma besogne, je m'étais mis à genoux devant le foyer. En retournant cette masse, qui jetait plus de fumée que de flamme, je parvins à faire glisser entre mes genoux quelques papiers qui, se trouvant au centre, n'avaient pas encore été atteints du feu, et ils furent ainsi soustraits à la vue de ces messieurs (M. du Châtelet and his brother), dans un moment où elle n'était pas tournée sur moi. Après ce déplorable incendie, étant sorti de l'appartement, je n'eus rien de plus pressé que de savoir ce que j'avais fait entrer furtivement dans ma poche; c'était un cahier de papier à lettres, qui contenait, en écriture fort menue, un *Traité de Métaphysique;* et le reste consistait en plusieurs lettres détachées. Je vis que, dans quelques-unes de celles-ci, on parlait de M. *de Voltaire* avec fort peu de ménagement. Je les conservai avec soin, et elles me servirent dans la suite, somme on le verra ci-après, à calmer l'extrême douleur qu'avait causée à M. *de Voltaire* la mort prématurée de madame *du Châtelet.* (II. 256–7).

11. Condorcet to Ruault, *ca* September 1780. n.a.fr.24338, f.380[r]; Decroix to Ruault, 20 May 1781, B.N.n.a.fr.13139, f.216[v].

This passage has been taken to imply that the Kehl text of the *Traité* is that of a presentation copy of his essay which there is reason to think Voltaire gave to Emilie and which she preserved; and Professor Wade has argued, on internal evidence, that the presentation must have been made in early 1736, and that the *Traité* as we know it therefore represents Voltaire's views at that date[12].

Unfortunately, we are once again in the presence of a piece of editorial embroidery by Decroix. Longchamp's autograph account of what happened when the Marquis du Châtelet insisted, against his brother's advice, on opening the forbidden packet reads merely as follows:

> ...malgré les remonstrances de son frère, le marquis l'ouvrit. Il tomba d'abord sur des lettres qui ne lui firent surement pas de plaisir, parce qu'il se mit en fureur et a jurer comme un payen. Sur cela son frere lui dit que c'etoit bien fait, qu'il êtoit payé de sa curiosité et qu'il méritoit bien cela et dans le même instant son frere ayant demandé de la lumiere, et ayant porté lui même ce paquet dans le foyer de la chaminée y mit lui même le feu. M'ettant approché pour le faire brûler en le remuant avec les pincettes j'appercus quelques lettres qui parloient de Mr de Voltaire. J'en escamotai trois où il êtoit traité indignement et qui ont servi dans la suitte à le guerir de l'attachement qu'il avoit conservé pour cette dame comme je le dirai après. (f. 66^v)

The discrepancy here between D and A can perhaps be accounted for without attributing too much to the mythopoeic impulses to which Decroix seems to succumb elsewhere. Longchamp's autograph narrative breaks off at f.89 after a group of anecdotes relating to Voltaire's time in Berlin in 1750—52; that is, at the point when their relationship came to an end. This is followed in the manuscript by a series of copies in Longchamp's hand of several poems by Voltaire and of a letter of his to

---

12.   I.O. Wade, *Studies on Voltaire*, New York, 1967, pp. 68—78. Mrs. H.T. Patterson makes similar assumptions in her edition of the *Traité* (2nd edition, Manchester, 1957, p.v).

Mme Denis of 9 July 1753 (ff. 90–102); and the manuscript is then rounded off by copies of two pieces of verse on Voltaire's death, and Longchamp's own indignant account of the scandalous difficulties concerning his burial (ff. 103–4). It thus seems clear that all but these last few pages were set down by Longchamp during Voltaire's lifetime, in all probability not long after the end of their association in the early 1750s, and that it was only the occasion of Voltaire's death that led him to return to his notebook. When he came to sell the *Traité de métaphysique* to the Kehl editors in 1780 he may well have thought of using his perhaps by then somewhat hazy recollections of what he rescued from the fireplace at Lunéville in 1749 to provide the basis of a plausible story to account for his possession of the manuscript; and such a story would certainly have reached the ears of Decroix. By 1786, when Longchamp sold Decroix his memoirs, he is scarcely likely to have noticed that his text did not confirm the story he had told; but Decroix, remembering it, would no doubt have felt perfectly justified in adding a reference to the *Traité* (which had passed through his hands) when he came to refurbish Longchamp's account of the incident in question.

Longchamp's testimony can thus no longer be reliably adduced in support of the view that the *Traité* as we know it is a work which Voltaire presented to Mme du Châtelet in 1736, and which therefore is in a form that he regarded as in some sense definitive. The Kehl text of the *Traité* may, more probably, derive from a copy made by Longchamp from a document found among Voltaire's papers at some time in the years 1746–1752, when he had access to them. Such a possibility calls for a reassessment of the problems of the genesis of the *Traité*, since existing accounts, notably that by Wade[13], rest upon the acceptance of Decroix's version of the *Mémoires*. In particular, it may prove to be misleading to regard the *Traité* as in any sense

13. *op.cit.*, pp. 56–114.

a finished work, rather than a draft preserved at random and representing a merely transitional stage in the development of a project subsequently abandoned. I hope to be able to explore these matters further in my forthcoming edition of the *Traité* in the *Complete Works* of Voltaire.

If one can speculate more or less plausibly about what may lie behind Decroix's embroidery on Longchamp's narrative where the *Traité de métaphysique* is concerned, the two earlier examples we have discussed, and some other cases not included here, are much more difficult to account for. Given the circumstances and the literary attitudes of his day, one can sympathize with Decroix's editorial itch to transform Longchamp's bald, clumsy and sometimes barely literate prose into something more elegant, and understand his desire to give the narrative a shape designed to hold the interest of the readership at which he was aiming. His gratuitous additions, however, are really the heart of the problem, from the standpoint of modern scholarship. Here one should perhaps remember that Decroix was the working editor throughout the publication of the Kehl edition, continually at the centre of things where the collection of material and its preparation for the press were concerned, a likely recipient from all quarters of anecdotes and information about Voltaire, and moreover that he was in personal touch with two of Voltaire's biographers, Condorcet and the notoriously unreliable Duvernet. In such circumstances it is not perhaps surprising that he should have thought fit to embellish Longchamp's pedestrian account of Voltaire's weeks in hiding at Sceaux with an attractive piece of hearsay about clandestine readings of the *contes* and their subsequent acclaim by the duchess's elegant circle of courtiers; nor that he should have taken a plain factual description of a road accident on a frosty night as the occasion for inserting a piece of embroidery reminding his readers of the high-minded scientific and philosophical enthusiasms of which Voltaire and Mme du Châtelet were capable. But such adornments are not much help to scholars. *Caveat emptor*!

LE CURÉ MESLIER AU THÉÂTRE – UNE PIÈCE D'ARTHUR FITGER (1894)

R. Desne

A vie de Jean Meslier, homme double, travaillant en secret à démentir le personnage qu'il doit jouer dans la société, semble pouvoir offrir matière à un roman, une pièce ou un film. De fait, on connaît une œuvre de fiction inspirée par le cas Meslier; mais on n'en connaît qu'une seule. Il s'agit d'un drame écrit par un auteur allemand aujourd'hui oublié, Arthur Fitger, et jamais traduit en français[1]. Ce texte mérite de retenir l'attention comme un témoignage, unique en son genre, sur la fortune de Meslier à la fin du 19ème siècle.

Œuvre singulière mais qu'on ne doit pas s'étonner de trouver à sa date et en son lieu. C'est d'abord en Allemagne que Meslier a bénéficié du renouveau d'intérêt que pouvait susciter la publication intégrale du *Testament* par Rudolf Charles, à Amsterdam en 1864. David-Friedrich Strauss est le premier à tirer parti de l'édition hollandaise dans une étude solide, annexée à son *Voltaire* (Leipzig, 1870). Cette étude est, peu après, publiée en feuilleton (six livraisons) dans les premiers numéros du *Volksstaat-Erzähler* (1873–1874), supplément littéraire hebdomadaire du *Volksstaat* - le journal de Bebel et Liebknecht-, l'organe central du Parti Social-démocrate. Dix ans plus tard

---

1. *Jean Meslier*, eine Dichtung von A. Fitger. Leipzig, A.G. Liebeskind, 1894. [IV] + 127 p.

Georg Adler, dans un hebdomadaire littéraire berlinois, invite à voir en Meslier 'un précurseur oublié du socialisme' (*Die Gegenwart*, 1884 (n° 38)). En France, où le *Voltaire* de Strauss a été traduit en 1876, la curiosité est ranimée par un article de l'Autrichien Carl Gruenberg dans la *Revue d'Economie politique* (mai-juin 1888) et un autre, de Benoît Malon, dans la *Revue socialiste* (août 1888); Meslier retient l'attention. L'année où Fitger publie sa pièce, on lui donne sa place dans le *Handbuch des Socialismus* de Stegmann et Hugo (Zurich, 1894, p.505–512), et, l'année suivante, dans la *Geschichte des Sozialismus* de Bernstein et Kautzky (Stuttgart, 1895, I, p. 792–810). Il n'est donc pas surprenant qu'un dramaturge de Brême se soit risqué alors à porter Jean Meslier à la scène et à dédier son ouvrage à un prince protecteur du théâtre, le duc Georges II de Saxe-Meiningen[2].

On est assez bien renseigné sur Fitger par les biographes allemands[3]. Né en 1840 à Delmenhorst (Oldenburg) et mort à Horn bei Bremen, en 1909, il était le fils d'un père fonctionnaire des postes et d'une mère issue d'une famille d'avocats. Après des études à Munich, Dresde, à Anvers, en Italie (1863–1865), à Vienne, il s'est fait connaître comme peintre, poète et dramaturge. Lui-même se considérait d'abord comme un peintre. Installé à Brême à partir de 1860, il a décoré les principaux bâtiments publics de la ville ainsi que ceux de Hambourg et de nombreux intérieurs de grandes maisons bourgeoises. Il a publié, de 1875 à 1894, trois recueils de poèmes. Au théâtre, il s'est distingué avec surtout deux pièces : *Die Hexe* (La Sorcière) (1876) — dont l'héroïne est une athée du 17ème siècle, jouée à

2.   Sur le rôle important joué par Georges II (1826–1914) et son théâtre de Meiningen dans la vie culturelle allemande et européenne, voir l'article de la *Neue deutsche Biographie*, Berlin, VI, 1964, p. 228–229.
3.   Voir l'article de H. Tardel dans la *Bremische Biographie des neuenzehnten Jahrhunderts*, Bremen, 1912, p. 133–145 et celui, plus succinct, d'A. Elschenbroich dans la *Neue Deutsche Biographie*. V, 1961, p. 216.

Leipzig en 1879 et sur plusieurs scènes allemandes, traduite en danois, en néerlandais, en hongrois et en anglais; et *Von Gottes Gnaden* (Par la grâce de Dieu) (1883) —satire du despotisme des princes des petits états allemands, jouée seulement à Brême et Hambourg, interdite à Berlin. A sa production théâtrale, qui comporte plusieurs autres titres, s'ajoutent des essais, des articles, des fragments autobiographiques. Il se dégage de cette œuvre une personnalité littéraire assez confuse, qu'on pourrait situer parmi les épigones du romantisme. Idéologiquement, Fitger s'est opposé au christianisme. On observe que son frère Emil (né en 1848), journaliste, a été un libre penseur, dirigeant du Freisinnigen Volkspartei, parti libéral où se retrouvaient de nombreux Francs-Maçons (mais aucun des deux Fitger n'est mentionné dans le *Freimaurer Lexikon*). Séduit par l'évolutionnisme darwinien, Arthur Fitger paraît avoir oscillé entre l'athéisme et le panthéisme, accentuant une tendance au pessimisme dans ses dernières années, tendance marquée dans son recueil poétique, *Requiem aeternam dona ei* qui paraît la même année que son *Jean Meslier*.

    Jean Meslier, drame en cinq actes, a été publié à Leipzig en 1894. Des exemplaires de cette unique édition se trouvent rarement dans les bibliothèques [4]. D'après la *Bremische Biographie,* la pièce aurait eu un grand succès lors de sa création au théâtre municipal de Brême le 14 février 1901; mais, d'après Helmut Wocke, auteur de la seule monographie consacrée à Fitger, *Jean Meslier* aurait partagé le sort des deux autres productions des dernières années de l'auteur (*Die Rosen von Tyburn,* 1888 et *San Marcos Tochter,* 1902) : ces pièces n'auraient pas été estimées à leur valeur ni reçu l'accueil

---

4.   On n'en trouve ni à la Bibliothèque nationale de Paris ni à la Staatsbibliothek de Berlin. Nous devons à l'obligeance de Martin Fontius d'avoir pu consulter l'exemplaire de la Bibliothèque municipale de Berlin (Berliner Stadtbibliothek, cote B 6460).

réservé à *Die Hexe* et à *Von Gottes Gnaden*[5].

Notre propos n'est pas ici d'étudier la pièce de Fitger dans le contexte littéraire allemand des années 1890–1900, mais d'en dégager la vision que le dramaturge propose de Meslier, de son milieu et de son époque.

Fitger a mis en scène les deux dernières journées vécues par le curé d'Etrépigny, entre la messe d'un dimanche matin (jour de la Saint-Jean) et son suicide, le lendemain soir.

Le 1er acte (p. 1–28) s'ouvre sur la sacristie. Des villageois pauvres, jeunes et vieux, accueillent le curé qui vient de finir sa messe, lui souhaitant sa fête et témoignant leur admiration et leur reconnaissance. Arrive le meunier Arnaud acculé à la famine par le seigneur du lieu, le marquis de Bonpère qui, en ces jours de sécheresse, détourne l'eau du moulin pour alimenter ses bassins et ses fontaines. Entre ensuite le marquis, touché par le prône de curé : il apporte de l'argent à Meslier pour ses pauvres et promet de ne plus retenir l'eau de la rivière. On annonce alors l'arrivée au château du chanoine (Domherr), 'Monseigneur der Graf von Clairy', en brillante compagnie. Le marquis s'en va pour fêter ses hôtes. Resté seul, Meslier, dans un long monologue, exprime son hostilité au christianisme; il voit dans l'arrivée du chanoine qui est pour lui un 'ami cher' et un supérieur bienveillant, 'un signe du destin' : il tire d'un placard dérobé le troisième exemplaire de son manuscrit et décide de le faire porter au chanoine par le sacristain, Frater Justinius, avec une lettre d'accompagnement qu'il rédige sur-le-champ. Mais le sacristain découvre sur le seuil de la porte Arnaud évanoui et mourant de faim, n'attendant plus que l'extrême-onction. Le curé renonce alors à se dévoiler : il continuera le jeu du 'pieux mensonge' afin de ne pas ôter au malheureux sa dernière consolation.

Dans la rue du village (acte II, p. 29–53), on voit Servant, le médecin, expulsé de l'auberge, faire profession d'incrédulité

5.   H. Wocke, *Arthur Fitger. Sein Leben und Schaffen*, Stuttgart, 1913, p. 12. Sur *Jean Meslier*, voir p. 65–70.

et pousser Arnaud à la violence contre le marquis.
Révolutionnaire, il prêche à Meslier 'la liberté, l'égalité et la
fraternité'. Mais le curé s'oppose vivement à ces discours qui ne
sont que 'tromperie' ; il traite Servant de 'mauvais hérétique', de
'vilain rêveur' et il invite Arnaud à laisser 'ce malheureux corbeau
à ses croassements'. Un message annonce que le marquis a
finalement décidé de faire marcher ses fontaines en l'honneur
de ses invités; il apporte au meunier une forte somme d'argent
offerte par le marquis. Arnaud la refuse violemment et s'en
retourne en colère.

Sur la terrasse du château (acte III, p. 54–77), Meslier
tente vainement de faire revenir le marquis sur sa décision. Il
décline l'invitation de se joindre à la fête car il doit conduire une
procession pour la pluie. La fête se prépare. Voltaire est parmi
les invités. Les réjouissances sont troublées par les clameurs des
paysans qui se sont attroupés après la procession et qui, sous la
direction d'Arnaud, commencent à saccager le parc. Arnaud
détruit la précieuse Vénus de Bouchardon; le marquis le blesse
d'un coup de pistolet. Meslier arrive, sermonne les uns et les
autres ('vous vivez comme des païens'), fait s'agenouiller les
deux adversaires 'devant le dieu présent', et les réconcilie.
L'attendrissement général est de brève durée : Meslier ne peut
supporter l'admiration dont il est l'objet. Il jette sa mitre (sic)
et son étole, déclare qu'il n'est qu'un païen 'qui a joué le
chrétien', qu'il va envoyer un livre, son 'Testament où on pourra
lire que le saint prêtre d'Etrépigny est l'antéchrist en personne'.
Consternation générale. Meslier s'enfuit.

Le lendemain, dans le bureau ('zimmer') du curé (acte
IV, p. 78–100), Antoinette, une chanteuse venue elle aussi pour
la fête du marquis et qui a été autrefois recueillie et élevée par
Meslier, apprend du sacristain que le testament a été transmis
au chanoine. Meslier sort de sa chambre. Antoinette, qui a
toujours été amoureuse de lui, propose qu'ils partent tous deux
en exil. Meslier refuse, tout en lui avouant qu'il l'aime 'outre

mesure'. Survient le chanoine qui exhorte Meslier à ne pas persister dans son défi ('un procès contre Jean Meslier serait un scandale pour toute la France') : qu'il accepte d'être relevé de ses fonctions et de profiter d'une sinécure, il pourra s'installer à Paris dans un hôtel particulier que le chanoine met à sa disposition, et là vivre avec Antoinette , parmi les philosophes et publier son testament 'comme un ouvrage purement philosophique'. Meslier est troublé. Il se remémore la tentation du diable sur la montagne.

Plus tard, dans le même bureau vide de la plupart de ses meubles (acte V, p. 101—127), des pauvres s'emparent de divers objets. Meslier entre, un sac de voyage à la main; il distribue des dons à ses paroissiens. Arrivent Arnaud et Servant. Meslier tente d'expliquer au meunier qu'il a prêché des mensonges pour détourner les villageois de la révolte dangereuse où les 'aurait attirés la langue empoisonnée de Servant'. Arnaud ne veut plus écouter le curé et annonce son intention de brûler le château. Arrive ensuite le marquis, furieux d'avoir été trompé par Meslier, et résolu, désormais, à faire valoir ses droits de seigneur. Ni lui ni Arnaud ne veulent croire à ce que le curé pourrait leur dire pour les réconcilier. Seul, Meslier se rappelle la fable du berger menteur. Il boit le flacon d'opium (que le médecin avait apporté, comme somnifère, au début de l'acte I) et s'agenouille dans une prière à 'l'Inconnu'. Un orage éclate. Entre le sacristain qui annonce l'arrivée de Voltaire. Celui-ci rapporte à Meslier son manuscrit, lui dit son admiration enthousiaste pour cette oeuvre ('comme une épée tranchante, elle fauchera dans les rangs de la prêtraille'). Mais ces paroles 'font honte' à Meslier. Il souhaite que ses 'pauvres feuilles' disparaissent avec lui ('l'hypocrite va enfin se taire'). Voltaire a juste le temps de persuader le moribond de lui remettre son manuscrit, avant de rendre le dernier soupir.

Malgré quelques longueurs et des complaisances pour le mélodrame, la pièce est bien construite; les scènes à effet sont nombreuses, les dialogues parfois vifs et les personnages fermement dessinés. Fitger a pu greffer le conflit intérieur (Meslier se déclarera-t-il?) sur le conflit social qui met aux prises le meunier et son seigneur. A-t-il, pour autant, réussi à restituer la véritable personnalité de son modèle comme le laissait attendre la référence explicite à l'édition R. Charles sur la page de titre?[6]

Fitger a retenu de l'histoire un certain nombre de données qu'on identifie aisément, sans savoir cependant quelle a pu être l'étendue de sa documentation. D'abord, le personnage même du curé acceptant d'assumer une fonction en opposition totale avec ses convictions et l'assumant de façon exemplaire. (En en faisant un 'saint' et un martyr de la bienfaisance, le dramaturge rehausse encore l'image du prêtre dévoué et généreux transmise par la biographie voltairienne). Fitger connaît l'existence des manuscrits : c'est le 'troisième' que le curé dissimule dans la sacristie; les deux autres ayant été 'déposés prudemment dans des archives sûres' (p. 25). Il sait que Meslier possédait un Montaigne (p. 102). Il lui fait rédiger une lettre au chanoine pour la joindre à son manuscrit, parce qu'il a lu, probablement, que Meslier avait écrit des lettres aux curés du voisinage. Le seigneur du village, sous le nom du marquis de Bonpère, paraît avoir pour modèle le seigneur Antoine de Toully de Cléry avec qui Meslier eut maille à partir. Et le chanoine fait penser au grand vicaire Lebègue, envoyé sur les lieux à la mort de Meslier (est-ce par une confusion involontaire que Fitger donne à ce chanoine le nom du seigneur, 'Clairy'?). Pour la plupart de ces informations utilisées, le dramaturge pouvait

6. 'Jean Meslier, Pfarrer von Etrépigny, starb im Jahre 1736. Bruch- stücke seines Testament, welches handschriftlich 'im Geheimen circulirt hatte, wurden zuerst 1762 von Voltaire in Holland herausgegeben. Die erste vollständige. Ausgabe ist durch Rudolf Charles 1864 bei R.C. Mejer in Amsterdam veranstaltet'.

s'en tenir à la préface de l'édition de Rudolf Charles[7]. Il n'est pas impossible qu'un détail anecdotique rapporté dans une note du curé Aubry (1783) publiée dans la *Revue de Champagne et de Brie* (1881) lui ait inspiré de faire sourire son personnage 'depuis quelque temps' (d'après ce que dit le sacristain) 'd'un sourire plus douloureux que la plus haute lamentation' (p. 9)[8].

On a dit que, dans son théâtre, Fitger aimait choisir un sujet historique qu'il transformait et développait de façon indépendante[9]. Incontestablement la matière que lui fournit l'histoire de Meslier subit entre ses mains des transformations notables.

Celles-ci portent d'abord sur le cadre : l'église spacieuse, avec des orgues, le somptueux château 'dans le style de Versailles' (sur la colline!), la rivière et son moulin ou l'auberge 'Au raisin doré', autant d'inventions qui nous éloignent du petit village d'Etrépigny.

Les transformations portent aussi, et plus gravement, sur le moment. Passons sur l'erreur de date qui fait mourir Meslier en 1736[10]. Plus insolite est la présence de Voltaire à Etrépigny (et auprès du curé mourant!), Voltaire déjà fermement résolu à

---

7. *Le Testament de Jean Meslier*, Amsterdam, 1864, I, p. XXXVI-XXXIX. R. Charles citant la notice biographique de Boulliot (1830) nomme le seigneur, M. de Clairy.

8. En parlant sur certains sujets de religion, 'il avait un geste, affecté sans doute, couvrant de la main droite partie de son visage, pour qu'on s'aperçût moins d'un sourire dont on ne connaissait pas alors toute la méchanceté' (note du curé Aubry) dans : Jean Meslier, *Œuvres complètes*, Paris, 1970–1972 , III, p. 398. On peut se demander si ce sourire tient de l'histoire ou de la légende. Selon Fitger, Meslier est surtout enclin à pleurer beaucoup (p. 9).

9. H. Wocke, ouvr. cité p. 47.

10. Coquille probable pour 1733. Depuis 1830 (article de la *Biographie ardennaise* de Boulliot) on pouvait savoir que Meslier était mort en 1729. R. Charles qui cite longuement Boulliot a néanmoins maintenu sur la page de titre de son édition la date de 1733 'comme la plus généralement acceptée' (*le Testament*, éd. cit. I, p. XXXVIII).

'écraser l'infâme'[11]. L'affabulation tire Meslier vers la deuxième moitié du siècle. Le décalage est accentué par les personnages de Servant et d'Arnaud qui parlent comme s'ils étaient à la veille de 1789 ou de 1793. Servant veut offrir 'un pays de liberté, d'égalité et de fraternité' (p. 47) et, à l'acte V, incitant Meslier à le suivre à Paris, il lui dit : 'vous serez le premier à qui la nouvelle France décrétera une statue' (p. 107), allusion évidente à la proposition faite à la Convention, en novembre 1793, par Anacharsis Cloots[12].

Par ses appels à la conciliation et à la résignation, le curé apparaît alors comme désirant freiner un mouvement révolutionnaire qui se développe autour de lui, et contre lui, un mouvement qui a déjà ses chefs ambitieux comme le médecin Servant et ses recrues (Arnaud). Meslier peut dire au marquis : 'ma comédie a sauvé votre parc et votre château' (p. 115).

Nous touchons là à la transformation essentielle, celle que subit la pensée de Meslier. Certes le curé a pu jouer au sein de sa paroisse un rôle modérateur, comme on le voit faire, en 1721, dans une querelle qui oppose deux villageois à un domestique du seigneur (d'après un document d'archives que Fitger n'a certainement pas connu[13]); mais cette affaire est postérieure au conflit de 1716 qui dresse le curé défenseur de ses paroissiens contre le seigneur d'Etrépigny et lui attire la réprimande de l'archevêque[14]. Aucun incident de ce genre n'est concevable

11. L'expression 'Ecrasez l'infâme' figure, en français, dans l'une des répliques de la dernière scène (p. 125). Signalons que la pièce de Fitger n'est mentionnée dans aucune des bibliographies consacrées à Voltaire. M.M. Barr, dans *A bibliography of writings on Voltaire*, New York, 1929, n° 1441 signale un texte d'A. Fitger : 'Eine Fabel von Voltaire', *Die Nation*, Berlin, 5 mai 1906. .
12. Voir J. Meslier, *Œuvres complètes*, III, p. 500–504.
13. Voir *ibid.*, p. 429–430.
14. L'anecdote répandue par la biographie éditée par Voltaire ('Abrégé de la vie de l'auteur') est confirmée par les archives du diocèse. Voir *ibid.*, p. 388–394 et 416–421.

dans la paroisse décrite par Fitger : le curé y est un 'saint' également vénéré par le marquis et par les villageois; le seul à s'opposer au curé étant Servant, le médecin incrédule et républicain. On ne trouve pas trace dans les propos de Meslier, même dans ses monologues, de l'esprit de contestation politique et sociale qui anime plus d'une page du *Mémoire*. Très caractéristique de cet affadissement du personnage est la lettre écrite par Meslier au chanoine et qu'on peut comparer aux lettres réelles adressées aux curés du voisinage (que Fitger n'a vraisemblablement pas lues[15]). Qu'il nous suffise d'en citer le début et la fin (p. 26–27) : 'Monseigneur! Que votre Eminence veuille bien trouver dans ce manuscrit que j'ose mettre respectueusement sous ses yeux la preuve que la paroisse d'Etrépigny est, depuis vingt ans, administrée par un homme qui n'est pas un chrétien, mais un hérétique, un antéchrist [...] Je dois en finir avec cette bouffonnerie, vous dévoiler mon âme dans ces pages, et attendre le verdict que vous allez prononcer'. Il est difficile de dénaturer davantage l'appel serein et hautain, souvent ironique, adressé par Meslier à ses confrères pour les inviter à éclairer et à guider le peuple ('...si vous m'en blâmez, je le dis franchement, je m'en soucie peu, d'autant que c'est pour la justice et pour la vérité que je parle', éd.cit. III, p. 200). Tout se passe comme si Fitger avait créé, à partir du Meslier historique, deux personnages : le curé infidèle qui a pris le christianisme en haine, 'antéchrist' malheureux dont la souffrance inspire la compassion, et Servant le révolté mégalomane qui se compare à Brutus et à Cromwell et qui déchaîne chez le meunier les instincts de vengeance et de

15. Louis Paris avait reproduit la plus courte de ces lettres et deux fragments de l'autre dans *Le Cabinet historique* (janvier 1856, p. 16–24). A l'exception de cette publication, il a fallu attendre l'édition des *Œuvres complètes* de Meslier (Paris, 1970–1972), pour avoir une édition de ces lettres aux curés (III, p. 181–206). C'est à cette édition que nous renvoyons pour les citations des textes de Meslier.

violence ('vous êtes enragé' dit Meslier à Arnaud, p. 114).
Le Meslier de Fitger est ainsi l'homme d'un drame de
conscience. Desservant sa paroisse depuis vingt ans (et non
quarante comme dans la réalité), il est entré par vocation dans
l'Eglise : c'est avec une 'foi fervente' qu'il a reçu les ordres
(p. 26); il a 'lutté durement avant de sombrer dans l'incroyance'
(*ibid.*). Le vrai Meslier n'a pas eu à lutter; il n'a pas perdu la
foi : il ne l'a jamais eue [16]. Vénéré par tous ceux qui l'entourent
('vous êtes tout pour nous' lui déclare un pauvre paysan (p. 6);
pour 'ces messieurs du chapitre', à en croire le chanoine, c'est
'un savant, un ami et un saint' (p. 90)), le personnage de Fitger
est déchiré entre la volonté de répondre à la confiance qu'on lui
porte et le désir de dire la vérité, d'en finir avec une vie de
mensonge, de 'comédie', de 'mascarade' etc. A cela s'ajoute
l'épreuve d'un amour impossible : Meslier, autrefois, a sacrifié
l'amour d'Antoinette à son devoir de prêtre; maintenant il le
sacrifie à la cause de la vérité ('Je porte un drapeau que même
l'ombre d'une tache ne doit pas salir' (p. 88)). Or Meslier, pour
dire la vérité, doit se démasquer comme hypocrite et ainsi
perdre l'espoir d'être jamais compris par ceux qu'il a si bien et
si longtemps trompés : pourquoi la parole de Meslier philosophe
serait-elle plus sincère, plus vraie que la parole de Meslier
prêtre? Là est la tragédie du héros, soulignée par l'orage qui
accompagne son suicide. Mais cette tragédie n'est visible au
théâtre que par une nouvelle entorse à l'histoire : le Meslier réel
n'a pas tenté de proclamer publiquement ses idées. Il s'est
laissé mourir en en préparant la révélation posthume.

Ces idées, nous l'avons dit, ne sont que partiellement
reprises par le personnage de Fitger. Le curé qu'il met en
scène justifie le recours au mensonge de la religion par les
nécessités de la bonne entente sociale. Si le mal existe, et c'est

---

16.   'Dès ma plus tendre jeunesse, j'ai entrevu les erreurs et les abus...'
(éd. cit., I, p. 7). Il s'est fait prêtre pour 'complaire à [ses] parents'
qui voulaient pour lui une situation 'honorable' (*ibid.*, p. 26–27).

cette existence du mal qui constitue son argument essentiel en faveur de l'athéisme (ou de l'agnosticisme) dans une longue réplique au chanoine (p. 95–96), il tient à un mystère de la nature. Reconnaissons que la souffrance et l'injustice sont des choses inévitables, incompréhensibles, et travaillons, du mieux que nous pouvons, à établir la fraternité parmi les hommes en cultivant des vertus fondées non sur la croyance religieuse mais sur les exigences de la société établie. Telles seraient, en somme, les convictions de Meslier. Certes le sacristain rapporte que le curé, en tirant le manuscrit de sa cachette, lui a dit que le moment du combat est venu : 'le combat avec le chanoine, avec le capital, avec l'archevêque et peut-être même avec le pape' (p. 80). Mais on ne saura pas comment Meslier concevait cette lutte contre le 'capital' (sic).

Qu'il ait lu ou non le *Mémoire* dans la version complète de Rudolf Charles, Fitger a donc retenu une vision de Meslier commandée avant tout par l'interprétation voltairienne, celle-ci étant toutefois débarrassée du credo déiste. Trois fois, Meslier se désigne comme 'l'antéchrist' (p. 26, 77 et 122) mot sans doute inspiré par la lettre de Voltaire à d'Alembert (Best. D. 10323), citée dans de nombreuses éditions du *Bon sens du curé Meslier,* depuis le début du 19ème siècle, et reproduite dans la préface de Rudolph Charles : 'Je vous enverrai un exemplaire de ce testament de l'antéchrist...' écrivait Voltaire à son correspondant. 'Prêcher le pauvre testament de l'antéchrist...' dit le curé dans son dernier monologue (p. 122). Le seule citation de son manuscrit faite par Meslier dans la pièce (lorsqu'il déclare dans son monologue de l'acte I que 'le dernier trait est tiré') est une traduction de la note. finale ajoutée par Voltaire à son *Extrait* : 'Dies ist das Testament von Jean Meslier, Pfarrer von Etrépigny' (p. 25). Ajoutons que l'intervention de Voltaire lui-même, au dénouement, félicitant curieusement Meslier d'être 'le grand précurseur' ('dem grossen Vorkämpfer...' (p. 125)) du combat contre 'l'infâme', souligne la position du curé dans une tradition foncièrement anticléricale. Mais en l'absence de tout déisme clairement affirmé (Voltaire dit seulement, dans sa dernière réplique, que l'œuvre de Meslier permettra d'édifier un temple digne de dieux plus nobles' (p. 127)), la doctrine anti-chrétienne, néo-païenne du héros de Fitger pouvait se concilier avec celle du *Bon sens* de d'Holbach attribué à Meslier depuis 1791. En définitive, ce Jean Meslier de 1894 doit beaucoup à l'image propagée au 19ème siècle par l'*Extrait* de Voltaire et le *Bon sens* de d'Holbach, et fort peu à l'œuvre éditée par Rudolf Charles. Les compatriotes de Fitger étaient d'ailleurs plus à même de connaître l'*Extrait* et le *Bon sens* (au moins quatre éditions allemandes de 1856 à 1880)[17] que le *Testament* complet, jamais traduit en allemand.

Fitger a probablement projeté dans cette interprétation ses propres convictions. Sympathie pour les humbles, non sans paternalisme, haine du mensonge, aspiration à la fraternité, hostilité envers l'égoïsme et la morgue des possédants, envers les mœurs relâchées des dignitaires de l'Eglise, refus de la violence révolutionnaire, une philosophie athée ou sceptique fortement teintée de pessimisme, tels sont les grands traits de la leçon portée au théâtre par un dramaturge qui montre en Meslier une victime plus qu'un coupable.

Malgré la référence indiquée sur la page de titre, Fitger ne semble pas s'être soucié de faire œuvre historique. De formation protestante - et le dédicataire de sa pièce est Georges II, un prince luthérien, il place comme il peut des touches de couleur

---

17.   Voir la bibliographie dans Meslier, *Œuvres complètes*, III, p. 585 et
        587. On remarque que Louis Büchner introduit des références à
        Meslier dans la 15ème édition (Leipzig, 1883) de son *Kraft und
        Stoff* (1ère éd., 1855); les citations produites sont toutes extraites
        du *Bon sens*. L'ouvrage de Büchner est réédité en 1887, 1892,
        1894, 1898 et 1902. Fitger l'a probablement lu. Une traduction
        française (*Force et matière*) a paru en 1884 et 1895.

locale catholique : on entend, à la messe, les premiers vers latins du *Gloria* (p. 11); il arrive à Meslier de répliquer au chanoine par une citation latine (p. 94). Le sacristain commente sévèrement la négligence du curé envers 'la substance' des sacrements : il est resté un grumeau d'hostie sur la patène et une goutte de vin a tourné au fond du calice! (p. 9–10); et son commentaire sur l'attitude de Meslier ('indifférent comme un hérétique' (p. 10)) ne peut que valoir à celui-ci la sympathie d'un public protestant. Le personnage du chanoine, type parfait du prélat riche et corrompu prêt à tous les accommodements, tout en faisant ressortir, par contraste, la qualité humaine du curé, est conforme à une tradition protestante de satire anticatholique. Mais Fitger connaît mal la liturgie et les usages catholiques. Les tout premiers mots de la pièce ('Il a déjà dit le dernier *amen*') laissent entrevoir une confusion probable entre *amen* et *ite missa est.* Antoinette chante divinement à la messe le *Miserere,* psaume réservé à l'office des morts ou aux vêpres. Le costume et l'attitude du prêtre dans la procession du Saint-sacrement, très sommairement décrite, ne correspondent pas aux nécessités de cette cérémonie (p. 72, 74, 76). Le chanoine est bizarrement désigné par le titre civil de 'comte de Clairy' ('Monseigneur der Graf von Clairy' (p. 21, 26)). La sacristie est munie d'un 'vestiaire' ('vestiarium') (p. 1) qu'on trouve dans les temples luthériens. Frater Justinius jargonne comme un sacristain protestant, nourri de lectures de la Bible (p. 3, 8, 33 etc). On remarque aussi que les paroissiens mis en scène, et ce sont apparemment les plus zélés, attendent dans la sacristie que le curé ait fini de dire sa messe comme s'ils avaient la liberté, qu'accorde le culte luthérien, de ne pas assister à l'office dominical! Détail amusant : les citations bibliques (sans références) dont Meslier orne ses propos sont prises littéralement dans la Bible de Luther![18]

On ne sait comment le *Jean Meslier* de Fitger a été reçu

par le public allemand. La coloration protestante de la pièce
a-t-elle permis d'étendre au protestantisme la révolte du curé
'antéchrist'? Ou n'a-t-on pas retenu, plutôt, les traits visiblement
anticatholiques pour se persuader que la tragédie d'un Meslier
n'était concevable que dans l'univers du catholicisme? L'enquête
sur l'accueil de la pièce par la critique allemande de l'époque
reste à faire et elle pourrait révéler l'idée (s'il en existait une)
qu'on se faisait de Meslier Outre-Rhin [18 bis].

On peut toutefois constater que Fitger place son *Jean
Meslier* à contre-courant de l'évolution des intérêts de tout
un public. Sans doute, esthétiquement, son oeuvre s'attarde
dans un romantisme dépassé au théâtre par le mouvement
réaliste que stimulent alors les exemples français[19]; H. Wocke
explique par là l'échec relatif des derniers drames de Fitger.
Mais nous voulons parler ici d'un autre décalage, idéologique.
Son *Jean Meslier* pose - peut poser - le problème religieux et
celui de la libre-pensée dans le sillage du Kulturkampf à une
époque où Meslier est déjà considéré comme un vigoureux
contempteur de l'inégalité sociale et revendiqué comme un
précurseur par les historiens et les théoriciens du socialisme,
en Allemagne comme en France. Dès 1870, D.F. Strauss
affirmait que 'notre curé révolutionnaire est en même temps
communiste'[20]. 'Jean Meslier, communiste et révolutionnaire',
tel est le titre de l'article de Benoît Malon en 1888. C'est de ce
point de vue qu'il figure - en cette année 1894 - dans le manuel de

18.   Il s'agit de Job 1.21 (p. 6), Luc 16. 19–22 (p. 73) et Matthieu
       4. 8–9 (p. 100). Cet aperçu sur les traits religieux de la pièce de
       Fitger doit beaucoup à l'aide de Jean-Robert Armogathe.
18   H. Wocke (ouvr. cit.) mentionne, dans sa bibliographie, un article
bis.   paru dans le *Berliner-Börsen-Courier* (19 fèvrier 1901) que nous
       n'avons pu consulter.
19.   Voir dans Fernand Mossé, *Histoire de la littérature allemande* (Paris,
       1959) le chapitre sur la période considérée, p. 758–784 (780–784).
20.   'Le curé Meslier et son Testament' dans D.F. Strauss, *Voltaire*,
       traduction Louis Narval, Paris, 1876, p. 366.

Stegmann et Hugo et l'année suivante dans le tome I ('Die Vorläufer des neuren Sozialismus') de la *Geschichte* de Bernstein et Kautzky. Fitger a-t-il voulu maintenir le souvenir du curé incrédule dans une tradition libérale *contre* la tendance du mouvement socialiste à l'intégrer dans sa lointaine histoire? Avec lui, de toute manière, se survit une image de Meslier transmise par le 18ème siècle alors que l'édition de Rudolph Charles a commencé de faire découvrir (non sans simplification et naïveté) une toute autre dimension de l' œuvre du curé athée.

On ne peut savoir quelle est la part de l'ignorance et celle du choix délibéré dans le parti adopté par le dramaturge[21]. L'interprétation retenue lui a-t-elle paru la seule convenable pour une représentation scénique? Poser cette question conduit à s'interroger sur la validité et la possibilité d'une exploitation dramaturgique du cas Meslier.

Bornons-nous à constater que le drame (historique) du curé d'Etrépigny ne se prête pas facilement à une adaptation théâtrale. Le danger, que n'évite pas toujours Fitger, est de placer dans des monologues ou de longues tirades les explications propres à faire comprendre le personnage. Sans doute est-il excessif d'affirmer que dans cette pièce 'le héros se contente de parler, et toujours de parler'[22]. Mais c'est un fait qu'il soliloque beaucoup. Si, cependant, il joue son rôle dans une pièce assez bien menée, c'est, nous l'avons vu, au prix de deux infidélités majeures à la vérité historique. D'une part le héros décide de faire connaître son 'testament' et, à cause de

21. La Bibliothèque d'Etat de Brême (Staatsbibliothek, Bremen, Breitenweg 27) conserve deux dossiers de correspondance et papiers personnels de Fitger (renseignement communiqué par Jürgen Voss). On y trouverait peut-être des indications sur la genèse de la pièce, les intentions de son auteur et la réaction des spectateurs et des lecteurs.

22. Fritz Mauthner, *Der Atheismus und seine Geschichte im Abendlande* Stuttgart, et Berlin, 1922, III, p. 77. Cet ouvrage contient la seule étude sur Meslier où la pièce de Fitger fasse l'objet d'un commentaire.

cette décision, se trouve acculé au suicide, alors que le vrai
Meslier ne s'est pas démasqué et a confié seulement à son
manuscrit ses hésitations à garder le silence ('j'ai été cent et
cent fois sur le point de faire indiscrètement éclater mon indignation' (éd. cit., I, p. 33)). D'autre part, la contestation de
l'injustice n'est pas le fait du curé mais de personnages qui
s'opposent à lui comme le médecin et le meunier. Le conflit
dramatique qui donne à la pièce son mouvement dans les trois
premiers actes se joue entre Arnaud et le marquis. Le propre
drame de Meslier n'occupe pleinement que les deux derniers
actes, encore faut-il le secours d'une héroïne amoureuse pour
meubler l'acte IV.

Dans ces conditions, on peut se demander si une mise en
scène respectueuse des données historiques (biographiques et
textuelles) de l'aventure de Meslier est possible. Dans l'optique
d'une dramaturgie romantique (ou post-romantique) cultivant
l'intrigue et les effets de surprise, l'exemple de Fitger oblige
à répondre par la négative. Comment transposer en une série
de scènes spectaculaires ce qui a été vécu comme un drame
intérieur? ou, plus probablement, comme une expérience
paisible d'un brave curé de campagne partagée, selon une
organisation bien réglée, entre les devoirs de sa fonction et le
travail solitaire du philosophe? Mais il n'est pas interdit de
penser qu'un autre théâtre pourrait trouver dans la vie de Meslier
le sujet d'une interprétation fidèle et captivante.

DIDEROT ET LES SIX TENTATIONS DU MATÉRIALISME DES LUMIÈRES

J. Ehrard

E 18ème siècle français est-il matérialiste? Certainement pas, si l'on tient compte de l'emprise que conservent les croyances religieuses sur les mentalités collectives, et si l'on s'interdit de confondre 'Lumières' et 'Philosophie'. A considérer seulement celle-ci le matérialisme y apparaît encore comme extrêmement minoritaire : le théisme à la Rousseau, le déisme à la Voltaire, le christianisme ouvert et tolérant de Montesquieu sont, sans nul doute, plus représentatifs de l'attitude moyenne des esprits 'éclairés' que l'athéisme du groupe d'Holbach. Mais une chose est l'opinion dominante d'une époque - phénomène massif et visible -, une autre les forces et les tendances qui la travaillent en profondeur : à cet égard le plus fréquent est rarement le plus caractéristique. Statistiquement, le matérialisme du 18ème siècle n'est pas représentatif. On peut pourtant le considérer comme la pointe extrême du mouvement philosophique : les penseurs qui s'en réclament vont plus loin que la plupart des autres philosophes, mais ils vont dans le même sens. Ou plutôt dans deux grandes directions parallèles : la réduction du surnaturel au naturel, par la critique du miracle et de l'idée de Création ; la réduction du spirituel au matériel, selon le choix du déiste Voltaire utilisant Locke, en 1734, pour suggérer que Dieu a pu douer la matière de la faculté de penser.

Reste que ce double effort poussé par quelques-uns jusqu'aux dernières audaces aboutit à un échec. Malgré Helvetius et surtout d'Holbach, le 18ème siècle des Philosophes n'a pas réussi à construire la synthèse matérialiste vers laquelle le portait sa propre logique. Chacun a, bien entendu, le droit de méditer à sa guise et selon ses propres options sur cette impuissance. Plus modestement, l'historien n'a-t-il pas intérêt à analyser les conditions et le processus de l'échec ? Depuis Bachelard et Koyré l'histoire des sciences est autant et plus l'histoire des obstacles mentaux au développement positif du savoir que celle de ce savoir lui-même. Il me semble que l'histoire des idées peut avoir profit à s'interroger de façon analogue sur les difficultés internes de la pensée des Lumières dans ses voies plus hardies : tendance structurelle du mouvement philosophique, la recherche matérialiste du 18ème siècle porte en elle-même les raisons de son insuccès ; mais d'autre part elle n'est jamais aussi vivante que lorsqu'elle prend conscience des tendances contradictiores qui la travaillent. Sur ce double caractère l'oeuvre de Diderot nous apporte, je crois, un témoignage privilégié.

* * *

Il n'est pas question de résumer ici l'histoire du matérialisme français du 18ème siècle. Je me bornerai à rappeler qu'au tournant du siècle, passé l'âge de la marginalité - celui d'un Meslier et de quelques cercles érudits - il bénéficie du nouvel élan des sciences positives. Naguère celles-ci freinaient la pensée spéculative, en disant leurs propres limites et en avouant leur impuissance à rendre compte de trois données originelles : le mouvement, l'ordre du monde, la vie. Désormais les conséquences imprévues de la révolution newtonienne, tardivement assimilée, le critique de l'abstraction et de la stérilite des mathématiques développée par Buffon et Diderot, l'essor des sciences concrètes, géologie, chimie, physiologie, biologie naissante, enfin la prétention neuve de l'histoire naturelle à devenir vraiment l'histoire de la nature font que la science stimule au contraire l'audace de la pensée et qu'une tentative de systématisation devient possible. Les années 1760 et 1770 vont voir l'apogée du matérialisme des Lumières, avec cette conséquence importante que la bataille des idées y sera triangulaire : Voltaire contre Nonnotte, mais aussi contre la ' coterie holbachique'.

Dans l'histoire des idées les événements les plus intéressants ne sont cependant pas toujours ceux qui font le plus de bruit. En 1758 l'affaire du livre *De l'Esprit* avait été particulièrement retentissante ; après 1770 les assauts du groupe d'Holbach ne laissent guère de trève à la 'superstition', le *Dictionnaire philosophique,* les *Questions sur l'Encyclopédie* marquent publiquement que Voltaire combat désormais sur deux fronts, et soulignent la scission intervenue parmi les Philosophes : scission au moins aussi grave que la rupture entre Rousseau et les encyclopédistes. Mais la dénonciation bruyante du 'fatalisme' moderne, qu'elle soit déiste ou chrétienne, nous éclaire moins sur celui-ci que ne le fait la réflexion critique à laquelle Diderot le soumet plus discrètement, et de l'intérieur.

Les progrès de la recherche érudite, l'édition en projet des œuvres complètes du baron d'Holbach permettront peut-être un jour de rendre à Diderot ce qui lui revient, en particulier dans le *Système de la Nature.* Cependant, si l'étendue de sa collaboration reste à circonscrire, son adhésion aux thèmes essentiels du livre ne fait aucun doute. En 1774 il regrette que l'ouvrage ne soit pas 'aussi bien fait qu'il pouvait l'être', mais répète que *Dieu* et l'*âme so*nt des 'mots vides de sens' *(Commentaire sur Hemsterhuis,* in O.C., édit. Roger Lewinter, T. XI, 1971, p. 93 et *passim).* A la même époque il oppose la fermeté 'tout d'une pièce' du *Système* à la 'circonspection pusillanime'

dont lui paraît quelquefois marqué le livre *De l'Homme :*
'j'aime une philosophie claire, nette et franche, telle qu'elle
et dans le *Système de la Nature* et plus encore dans le *Bon
Sens' (Réfutation d'Helvétius, ibid.,* p. 592). Mais lorsqu'il
écrit pour lui-même il se garde d'adopter la forme du traité:
au didactisme trop voyant qui est commun à Helvétius et au
baron il préfère 'l'ordre sourd' du dialogue, du conte ou du
roman, voire le pointillisme du commentaire en marge
(Réflexions sur le livre 'De l'Esprit', ibid., t. III, 1970, p. 246).
Non par laisser-aller ni par coquetterie, mais par exigence
intellectuelle : le 'je ne prononce pas, j'interroge...' que lui
inspire l'ouvrage posthume d'Helvétius *(op. cit.,* p. 581) traduit
remarquablement l'attitude d'esprit qui est familière dans les
quinze ou vingt dernières années de sa vie; attitude interrogative,
heuristique - selon le mot de R. Mortier - qui justifie le recours
à des formes d'expression originales et à la fiction là où l'énoncé
abstrait se révèle inefficace. Il faut lire dans les textes que
Diderot compose dans cette période non pas l'abandon du
'fatalisme', ni le reniement d'un engagement ancien, mais
l'inventaire lucide des obstacles rencontrés, le bilan critique
des difficultés, ou plutôt des tentations que la pensée
matérialiste rencontre alors nécessairement.

* * *

Il est d'autant plus facile à d'Holbach de proposer une
cosmogonie matérialiste qu'il se contente le plus souvent
d'affirmations générales et ne se hasarde guère à parler du
comment de cette genèse universelle. Les problèmes de la vie
ne le retiennent guère et la science dont il se réclame est plutôt
la chimie - la vieille chimie des 'éléments' - qu'une biologie
à peine balbutiante. Or c'est le passage du non-vivant au vivant

qui, depuis les années 1750 où il méditait Maupertuis et Buffon, ne cesse de fasciner la réflexion de Diderot. On sait par quel audacieux renversement le géomètre du *Rêve de d'Alembert* fait disparaître la difficulté. Mais il ajoute lui - même: 'cela est dur à croire'. Indispensable, grandiose, l'hypothèse de sensibilité universelle - avec son corollaire paradoxal, l'idée de 'sensibilité inerte' - gêne l'esprit critique du philosophe : n'est-elle pas un retour aux vieilles doctrines animistes que Descartes et le rationalisme moderne croyaient avoir enterrées ? Curieux de la pensée des anciens théosophes, comme l'a montré J. Fabre[1], Diderot admire le génie d'un Paracelse ou d'un Van Helmont, mais il voudrait retenir leurs intuitions 'sublimes' sans céder à leurs 'extravagances' *(Encyclopédie,* art. 'Théosophes'). On le voit de même se prémunir contre une interprétation abusive du 'fatalisme' moderne. La comète qui trouble en 1769 les esprits les plus 'éclairés,' - Sophie, d'Holbach lui-même (Georges May, 'L'année de la Comète', in *Dix-huitième siècle,* n⁰ 1, 1969) - lui inspire une 'réflexion singulière' dont il fait part à Madame de Maux: 'c'est que l'athéisme est tout voisin d'une espèce de superstition presque aussi puérile que l'autre' *(Correspondance,* édit. G.Roth, t. IX, pp.94 et 154). On dirait que Diderot pressent l'aboutissement ultime du mouvement philosophique, le glissement des Lumières à l'illuminisme, qui marquera bientôt toute la fin du siècle.

Du moins résiste-t-il efficacement à cette deviation occultiste. Il échappe moins facilement à sa contre-partie, le pyrrhonisme, écueil sur lequel échouent au 18ème siècle, de La Mettrie à d'Holbach, les plus grandes audaces de pensée. En 1750 La Mettrie empruntait à Fontenelle l'image de la Nature-Opéra, mais pour conseiller de jouir du spectacle sans plus se

---

1.   'Diderot et les Théosophes', in C.A.I.E.F., n⁰ 13, 1962, pp. 203—222. Voir aussi, *ibid.,* pp. 189—202, J. Ehrard, 'Matérialisme et naturalisme : les sources occultistes de la pensée de Diderot'.

préoccuper d'une machinerie interdite au public *(Système d'*
Epicure, in *Œuvres,* Berlin, 1796, t. II, pp. 3–4). 'Nous sommes
de vraies taupes dans le chemin de la Nature', proclamait de
même l'*Homme Machine* (édit. Maurice Solovine, Paris, 1921,
p. 142). A son tour d'Holbach souligne la disproportion entre
la faiblesse de l'esprit humain et la puissance de la Nature:
disproportion d'autant plus grande que la Nature est mouvante
et que le changement - toujours imprévisible - est sa seule loi.
Parler à ce propos d'évolutionnisme, c'est oublier que pour
l'auteur du *Système de la Nature* l'évolution est inintelligible: 'Il
n'y a nulle contradiction à croire que les espèces varient sans
cesse, et il nous est aussi impossible de savoir ce qu'elles
deviendront que de savoir ce qu'elles ont été' (nouvelle édition,
Londres, 1771, t. I, Première partie, ch. $\overline{VI}$, p. 92).De même les
visions du *Rêve de d'Alembert* évoquent-elles moins Lamarck ou
Darwin que les *Métamorphoses* d'Ovide : un auteur que d'Holbach
cite du reste plus d'une fois *(ibid.,* ch. II, III etc.), pour renvoyer
à travers lui au pythagorisme. Dans un monde ou tout change
incessamment et où les espèces n'ont aucune réalité, même
provisoire, aucun savoir ne peut penser le devenir de la Nature
(J. Roger, *Les Sciences de la vie dans la pensée française du
XVIIIe siècle,* Paris, 1963, pp. 666–667). Dans un monde où
tout est possible, n'est-ce pas la science qui devient impossible ?
Des *Pensées* de 1754 (LVIII, 1) aux *Eléments de Physiologie*
cette inquiétude traverse toute la réflexion philosophique de
Diderot : 'Qu'aperçois-je ? Des formes, et quoi encore ? des
formes, j'ignore la chose. Nous nous promenons entre des
ombres, ombres nous-mêmes pour les autres, et pour nous'
(Eléments, édit. Jean Mayer, Paris, 1964, pp. 307–308).
Désenchantement justifié par les propos prêtés en 1769 à
l'homme de science qu'était Bordeu, propos dont le tour
conditionnel n'atténuait guère la gravité : 'les lois les plus cons-
tantes de la nature seraient interrompues par des agents
naturels' *(Rêve de d'Alembert,* édit. P. Vernière, Paris, 1951,

pp. 78–79). Quelle prise une nature *sans lois* offre-t-elle à la connaissance scientifique ? En dissolvant l'idée de loi naturelle le matérialisme des Lumières menace toute notion de rationalité et retourne donc contre elles-mêmes ses propres ambitions explicatives. Comme l'homme de Pascal, celui de Diderot et de son ami d'Holbach est perdu dans un univers opaque : l'effort matérialiste dévie en un naturalisme sceptique.

Or les difficultés sont encore plus pressantes sur le plan moral et social. Et là encore c'est Diderot qui explore le plus lucidement les antinomies du 'fatalisme'. Système humaniste, celui-ci soustrait l'homme à l'arbitraire du surnaturel, de même qu'il le disculpe de la faute originelle : ni grâce, ni péché, mais une nature qui 'ne fait les hommes ni bons, ni méchants' (D'Holbach *op. cit.* Première partie, ch. IX, p. 160). Mais, simultanément, le 'fatalisme' n'est-il pas la négation de tout humanisme? Si l'homme est immergé dans le Grand Tout, simple maillon de la chaîne des êtres, nul ne peut être différent de ce que la nature lui impose. Dans cette hypothèse il n'y a plus que des 'idiotismes moraux' et l'idée d'une morale universelle perd toute crédibilité : cela justifie le cynisme du Neveu de Rameau, en attendant les aphorismes destructeurs de Sade. Pour éviter cette conclusion le philosophe peut se tourner vers la société, faire confiance à 'l'education', c'est-à-dire à la pression du milieu ; mais une morale imposée ne risque-t-elle pas d'être oppressive ? Si la nature est amorale, la morale ne peut que lui faire violence ; quant à l'ordre social, son établissement et son maintien exigent l'intervention d'une 'puissance coactive' susceptible de *tempérer* les 'intérêts opposés', selon la formule que l'*Encyclopédie* retenait de Hobbes (art. 'Hobbisme'). Cependant, concéder à l'auteur du *Léviathan* que 'ce n'est pas la vérité, mais l'autorité qui fait la loi' *(ibid.)* revient à justifier l'existence d'un pouvoir sans frein. C'est ce que fait Helvétius lorsqu'au paradoxe de l'égalité des aptitudes - paradoxe qui autorise 'l'éducation' à prétendre obtenir de n'importe qui

n'importe quoi - il ajoute, au scandale de Diderot, une apologie
du 'gouvernement arbitraire' empruntée à Frédéric II *(Réfutation d'Helvétius, op. cit.,* p. 574). Non seulement Diderot
répète que Frédéric est un 'tyran', mais il finit par constater
que la fausse sagesse d'Helvétius rejoint la folie de La Mettrie :
tentation du pouvoir fort et amoralisme cynique, ce Charybde
et ce Scylla du matérialisme se confondent en un même écueil
puisque l'auteur de *L'Art de jouir* et de l'*Anti-Sénèque* a pu
trouver refuge auprès du roi de Prusse. D'où l'injuste diatribe de
l'*Essai sur Sénèque* (Livre Second, *Des Lettres de Sénèque,* VI)
par laquelle Diderot règle son compte à cet homme 'dissolu,
imprudent, bouffon, flatteur [...] , fait pour la vie des cours et la
faveur des grands'.

L'amoralisme a sa logique, qui scandalise le Philosophe.
Mais sur quel principe celui-ci fondera-t-il son culte de la
justice et de la vertu? Lui faudra-t-il revenir à un innéisme plus
ou moins honteux ? C'était l'attitude, inconséquente mais
facilement explicable, des pionniers du matérialisme des Lumières,
un Meslier ou un Fréret. Le second dénonçait dans les notions
de justice et d'injustice des idées 'absolument arbitraires et
dépendantes de l'habitude' *(Lettre de Thrasybule à Leucippe,*
Londres, 1768, p. 228), mais il n'en affirmait pas moins que
l'homme est naturellement sociable, en fonction du plaisir
'naturel' que lui procure le commerce de ses semblables (p.
220[2]). Quant à Meslier, il ne manquait pas d'opposer aux
'fausses maximes' des religions 'les règles de la probité, de la
justice et de l'équité naturelle' *(Œuvres complètes,* édit.
Jean Deprun, Roland Desné, Albert Soboul, Paris, t. I, 1970,
Avant-Propos, p. 35); et il condamnait avec véhémence

---

2.   La rédaction de ce texte remonterait à 1722. Son attribution à
      Fréret est généralement admise. Sur le double aspect de la morale
      de Fréret, voir J. Ehrard, *L'Idée de nature en France dans la
      première moitié du XVIIIe siècle,* Paris, 1963, pp. 383–384.

l'excès d'inégalité au nom du 'droit de la nature' *(ibid.,* t. II, 1971, *Sixième Preuve,* 42, p. 18), mais sans jamais se demander si cette 'nature' normative qu'il invoquait était bien la même que celle dont il donnait par ailleurs une définition matérialiste ... En fait l'ambiguité du mot permet constamment au 18ème siècle de réintroduire de façon subreptice à l'échelle de l'homme la finalité que l'on refuse au système général du monde. D'Holbach cultive lui aussi une équivoque bien commode lorsqu'il prétend asseoir sa morale 'sur les rapports éternels des choses' *(op. cit.,* Première partie, ch. IX, p. 146), c'est-à-dire l'*utilité* ou l'*intérêt* : car dans son abstraction cette morale utilitariste escamote les conflits possibles, sinon inévitables, entre les passions de chacun et la raison collective. Il *suffirait* de 'ramener l'homme à la nature' *(Préface)* pour retrouver une sorte d'harmonie préétablie entre l'intérêt individuel et les vertus sociales.

Le naturalisme des Lumières juxtapose volontiers à sa vision d'un univers déshumanisé et à son refus de toute cosmologie anthropomorphique une confiance inaltérable en l'ordre spontané des choses. Tout au plus l'éducateur, le législateur sont-ils appelés par d'Holbach à donner ici ou là un petit coup de pouce pour que dans les relations humaines l'intérêt bien compris l'emporte sur l'égoïsme aveugle : 'La raison, fruit de l'expérience, *n'est que* l'art de choisir les passions que nous devons écouter pour notre propre bonheur *(op. cit.,* Première partie, ch. XVII, p. 186 - Voir R. Mauzi, *L'Idée du bonheur au XVIIIème siècle,* 1960, ch. XII et XIII). On trouverait également chez Diderot plus que des traces d'un optimisme aussi rassurant que peu conséquent. Mais surtout sur le mode de l'utopie : il faut gagner la Nouvelle Cythère pour découvrir un pays où la pleine liberté sexuelle coïncide avec l'intérêt de l'espèce, la loi du plaisir avec les exigences de la procréation. Encore y subsiste-t-il quelques interdits: les 'voiles noirs'

et les 'voiles gris'. Bien plus, l'évocation utopique est prise en
charge par un dialogue qui en transforme l'euphorie en interro-
gation critique : sur le bonheur comparé du sauvage et du
civilisé, sur la responsabilité du mâle envers la femme, victime
née du libertinage masculin *(Supplément au voyage de Bougain-
ville,* édit. Dieckmann, Genève et Lille, 1955, pp. 61 *et seq.).* C'est
que selon le philosophe la nature humaine ne se définit pas
seulement par un ensemble d'appétits. 'Fut-il un temps où
l'homme put être confondu avec la bête? Je ne le pense pas'
(Réfutation d'Helvétius, op. cit. p. 591). L'erreur d'Helvétius
est de réduire l'humanité à l'animalité : il est faux que la
sensibilité humaine soit toute physique, 'qualité qui constitue
l'animal et non l'homme' *(ibid.,* p. 527) ; il est faux, en
conséquence, que la justice se réduise aux lois établies : c'est
elle au contraire, 'aveu préliminaire de la conscience', qui
fonde la loi (p. 590). Et lorsque Helvétius soutient sommairement que 'sentir, c'est juger', Diderot réplique : 'je suis homme,
et il me faut des causes propres à l'homme' (p. 490). Ce n'est
pas de sa part retour inavoué au spiritualisme, mais protestation
contre une philosophie simpliste qui ignore les caractères
distinctifs de la 'machine', ou plutôt de 'l'organisation'
humaine.

En s'orientant dans ses dernières années vers un néo-
stoïcisme à la fois 'fataliste' et volontariste Diderot suit sa
pente propre, et pas seulement celle de son siècle. Du *Rêve de
d'Alembert* à l'*Essai sur Sénèque,* en passant par les *Eléments de
Physiologie,* la *Réfutation* d'*Helvétius,* le *Paradoxe sur le
Comédien,* les observations qu'il rassemble sur le système
nerveux et les rôles respectifs du cerveau et du 'diaphragme',
aussi bien que sa réflexion esthétique, morale et politique
convergent vers un même objectif : assurer solidement un
humanisme matérialiste qui restitue à l'homme, avec sa nature
propre, une marge pratique d'autonomie dans la chaîne des
êtres et des événements : ni simple faisceau d'instincts, ni être

'qu'on modifie' *(Correspondance, op. cit.,* I, p. 214), mais être
qui *se* modifie. Par là se trouverait dépassée, avec toutes ses
conséquences fâcheuses, l'opposition statique entre *organisation*
et *éducation,* où s'enfermait en 1756 la pensée de Diderot. On
comprend qu'après 1770 la politique l'attire de plus en plus,
puisqu'elle est le moyen d'intégrer à l'histoire la petite marge
d'initiative que par la réflexion et la maîtrise de soi tout homme
véritable sait se donner. Dès lors il n'est plus question que le
sage se résigne à laisser aller simplement le monde comme il va,
quitte à chercher la sérénité dans le tonneau de Diogène,
comme en était tenté l'interlocuteur du Neveu de Rameau. La
sagesse est d'imiter plutôt Sénèque, d'accepter de demeurer
parmi les hommes, pour y jouer son rôle dans la cité. Mais en
prenant délibérément le risque de s'y compromettre Diderot ne
cède pas à une nouvelle illusion. Il ne croit pas que l'homme
parvienne jamais à dominer pleinement ni durablement le
flux des choses : ni par la pensée, ni par l'action. A la conclusion
désabusée des *Eléments de Physiologie* sur les limites de la
connaissance fait écho la page de l'*Essai sur Sénèque* qui met
en garde les insurgents d'Amérique contre ce qui menace
inévitablement leur révolution victorieuse. Cette société nouvelle
et juste, à peine édifée il la voit déjà détruite par l'inégalité et
par les ambitions de quelque César. Ainsi la mélancolie se glisse-
t-elle dans l'enthousiasme : seule une ironie lucide, l'ironie de
Jacques le fataliste, préserve finalement Diderot du pessimisme.

Le pessimisme : encore une tentation constante du
matérialisme au 18ème siècle. Meslier a beau proclamer que la
méchanceté des hommes vient des 'mauvaises lois', et prêcher
de toute sa vigueur la révolte et le tyrannicide *(Conclusion,*
t. III, 1972, p. 166), il dit aussi 'la vanité des choses humaines'
(p. 169) ; prophète d'un monde plus juste, il n'en trouve pas
moins, contre les 'Déicoles' son suprême argument dans
'la nécessité inévitable du mal' *(Huitième preuve,* 94 - dans le
titre -, *ibid.,* p. 120); car si 'excellente ouvrière' que soit la

nature *(Septième preuve,* 76, t. II, p. 356), elle ne peut se dispenser de mêler la mal au bien ; la maladie, la mort, la guerre sont nécessaires à son renouvellement et à son équilibre (t. III, *loc. cit.,* p. 121). De même le naturalisme astrologique d'un Boulainvilliers disait-il, à l'aube des Lumières, l'impuissance de l'homme devant la destinée *(Astrologie mondiale,* édit. R. Simon, Garches, 1949, p. 223), et son incapacité à sortir de 'l'âge de fer' (manuscrit de l'*Abrégé de l'Histoire universelle* cité par R. Simon, *Henri de Boulainviller...,* Paris, 1939, p. 265).

Thèmes archaïques, vestiges d'une autre mentalité? Mais à l'apogée du mouvement philosophique ils continuent à miner sourdement l'optimisme militant d'un d'Holbach. A l'apostrophe finale du *Système de la Nature* (Deuxième partie, ch. XIV, p. 443) répond d'avance l'affirmation que dans 'cette nature dépourvue de bonté comme de malice' (Première partie, ch. I, p. 6), l'homme est 'un instrument passif de la nécessité' *(ibid.,* ch. VI, p. 81), et qu'il 'n'a point de raison pour se croire un être privilégié' (p. 95). Enfin la confiance du baron en une 'Politique naturelle' qui aiderait l'humanité à sortir de l'enfance (p. 9) bute, elle aussi, sur la conviction qu'aucune société n'échappe à la loi des universelles vicissitudes *(Politique naturelle,* disc. IX, texte cité par P. Naville, *D'Holbach et la philosophie scientifique au XVIIIe siècle,* nelle édit., Paris, 1967, pp. 398–399). Pour d'Holbach, bien éloigné du messianisme de Condorcet, et dont l'esprit reste façonné par la vieille vision cyclique de l'histoire, la nature déjoue les efforts des hommes pour perpétuer leur bonheur. Le temps, qui produit tout, c'est un temps destructeur.

* * *

Toutes ces analyses, si sommaires qu'elles soient, nous permettent de dessiner l'espace intellectuel du matérialisme des Lumières : non pas un système clos, mais un ensemble qui ne parvient à trouver ni stabilité, ni cohérence, une configuration instable de forces centrifuges. Giraudoux parlait des 'cinq tentations' de La Fontaine. Nous avons analysé les six tentations permanentes de la pensée la plus hardie du 18ème siècle français : occultisme et scepticisme ; cynisme et despotisme; finalisme et pessimisme. Contre ces tentations par lesquelles il se nie lui-même, le matérialisme des Lumières se défend d'autant plus mal que leur émergence est inséparable de son développement. Il serait vain de s'en tenir ici à un catalogue superficiel de 'contradictions'. Ce qu'il faut comprendre, c'est le mouvement qui les engendre, qu'elles freinent et dévient à chaque moment de sa trajectoire, mais qui néanmoins les emporte, dans son unité contradictoire, vers un point M inaccessible, situé quelque part à l'horizon de la Philosophie. C'est pourquoi les oscillations de la pensée de Diderot, si souvent relevées avec ironie ou fausse indulgence, ne sont pas le fait de la girouette de Langres. Diderot n'est pas grand *malgré* ses contradictions, mais bien plutôt *par* elles. C'est par elles que ce génie lucide et inventif résume, exprime et dépasse son temps.

FALSE ATTRIBUTIONS OF THE
LETTRES PERSANES

A.W. Fairbairn

A S is known, when Montesquieu was ready to publish his *Lettres persanes* he prudently took all requisite measures in order to hide its true authorship. His secretary, the Abbé Duval, was sent off to Amsterdam, where, with due discretion, he arranged for its publication by Jacques Desbordes, a second generation Huguenot of the dispersion[1]. Since Desbordes kept his own involvement secret, the work appeared - in the spring or early summer of 1721 - not merely anonymously but with a title page bearing the almost transparently fictitious details *à Cologne, chez Pierre Marteau,* a figure who has elicited from Pierre-Gustave Brunet the comment: 'Il n'est aucun typographe imaginaire dont le nom ait été aussi souvent employé que celui-ci'.[2]

Thus abetted by that of his publisher, Montesquieu's initial self-effacement proved secure against even the most favourably placed of the preternaturally knowledgeable literary journalists. This is evident from the notices of the *Lettres persanes* contained in three of the numerous periodicals printed in Amsterdam: the *Maendelyke Uittreksels, of Boekzael der geleerde*

1. See R. Shackleton, *Montesquieu: A Critical Biography*, Oxford, 1961, p. 27.
2. *Imprimeurs imaginaires et libraires supposés*, Paris, 1866, p. 112.

Werelt of July and August 1721 (xiii. 27–47, 224–8); Jean Le Clerc's *Bibliothèque ancienne et moderne* of 1721 (xv. 461–3); and the *Mémoires historiques et critiques* of 15 January 1722 (I. 11–22), whose editors were Denis-François Camusat and Antoine-Augustin Bruzen de La Martinière.[3] Another such work of Dutch provenance, the *Journal littéraire* of The Hague, which suffered interruption for much of the 1720s but appraised the second edition of the *Lettres persanes* in its belated coverage of the earlier part of the decade (xi. 446–64; xii. 280–304), referred vaguely to 'l'auteur', as did Marivaux in the *huitième feuille* (dated 8 September 1722) of his *Spectateur français*. Likewise, John Ozell, in the introduction to his translation, which appeared at London in 1722, as *Persian Letters*, could write, clearly in equal ignorance of the author's identity but neatly making a virtue of necessity:

> I shall not pretend to inform the Public of the Name of the Author; if I knew I wou'd bury it in eternal Silence. He has threaten'd us with so severe a Penalty if we enquire him out, namely, that of being silent from the moment he is discovered, that the World would have no great Obligation to any body's impertinent Curiosity, that shou'd make them pay for so trifling an information with so invaluable a Loss.

Ozell's allusion was, of course, to Montesquieu's own introduction, which, if now taken for granted as a far from disingenuous explanation of the President's preference for anonymity, must at the time have enhanced the piquant mysteriousness of the work, whose author held out the promise of further letters, but only

> à condition que je ne serai pas connu: car, si l'on vient à savoir mon nom, dès ce moment je me tais. Je connois une femme qui marche assez bien, mais qui boite dès qu'on la regarde. C'est assez des défauts de l'ouvrage, sans que je présente encore à la critique ceux de ma personne. Si l'on savoit qui je suis, on diroit: 'Son livre jure avec son caractère; il devroit employer son temps à quel-

3. E. Hatin, *Bibliographie historique et critique de la presse périodique française*, Paris, 1866, pp. 40–1.

que chose de mieux: cela n'est pas digne d'un homme grave.'
Les critiques ne manquent jamais ces sortes de réflexions, parce
qu'on les peut faire sans essayer beaucoup son esprit.

Understandably, following the immediate success of the
Lettres persanes, Montesquieu's compatriots, far from imitating
Ozell's refusal even to attempt to pierce his incognito, must
have been quick to seize upon this one meagre clue to his
identity. Nor was it unnatural, in view of the outstanding
quality of the work, that their first supposition should be that,
whatever staid position in society explained his present reticence,
here was an already practised and established author. Apparently
some rumours to this effect had been developing during the
latter months of 1721; for, by the turn of the year, the
Mémoires historiques et critiques, after quoting amply from this
third paragraph of the introduction, could conclude with the
following animadversion on its final sentence:

> Il est vrai qu'il ne faut pas beaucoup d'esprit pour remontrer
> à un Chanoine Regulier (1) qu'il pourroit s'occuper à quelque
> chose de meilleur qu'à composer des Lettres Persannes: mais
> surement il y auroit beaucoup de jugement à donner cette
> leçon, et dans le siècle où nous vivons, on essaïe encore moins son
> jugement que son esprit.

> (1)   On attribuë communément les Lettres Persannes à celui
> qui nous a donné le *Système du cœur* et *les Agremens du
> langage.*

Those whose friendships or special interests had not made
them privy to the authorship of the two works mentioned in
this footnote (p. 22) would have required instead a good general
knowledge of the literary scene in order easily to identify the
regular canon (and thus the religious) who had allegedly abused
his monastic leisure by writing Persian letters. Admittedly, the
first edition of the earlier of the two works had seemed to pose
no serious problem of authorship. Published at Paris in 1704 as
*Systeme du cœur ou Conjectures sur la maniere dont naissent
les différentes affections de l'ame, principalement par rapport*

aux objets sensibles, its title page had also borne the words
'par Monsieur de Clarigny'. In keeping with this, the accom-
panying *privilège du roi* had been granted to 'le Sieur de
Clarigny'. However, this authorial indication had not been
retained in its second edition, which accordingly became an
anonymous work (albeit with an 'epître' by 'de Cxxx') when
it re-emerged in 1708, again at Paris but from a different
publisher, as *Systeme du cœur ou la Connoissance du cœur
humain.* Moreover, the other work specified in the footnote had
itself appeared anonymously. Entitled *Les Agrémens du langage
reduits à leurs principes,* it had been published at Paris in 1718.
The one intrinsic clue to its authorship had been that section of
its preface which discreetly hinted that the writer had also
been responsible for the *Système du cœur.*

Among the both uninitiated and ill-informed, those who,
on perusing the review which inaugurated the *Mémoires
historiques et critiques,* had access to the 1704 edition of the
Système du cœur, may well have concluded that the *Lettres
persanes* were being widely imputed to an ecclesiastic named
Clarigny. By contrast, to any who had recourse to the second
edition of the *Système du cœur* or to *Les Agréments du langage,*
or even to both, the putative author of the *Lettres persanes*
would have remained an anonymous figure.

There were no doubt others who, as sedulous readers of the
periodical literature of the time, felt immediately enlightened
as to the reputed author of the *Lettres persanes,* while yet
having no close acquaintance with either of the two works
mentioned. For it was from a periodical that the only public
information then available respecting the real identity of their
author had emerged. Thus although the *Journal des savants* for
November 1718, while accepting their common authorship in
its review of *Les Agréments du Langage,*[4] had referred merely

4.   Amsterdam edition, pp. 547–58.

to 'l'ingénieux anonyme', a few months later *L'Europe savante*
could be much more specific. Its issue for April 1719 had ended
a notice of the work by stating: 'On l'attribuë à M. l'Abbé DE
GAMACHE, qui a déja donné au Public le Sisteme *du Cœur'*
(viii. 204). More emphatically, the index to this issue had baldly
affirmed, *s.v. Agremens du langage:* 'M.l'Abbé de Gamache en
est l'auteur'. With this information, it would not be difficult to
identify him further as Etienne-Simon de Gamaches, a member
of the Patres Cruciferi *(pères croisiers),* an Augustinian order
whose Paris house, of which Sainte-Croix de la Bretonnerie was
the church, stood in the street of that name.[5] As the editors of
the *Mémoires historiques et critiques* evidently well knew, and
hoped their readers would know, Abbé de Gamaches - like all
French Crosiers of the time - had the formal title of *chanoine
régulier.*

Gamaches having gained a certain personal reputation
from his two works, notwithstanding the pseudonymity of the
one and the anonymity of the other, obviously it was to those
familiar with them that the *Mémoires historiques et critiques*
had especially addressed its cryptic comment on the authorship of the *Lettres persanes.* Paradoxically, among those who,
in 1722, could thus have named the author of the *Système du
cœur* and *Les Agréments du langage* was, in all likelihood,
Montesquieu himself. He not merely owned both works[6] but
clearly knew thoroughly at least the *Système du cœur,* as
witness the *Pensée* in which he nicely epitomizes what proved

5.   Germain Brice, *Nouvelle description de la ville de Paris,* 8e
      édition, Paris, 1725, II, 82. On the order to which Gamaches
      belonged see J.M. Hayden, 'The Crosiers in England and France',
      Clairlieu, 20 (1964), 91–109. On Gamaches himself A.Pizzorusso
      has written perceptively. See *La Régence,* edited by H. Coulet,
      Paris, 1970, pp. 66–72.
6.   *Catalogue de la bibliothèque de Montesquieu,* edited by L. Desgraves,
      Geneva and Lille, 1954, p. 114 and p. 133.

to be Gamaches's perennial attitude to the human condition.[7] Although Montesquieu's library catalogue does not list the *Mémoires historiques et critiques,* its review of the *Lettres persanes* may possibly have come to his attention. After all, despite the stoic opening paragraph of his introduction, and his strictures on the literary journalists in Letter 108, it seems that Montesquieu was, like almost any new author, hypersensitive to how his work had been received. For it is surely no accident that the only volume of the *Bibliothèque ancienne et moderne* which he appears to have possessed was that containing Jean Le Clerc's notice of the *Lettres persanes.*[8] It is by no means inconceivable, therefore, that its attribution to Gamaches became known to Montesquieu, who, if not abashed or even mortified by this, must at the least have been somewhat taken aback.

Easily though Montesquieu himself could have comprehended this first recorded guess at the authorship of the *Lettres persanes,* both the obliqueness and the ambiguity of the footnote in the *Mémoires historiques et critiques* were to the advantage of the otherwise ill-used Gamaches, who had reason to be thankful not to have been mentioned by name. He was, on balance, benefited too by the well nigh contemporaneous appearance of the first work to bear his name. Albeit dated 1721, this *Système du mouvement, par M. de Gamaches, Chanoine Regulier de Sainte Croix de la Bretonnerie* was presumably published after the turn of the year, in that its

7. *Pensée* 2079, in *Œuvres complètes* (Bibliothèque de la Pléiade), I, 1542. Compare *Système du cœur:* 'Les plus belles liaisons languissent avec le temps, quelque précaution que l'on prenne pour les garantir de cette dure fatalité' (p. 245); and *Système du philosophe chrétien,* Paris, 1746; 'Par quelle fatalité faut-il que j'ignore ce que j'aurois, ce semble, le plus d'intérêt de connoître' (p. 11).

8. Desgraves, p. 182.

privilège had not been registered until 24 December. Though cognate with the *Système du cœur,* and therefore a further clue to his authorship of both it and *Les Agréments du langage,* this scientific treatise, which the *Mémoires de Trévoux* reviewed in May 1722 (pp. 845–66), was timely evidence that Gamaches had not recently turned towards a very different type of literature.

Although the chain of reasoning which came to link Gamaches with the *Lettres persanes* cannot be reconstructed with any precision, it is possible to discern the more salient plausibilities which may have led to the work's attribution to him. Certainly the glimpse in its introduction of a writer who had a strong motive for wishing to remain anonymous well fitted someone such as a regular canon. And had not Gamaches shown a definite reluctance to avow his publications ? More specifically, did not their novelty, their ingeniousness, and their semi-philosophical character betoken a kinship with the *Lettres persanes*? Might not even the subtle diversities of its elegant prose be intended as an exemplification of those stylistic categories so confidently propounded, three years earlier, in *Les Agréments du langage*? Suggestive parallels such as these, emanating from an area of the republic of letters in which the fruits of Gamaches's literary avocation were known and respected, would not be lost on the general reading public. On the contrary, it would tend to be inordinately receptive to them, so keen must have been its desire to penetrate so challenging an anonymity as that of the author of the *Lettres persanes.*

Whether this attribution stemmed from some such *bona fide* hypothesizing or - less probably but not impossibly - from some Regency wit's perpetration of an ingenious *canard* at the expense of Gamaches, it emergence into print was bound to cause some repercussions of its own. Demonstrably this was so in Germany, where the prestige of French culture had created an imperative demand for up-to-date information about the literary scene in France. Among the agencies which satisfied this need was Johann Gottlieb Krause's *Neue Zeitungen von gelehrten Sachen,* a Leipzig periodical whose issue for 21 May 1722 summarized the contents of the first number of the *Mémoires historiques et critiques,* including its comment on the authorship of the *Lettres Persanes.* This Krause mediated to his compatriots as follows:

> Der Verfasser sagt, es brauche nicht viel Scharffsinnigkeit, zu sagen, dass ein *Canonicus Regularis* was bessers thun könne, als solche Briefe schreiben, aber diese Lection würde doch judiciös seyn. Dabey wird in der Anmerckung erinnert, dass man diese *Lettres* dem *Autori* des *Système du Cœur* und der *Agremens du langage** zuschreibe (pp. 406—7).

> *Der *Autor* hiervon soll *de Clarigny* heissęn, wie in unsern Zeitungen von 1718 p. 797 erinnert worden.

Unfortunately for Krause, his endeavour to eludicate the French original, by adding in a footnote the name under which the 1704 edition of the *Système du cœur* had appeared, was less than helpful to his readers. Even the more discriminating among them would be likely to associate the *Lettres persanes* with the name de Clarigny, *a fortiori* if, conscientiously consulting the *Neue Zeitungen* for 1718 they had encountered there a more positive statement of 'Herr de Clarigny's' responsibility for both the *Système du cœur* and *Les Agréments du langage.* And so, by an ironical coincidence, May 1722, which saw a review of the first work to bear Gamaches's name, was marked in Germany by the virtual ascription of an immeasurably greater work to his long discarded pseudonym.

In France, meanwhile, this rumour concerning the authorship of the *Lettres persanes,* far from being strengthened by its emergence into print, would seem to have been hastened to its natural death. Its verisimilitude mocked by the appearance of Gamaches's *Système du mouvement,* it became even more fossilized - so the absence of any subsequent mention (let alone rebuttal) of it would suggest - in what was soon the decent obscurity of the *Mémoires historiques et critiques,* which itself proved an ephemera. Thus the way was left clear for that more informed speculation by which the name of Montesquieu entered the mainstream of French literary history; and by which its bearer, gratified but not sated by the plaudits he had received in Bordeaux, went on to enjoy the more covetable delectation of being lionized in the capital. As the 1720s progressed, with the Regency ending and the lamentable intermezzo of Monsieur le Duc giving way to the Fleury era, Montesquieu had as much reason to be satisfied with the nature of his emergent connection with the *Lettres persanes* as with the corpus of always anonymous editions which was attesting its continuing success. Confirmed more and more in his position as its recognised - but not its avowed - author, he enjoyed a status which maximised the advantages, while minimising the drawbacks, of having written so delightful yet so iconoclastic a work. Nor, unlike the hapless Gamaches, was he exposed to the embarrassment of having his authorship of it publicly asserted for him in print. Even in the well-informed Paris bookseller and bibliographer Gabriel Martin's *Bibliotheca fayana* of 1725 (p. 330) - a sale catalogue in which the known authors of anonymous works were generally identified - and in his *Catalogue de la bibliotheque du chasteau de Rambouillet* of 1726 (p. 275), the *Lettres persanes* was unobtrusively listed as an innominate publication.

At length, however, Montesquieu's complacent perpetuation of a situation in which he neither avowed nor disavowed his authorship of the *Lettres persanes* threatened to become a serious liability to him. The death of Sacy on 26 October 1727 having created a vacancy in the Academy, Montesquieu offered himself as a candidate, notwithstanding his unflattering description of that body in the seventy-third *Lettre persane.* This letter, both embarrassing in itself and now maliciously set off against the easily exploitable anonymity of the work, constituted the most obvious weakness of his position, as Marais informed Bouhier on 24 November: 'On lui dit; "Si vous avez fait les *Lettres Persanes,* il y en a une contre le corps de l'Académie et ses membres. Si vous ne les avez pas faites, qu'avez-vous fait?' [9] Although, in the event, the horns of this dilemma proved a less pointed threat to Montesquieu's ambitions than did Fleury's declared animus against the *Lettres persanes,* particularly letter 22,[10] his adroit appeasement of the cardinal - the *sine qua non* of his election, by majority vote, on 20 December - did not deter his enemies within the Academy from continuing to make whatever capital they could out of the dubieties inherent in what was still his merely implicit claim to have written the *Lettres persanes.* Even during the ceremony of his installation, on 24 January 1728, the new Academician was unwelcomingly reminded of this anomaly in his position. Having made his *discours de réception,* he then had to listen with silent anger as Mallet, in his capacity as *directeur,* delivered a reply which verged on a riposte, its acidulous leitmotif being the anonymity of the *Lettres persanes.*[11] Nor was this the only, or even the most grievous, post-election manifestation of *odium academicum* of which he was the object. Four days later, another member, Valincourt, writing to Jean Bouhier of Dijor. ..aself recently installed in a *fauteuil académique*), reporte... i.Iontesquieu's adverse reaction to Mallet's words, and then continued:

> ... mais il y a bien pis les Ennemis du Candidat qui avoient voulu l'exclure de l'Academie comme Auteur des lettres persannes qui sont en effet un abominable ouvrage disent maintenant qu'il

9. *Journal et mémoires de Mathieu Marais,* edited by M. de Lescure, Paris, 1863–8, III, 501.
10. Shackleton, pp. 87–8.
11. *Recueil des harangues prononcées par messieurs de l'Académie françoise,* IV, Paris, 1735, pp. 475–9.

n a pas eu l'esprit de les faire mais qu'elles sont d'un homme de
Bordeaux qui les lui a données pour s'en faire honneur Si cela se
verifie ce sera bien le contraire de l'aventure de Virgile
hos ego versiculos feci tulit alter honores
car il faudra quil dise je ne les ay pas faites et jen ay eu toute
l'infamie voila ce que cest que la republique des Lettres et
que la nation des beaux Esprits Je voudrois bien quil ny eut
point dans le Royaume dautres diferens ni dautres interrests
plus dificiles a Concilier car quoy que je ne sois pas mechant
ce me seroit une espece de consolation durant mon rhumatisme
de voir ces M$^{rs.}$ la se dechirer les oreilles les uns aux autres
Vale et me ama.[12]

Unlike the patently *bona fide* ascription of the *Lettres
persanes* to Gamaches, the allegation that a fellow Bordelais had
complaisantly given the work to Montesquieu was a false attribution in more than just the factual sense of the adjective.
Little short of a deliberate untruth, its only cogent testimony
was to the brazen *volte-face* executed by his enemies, who,
perversely transmogrifying his fault of commission into one
of omission, were now intent on branding him as a literary
imposter. Knowing full well the circumstances in which this
charge had been laid, Valincourt presumably mooted the possibility of its subsequent verification more for the sake of introducing an apt quotation from Virgil than through any real
belief in his new colleague's guilt. To judge by the tone of his
concluding comments on this latest Academy election, which
he implicitly likened to a storm in a teacup, his more considered
judgement was that it had been a thoroughly personalized
episode, studded with ill-tempered, if not wild, accusations. The
best that can be said in favour of the blackballing faction's final
thrust at Montesquieu is that it did not do violence to all
verisimilitude. If then adduced, the name of Jean-Jacques Bel,
one of the President's closest Bordeaux friends and himself an
author of independent outlook, might well have obfuscated, if
only for a time, the true authorship of the *Lettres persanes,*

12. Paris, Bibliothèque Nationale, fonds français, 24420, ff. 442–442vo.

particularly as his advice had perhaps been sought during the composition of the work.[13] But whether Montesquieu's enemies were prepared to venture so precise a calumny is an open question.

What is indubitable is that, having secured the status of an Academician, Montesquieu had little need to fear any repetition of this mean-spirited attempt to cheat him out of the honour of having composed the *Lettres persanes*. Although its formal anonymity, in edition after edition, was to remain inviolate until the mid-century, the early 1730s provided abundant testimony to his continuing enjoyment of what was by now the strongest possible *de facto* recognition as its author. In 1732 he was expressly named - and eulogized - as such by Saint-Hyacinthe, whose acquaintance he had made during his visit to England.[14] And in 1734, on the occasion of his second major publication, the *Considérations sur les Romains,* its two Amsterdam editions bore title pages whose details, if read together, amounted to a weighty indication of his responsibility for the earlier work. The second issue of that published by Jacques Desbordes carried the initials L.P.D.M., an abbreviation which concealed, but perhaps also revealed, *le président de Montesquieu.* Complementing this, Pierre Mortier's edition advertised itself as being 'par l'auteur des *Lettres persanes',* a recommendation reiterated in the London and Dublin editions of the English translation, which was published later that year. In France meanwhile, there had been a heightened sense of expectancy among those aware of the forthcoming appearance of the *Considérations.* On 28 December 1733, the abbé Granet, after reporting to the marquis de Caumont that 'le Président de Montesquieu fait imprimer en Hollande des réflexions sur la décadence de l'empire romain', went on to remark: 'Comme il a

13. Shackleton, p. 27.
14. Shackleton, pp. 134–5.

l'art de traiter d'une manière originale les matieres les plus
communes, je suis persuadé qu'il y aura des idées neuves dans
cet ouvrage.'[15] Similarly, another of Caumont's correspondents,
d'Anfossy, writing from Versailles on 7 July 1734, when the
Paris version was about to go on sale, ended his allusion to it
by observing: 'Il est de Mr de Montesquieu auteur des lettres
persanes, et l'on doit s'attendre a des choses singulieres et
hardies'.[16] This confident prediction - and assuredly that of
Granet - shows clearly that the President's fellow countrymen
had ceased to harbour even lingering doubts about his authorship of the *Lettres persanes.* So too do some of the immediate
post-publication reactions to the *Considérations,* among them
that of Le Blanc - an acquaintance of Montesquieu - who, in a
letter dated 20 July, confided in Bouhier: 'Je ne crois pas qu'il
lui fasse autant d'honneur que les Lettres Persanes'.[17] Nor was
it long before the *Neue Zeitungen von gelehrten Sachen* made
amende honorable for the imbroglio inherent in its unfortunate
linking of 'Herr de Clarigny' with the *Lettres persanes.* In its
issue for September 1734 it reported that there was already
available an English version of the *Considérations,* 'davon der
Herr President Montesquieu Autor ist, welcher auch die Lettres
Persanes ehemals geschrieben hat' (p. 659).

This German epitome of Montesquieu's literary career
testifies to his remarkably sure-footed ascent from provincial
obscurity to European renown. Fêted in Bordeaux, in Paris,
and on the Grand Tour, he had become, *pari passu,* a member
of the French Academy, the Etruscan Academy of Cortona,
and the Royal Society. All this had devolved to him, essentially,
from the unabating popularity of a work whose title page had

15.   Avignon, Muséum Calvet, fonds Calvet, 2375, f. 331.
16.   Avignon, fonds Calvet, 2278, f. 154.
17.   H. Monod-Cassidy, *Un Voyageur-philosophe au XVIIIe siècle,*
       Cambridge, Massachusetts, 1941, p. 213.

yet to bear his name or even, in its French editions, that of an existent publisher. Nevertheless, he had not altogether escaped the vexations which can await the anonymous author of what proves to be a best seller. Having opted for self-concealment after resolving to publish the *Lettres persanes,* he could not, of course, complain at his admiring readers' eagerness to ferret out his identity. Even so, its attribution to a member of a religious order was a thoroughly paradoxical development, as was the embroilment created by Gamaches's use of the pseudonym Clarigny. But at least these were honest errors, and therefore not on a par with the calculated ascription of the work to an 'homme de Bordeaux', whose obtrusion in 1728 was palpably an act of spite on the part of the defeated faction in a hard-fought Academy election.

Although there were no subsequent misattributions of the work, to which the Amsterdam edition of the *Observations sur les écrits modernes* confidently alluded in 1735 as 'les inimitables *Lettres Persanes* du President de M...' (i. 235), it was not until the evening of his life that the name Montesquieu appeared on its title page. Breaching an anonymity which the continental and English book trade had respected, Robert Urie of Glasgow published an edition of the English version - there is a copy in the Bodleian, with the pressmark Vet. A 5 f. 1771 - which he described as 'Translated from the French of M. de Secondat, Baron de Montesquieu, Author of the Spirit of Laws'. Not inappropriately, this edition is dated 1751, the year of publication of the first volume of the *Encyclopédie.*

WHO WERE THE *IDÉOLOGUES?*

B.G. Garnham

N his article 'Who were the *Philosophes?* [1] Professor Lough raises, among many others, the following questions:

> ... one is bound to ask where one draws the line between *Philosophes* and *Idéologues*. So far in our list of *Philosophes* we have applied the term to two men as far apart in age as Voltaire who was twenty-one when Louis XIV died and Condorcet who was in the prime of life when the Revolution broke out in 1789. Men like Cabanis (b. 1757) and Destutt de Tracy (b. 1754) were only a dozen or so years younger than Condorcet and yet they generally bear a different label. And what of Volney (b. 1757) whose *Les Ruines* was published in 1791?

It is to these problems that this article is addressed, problems made all the more complex because the *Idéologues* are conscious of their rôles as inheritors of the Enlightenment, and see their contribution to philosophy as the development of ideas and attitudes expressed throughout the eighteenth century. They approach these ideas and attitudes in a critical spirit and impose upon them a new perspective, and so it becomes possible to draw a line, albeit tentatively, between *Philosophes* and *Idéologues*. But there are other considerations to be borne in mind when asking 'Who were the *Idéologues*?', for this is

1. *Studies in Eighteenth-Century French Literature presented to Robert Niklaus*, Exeter, 1975, pp. 139—150.

clearly a question of a different order from that raised by
Professor Lough. The contribution of the *Philosophes* to the
history of ideas cannot be doubted, and if the exact composition
of their ranks is a matter for debate, the term represents at least a
clear, if generalised image. The same is not true of their
successors. History has not been kind to them, and their works
have tended to arouse little real interest. One is therefore led
necessarily to discuss why philosophy took the course it did
during the Revolution, a course which, in more recent times,
has often been neglected and sometimes scorned.

Idéologie, technically speaking, did not exist before 1796:
it was in that year that Destutt de Tracy coined the name of the
'new science' (a name he declared to be 'très sage') in a
mémoire read before the second class of the Institut. By
Idéologie he meant, quite specifically, 'la science qui traite des
idées ou perceptions, et de la faculté de penser ou percevoir';
rejecting such names as *métaphysique* and *psychologie,* he
preferred *Idéologie* which, as the literal translation of the phrase
science des idées, demonstrated clearly that the science had
as its object an understanding of man through the analysis of his
intellectual faculties. It was, in Tracy's view, a fitting name for
the studies which in effect already occupied the first section of
the second class of the Institut and which were officially referred
to as *analyse des sensations et des idées.* In his *mémoire* Tracy
envisaged a three-part programme: 'état présent de la science
de la pensée; perfectionnement des instruments qu'elle emploie,
les langues; plan d'observations et d'expériences nouvelles' and
added: '... voilà, citoyens, ce que la philosophie attend de vous,
et ce qu'elle ne peut espérer que de vous'.[2] In the Institut the
science had a natural home, and, Tracy maintained, if its

2.   Destutt de Tracy, 'Mémoire sur la faculté de penser', *Mémoires de
      l'Institut national, Classe des sciences morales et politiques,* Paris,
      1798–1804, 5 vol., I, 320.

practitioners were prepared to apply the same methodology demonstrated by the Académie des sciences physiques et mathématiques after its formation in 1666, before long there would appear 'un Newton pour la science de la pensée' to enrich *Idéologie* with new discoveries and truths and render it increasingly able to contribute to the well-being and happiness of men.

Idéologie was conceived, then, as an academic discipline, and the term *idéologue* should be applied initially to those who, persuaded that all knowledge is derived through the senses, undertake an analysis of the mind and who seek an accurate account of the various phenomena of human consciousness. Tracy himself divides the science into two branches, the rational and the physiological; both branches place emphasis less upon the source of the data of experience and more upon the mechanisms of the mind receiving them. In this way the *Idéologues* are firmly in the tradition of Condillac, whom they acknowledge to be the true founder of their science.

All *Idéologues* are enthusiastic concerning the spirit and aims of Condillac's philosophy. They have the same priorities, in which the primary need is one to establish the way in which the mind gains knowledge and makes judgements, and they value Condillac above all as the first philosopher to have undertaken a study of the human mind in which its diverse operations, its limits and its capabilities are examined in detail, and in which causes and effects are carefully investigated, so that the chain leading from simple perception to complex thought can be established. Condillac was the first to pay attention to the multitude of different impressions which are made upon the human mind by the perception of external reality, and in his analysis of these impressions, and in his differentiations between them, he had raised the fundamental questions on which all further enquiry must be based. He may not have produced solutions to all the problems, but in his very treatment of them

he had opened up new avenues of investigation. Tracy affirms
that Condillac created *Idéologie* and insists that he himself is
merely continuing the work of Condillac, seeking to provide a
complete and systematic account of truths scattered throughout the earlier philosopher's works.

It is clear, however, that warm though such praise might
be, it is Condillac's method which *Idéologues* value, for they
are not without reservations when they come to examine his
ideas closely. They are critical on many points of detail, and
there is a fundamental difference which Bréhier characterises as
follows:

> L'idéologie proprement dite est une analyse des facultés
> humaines de même contenu mais d'une inspiration bien différente
> de celle de Condillac, avec qui il ne faut pas confondre les
> idéologues, si souvent qu'ils s'en réclament. Tracy n'est pas un
> 'généalogiste' qui cherche la genèse des facultés et l'on ne trouve
> rien chez lui de l'analyse réductrice du *Traité des Sensations.*[3]

Condillac, together with many eighteenth-century philosophers,
felt that the explanation of any phenomenon lay in its origins,
and consequently his work is dominated by his search for first
principles. Just as Newton's theory of gravitation sought to
explain all the phenomena of motion, so Condillac hoped to
find the basis of human understanding, and the laws governing
its development and assimilation of ideas, in a single principle.
Tracy and other *Idéologues* remain constant in defending the
notion of a series of basic and independent faculties in man.
Bréhier justifiably concludes that in this approach they show
a marked preference for observation of tangible reality over an
analysis which is fundamentally arbitrary, and Le Roy describes
the approach of the *Idéologues* as follows:

> Au lieu de poursuivre un idéal d'unité et d'identité logiques,
> on voulut apprécier la variété et l'hétérogénéité des faits, tels que

3. E.Bréhier, *Histoire de la philosophie*, Paris, Alcan, 1932, 2 vol.,
II, 602.

> l'observation les montre. On songea moins à une systématisation
> rigoureuse qu'à des descriptions exactes serrant le réel d'aussi
> près que possible.[4]

It is Destutt de Tracy who provides the most comprehensive
account of rational *Idéologie*. It is to be found in the various
mémoires he read before the second class of the Institut and,
more particularly, in his major work, *Eléments d'Idéologie*
(published 1801–1818), which was originally conceived as a
textbook for the course of general grammar in the écoles
centrales. Its different parts include the analysis of the four
faculties which he sees as fundamental to man (sensation,
memory, judgement and will) and the way in which these
contribute to the gaining of knowledge and the conception of
abstract and complex thought. Another account of rational
Idéologie, with particular emphasis upon the relationship between
thought and language and the need for language to stabilise
sensations in the mind and elaborate theories and complex
thoughts is to be found in the work of Degérando. Having won
the prize offered by the Institut in 1797 for an essay on the
subject 'Déterminer l'influence des signes sur la formation des
idées', he published three years later his major work, *Des Signes
et de l'Art de penser considérés dans leurs rapports mutuels.*
The third important figure in this field is that of Laromiguière,
a former priest who was to become *professeur de philosophie*
in the Faculté des Lettres from 1809 until his death in 1837.
He was an editor of Condillac, collaborating in the 1798
edition of his works, and the author of three important
mémoires read before the second class of the Institut, the
Paradoxes de Condillac (1805) and the *Discours sur la langue du
raisonnement* which appeared with his *Leçons de Philosophie*
in 1815.

4.   G. Le Roy, Introduction to Condillac, *Œuvres philosophiques,*
Paris, PUF, 1947–51, p. xxxii.

Among the *physiologistes* the most important writer is Cabanis, who in his *Rapports du physique et du moral de l'homme* (first presented as a series of *mémoires* to the Institut before being published as a single work in 1802) accepts that sensations are the necessary causes of our ideas and deduces from this that the mental is only the physical considered from another point of view. Like D'Holbach, he discusses sensations in terms of certain arrangements of matter, and treats personal characteristics and temperaments in terms of internal structure. He interprets so-called 'free' action as action springing from an ultimately involuntary modification of the brain, and again like D'Holbach, he gives cogent expression to that materialism which is inherent in any sensationalist doctrine.

To these four thinkers, Tracy, Degérando, Laromiguière and Cabanis, can be added several others whose works illustrate, to greater or lesser degree, the principles and methods of *Idéologie,* both rational and physiological: Garat, Jacquemont, Lancelin, Thurot, Maine de Biran, Pinel, Alibert, Bichat, Moreau ... - and there are indeed others. Most of these names have fallen into obscurity, and if what has so far been discussed represented the limits of *Idéologie,* it would not be difficult to see why, despite differences of detail, it might be regarded as 'the tail of Condillacism'.[5] If this were the case, the title *Idéologue* would refer to a limited number of philosophers engaged in research in a somewhat narrow and esoteric field.

But from the very beginning *Idéologie* is more than an investigation into human psychology. It is the means of discovering new principles relevant to education, legislation and the proper organisation of society. As Tracy puts it:

> (...) personne ni niera sans doute que la connaissance de la génération de nos idées est le fondement de l'art de communiquer

5.   C.H. Van Duzer, *The Contribution of the Ideologues to French Revolutionary Thought,* Baltimore, Johns Hopkins Press, 1935, p. 13.

> ces idées, la grammaire; de celui de combiner ces mêmes idées et d'en faire jaillir des vérités nouvelles, la logique; de celui d'enseigner et de répandre les vérités acquises, l'instruction; de celui de former les habitudes des hommes, l'éducation; de l'art plus important encore d'apprécier et de régler nos désirs, la morale; et enfin du plus grand des arts, au succès duquel doivent coopérer tous les autres, celui de régler la sociéte de façon que l'homme y trouve le plus de secours et le moins de gêne possible de la part de ses semblables.[6]

Knowledge is derived from the working of the mind, which operates in a consistent and identical manner whatever the material to which it is applied. If the mechanism of the mind can be grasped, then not only can error and prejudice be eradicated, but the key to all the sciences will have been discovered, for scientific progress ultimately depends upon correct methodology and clarity of language. Hence the unity of the sciences and the interrelation of the different branches of scientific enquiry which the *Idéologues* stress; *Idéologie* is the science of methods, the science of those relationships which unite all branches of knowledge in one synthesis, for all, in their particular development and application, have the same starting-point and the same end. In this way specialists in different fields can be associated with the general progress of knowledge.

This is demonstrated nowhere more clearly than in the organisation and working of the Institut, of which many of the *Idéologues* already named were members. The constitution of l'an III had made provision for a new higher seat of learning to replace the old academies which had been suppressed in 1793, and had laid down that there was to be 'un institut national chargé de recueillir les découvertes, de perfectionner les arts et les sciences'. The new body, set up by virtue of the law of 3 brumaire an IV (25 October 1795), was composed of three classes: physical and mathematical sciences, moral and political sciences and literature and the fine arts. Each class was divided

6.   'Mémoire sur la faculté de penser', *op. cit.*, p. 287.

into sections of six members each, and the total number of members of the Institut was 144. Provision was made for an equal number of non-resident associate members.

The primary aims of the Institut were to promote research and publish the results and to engage in correspondence with other learned societies abroad. It reflected in its organisation and in the close links between its different sections and classes the same attitude to the various branches of knowledge as the *Idéologues*. Although each member was designated to a particular section, he was free to attend meetings of other sections, and four times a year meetings were held at which all sections came together to discuss matters of mutual interest. The members were thus reminded that they were engaged upon a common enterprise and that in that enterprise private initiative should accommodate itself to collective advancement.

The most striking feature of the Institut, however, lies in the existence of its second class. There was no direct precedent for a class of moral and political sciences in the academies before the Revolution, and its creation in 1795 bears witness to the transformation which the Académie française had undergone in the eighteenth century. Where once philosophy was discouraged, or totally absent, and where philosophers, moralists and indeed historians could enter only on their literary merits, the Académie française, with the election of Voltaire in 1746, and d'Alembert in 1754; and subsequently of Marmontel, Saint-Lambert, Buffon, Condillac, Condorcet and others, had progressively become a philosophical academy. The Institut, and particularly its second class, was, in a sense, the rationalisation and the confirmation of what the Académie française had become. Philosophy, or more specifically, the analysis of sensations and ideas, was dominant; it not only took its place among the specialist sciences, but it gave to the whole organisation the foundation for its encyclopedic character.

Tracy, Laromiguière, Degérando, Cabanis and Garat were

all members or associate members of the first section, the analysis of sensations and ideas, together with Lebreton, Ginguené and Volney. Daunou, one of the principal authors of the law of 1795, was a member of the third section, social science and legislation, and members of the fourth section, political economy, included Sieyès, Talleyrand, Rœderer and Dupont de Nemours. While it would be idle to suggest that all members of the Institut must necessarily be termed *Idéologues,* it must be remembered that it was a living testimony to the value they placed on the gaining of knowledge and the pursuit of truth as the means of enlightening men and improving the quality of their lives. As the first truly organised centre of research and information, the Institut was, in the eyes of its supporters, a force of the greatest importance, providing a meeting-place and a platform for a large number of writers who, while not all concerned with an exposition of *Idéologie* as such, embody its principles in their works.

Inside the Institut and outside it, *Idéologie* goes beyond the study of man himself to become a science of methods applicable in many fields - legislation, political economy, education, medicine, mathematics and so on. Specialists in these fields are fed by the science and feed it in return: they apply *Idéologie's* principles to their work and help to spread its influence, and then provide detailed data which can be used to demonstrate the effectiveness and universality of *Idéologie.* Furthermore, the principles of *Idéologie* are defended and publicised in the press and in the national assemblies by many who accept them without being philosophers themselves. In this way the 'new science' breaks out of the narrow confines of a strict academic discipline and enters many fields of activity, and to those names already mentioned can be added many others: Jean-Baptiste Say, Marie-Joseph Chénier, Constant, Fauriel, Andrieux, and, as G. Gusdorf suggests, the leading scientists of the time:

> Surtout, les savants eux-mêmes, les plus grands noms de l'époque, se trouvent associés à l'entreprise: Lavoisier, Laplace, Monge, Berthollet, Lamarck admettent eux aussi les mêmes principes directeurs, réalisant une unanimité rare, et bientôt détruite entre les divers domaines de la connaissance.[7]

This view of what Gusdorf sees as a *reprise* of the Renaissance and of the collective effort of the *Encyclopédistes* is far removed from Tracy's precise and restricted definition of *Idéologie,* and there is an obvious danger that the net will be cast too wide and that the term will lose all real significance. Nonetheless it is true that in the last decade of the eighteenth century there was a striking conjunction of philosophy, scientific endeavour and social awareness. *Idéologie,* in the eyes of Tracy and his closest associates, had a practical end and a specific question to answer: 'les facultés d'une espèce d'êtres animés étant connues, trouver tous les moyens de bonheur dont ces êtres sont susceptibles'.[8] For Tracy there was a clearly established procedure, a chain of enquiry by which he sought to arrive 'par une suite de conséquences rigoureuses et non inter - rompues depuis l'examen de notre premier acte intellectuel jusqu'à la dernière de nos dispositions législatives'.[9] Maine de Biran ascribes an even more grandiose aim to Tracy and to Cabanis when he characterises their ambitions with the phrase 'l'idéologie doit changer la face du monde'.[10]

In the work of reconstruction which the Revolution represented, it is not surprising that many should wish to respond to such challenges, but what is most notable is the

7. *Introduction aux Sciences humaines,* Paris, Les Belles Lettres, 1960, p. 272.
8. Destutt de Tracy, 'Mémoire sur la faculté de penser', *op. cit.,* p. 288.
9. Letter to Thomas Jefferson, dated 21 October 1811. Reprinted in G. Chinard, *Jefferson et les Idéologues,* Baltimore, Johns Hopkins Press, Paris, PUF, 1925, p. 88.
10. Remark used by Biran, after his first meeting with Tracy and Cabanis, in a letter to l'Abbé de Feletz dated 30 July 1802: *Œuvres,* (ed. Tisserand), Paris, Alcan, 1920—49, 14v., VI, 140.

method of approach used by *Idéologues*. It is here that the intriguing paradox of their enterprise lies, and it is here that one can see most clearly what distinguishes them from the *Philosophes*. Whereas the *Philosophes* had little prospect of political power and remained essentially in opposition to authority, the *Idéologues* were writing at a time of social change which had yet to be properly defined and which was seeking its new direction. Many of the principles of the *Philosophes* seemed in large measure to have triumphed and were now to be translated into reality through laws and institutions. The *Idéologues* found themselves cast as creators, innovators and organisers at a time when all was urgency and novelty, and they did not shrink from these tasks. They played an active part in national assemblies and government commissions; they enjoyed official favour and political influence. And yet, although their work was conducted under the pressure of events, they never lost a wider vision or the sense of detachment which went with it. The reforms they advocated and the institutions they envisaged were the translation into social terms of philosophical concepts previously arrived at by speculation and theory. For they saw that 'philosophy in action' could not survive unaided. Any attempt to right particular wrongs and to create a new social and political framework could rely for a time upon its own vigour and enlightened self-interest. But sooner or later there would come the need for the verification and justification of the assumptions on which the vigour and self-interest were based. There was the need, as Van Duzer puts it, 'to determine the grounds of ultimate reference'.[11]

So the *Idéologues* went back to basic principles. They saw that little was to be gained by debating in detail the ideas of the *Philosophes,* but rather searched for a solid basis on

11.   *op. cit.,* p. 14.

which to build their enquiries which would lead to the establishment of a social science, the most advanced and worthy of
the sciences, and the sum total of them all. They were anxious
to prove the suggestion, drawn from Locke and Condillac, that
it was possible to establish truths in the moral and political
sciences which were as soundly based as those in the physical
sciences. The problems to be solved may well be concerned
with happiness, liberty, equality and justice, but the answers
were to be expressed in philosophical terms. They sought to
realise a close link between intellectual life and moral and
political life, and to make the former an instrument of the
latter.

It is useful to refer at this point to the description of the
Philosophe which Professor Lough draws from Condorcet:

> The whole outlook on the world of a *philosophe* will be based
> on reason; thanks to this guide he can think things out for
> himself, discard all prejudices and reject authority and tradition.
> In religion it is bound to lead him to reject orthodox Catholicism,
> but whatever his final attitude may be - whether he be deist,
> agnostic or atheist - he will preach the virtues of toleration and
> denounce intolerance and fanaticism wherever they appear. The
> *philosophe* is definitely outward-looking. He will examine criti-
> cally the society in which he lives and the government of his day,
> attacking all forms of tyranny and unnecessary restrictions on
> freedom, including the particularly important freedom of the
> press. He will denounce all forms of inhumanity such as war,
> miscarriages of justice, barbarous punishments and negro slavery.[12]

It is notable that this account is couched primarily in terms of
denunciation and criticism, rejection and attack. There is
little sense of the creation and stabilisation of a new order. And
yet much in the account could be applied to the *Idéologues*.
They accepted not only those currents in eighteenth-century
French thought which derived from its attachment to scientific methodology, but also those which derived from its

12. *op. cit.*, p. 142.

liberalism. They were imbued with the same love of liberty and the same hatred of theocratic and feudal institutions, together with the doctrines which were their foundation. They respected the concepts of tolerance and liberty, and accepted, at least tacitly, the principle of the perfectibility of man and the ethical utilitarianism which, in the eighteenth century, was destined to give new impulsion to it. They were, moreover, temperamentally inclined to favour those moral values fashioned by reason; they referred favourably throughout their works to those virtues which eschewed the extremes of passion, virtues such as industry, sobriety and honesty. These were, furthermore, virtues which carried with them a sense of social responsibility: the individual, in subduing passion, curbed the demands of personal satisfaction and thus contributed to the well-being of all.

But there is a significant difference. The *Idéologues* were not outward-looking. The society they discussed was an ideal one, arranged around a human type and shaped by principles which were the direct consequence of the constitution, mental and physical, of that type. They had no concept of history as a process of gradual evolution, and considered it instead as a catalogue of the different approaches made by societies to the ideal. They were not political or social observers, and consequently in their work deduction took precedence over observation and historical research. They were predisposed to analysis rather than to documentation, and they were attached to logic with a corresponding tendency to generalisation and abstraction.

Critics of the *Idéologues* have never been slow to decry this approach, none more stridently than Napoleon, whose bitter opposition ensured the rapid decline of their political influence. Even Taine, who went so far as to describe *Idéologie* as 'notre philosophie classique' and 'la vraie méthode de l'esprit français' [13]

13.   *Les Philosophes français au XIXe siècle*, Paris, Hachette, 1857, p. 19.

repeated the common jibe:

Jamais avec eux on n'est sur le terrain palpable et solide de l'observation personnelle et racontée, mais toujours en l'air, dans la région vide des généralités pures.[14]

Such criticisms do not in themselves invalidate the work of the *Idéologues,* the form of which was in such large measure determined by the circumstances in which it was undertaken. The Republic existed before republican customs and a republican spirit had been created, and there was a need for the establishment of solid foundations on which the future could be built. The *Idéologues* showed themselves genuine in their concern to change the world and to create a more just, tolerant and liberal society, in which inequalities of wealth and the resultant inequalities of power were destroyed and in which the individual could enjoy the greatest amount of freedom and happiness. Although constantly attached to the general principle and too easily persuaded that men are willing and able to follow the teachings of reason, the *Idéologues* were well able to master practical and at times intricate detail in their attempt to organise society; this is particularly noticeable in the field of political economy, legislation, education and physiology. Their influence was limited by their ignorance of social forces and the changing circumstances which brought forth new problems to be solved. It was also limited to the age to which they belonged, for, however detached they might have been from their contemporary scene, their attitudes are clearly moulded by that age. They are part of that generation educated in the eighteenth century and called upon to create the Revolution, and they answered the challenge by remaining faithful to the logical analysis of sensationalism. Whatever the ultimate validity of that method, it served to make of the *Idéologues* a bridge between the *Philosophes* and the social

14. *L'Ancien Régime,* Paris, Hachette, 1876, p. 263.

thinkers of the nineteenth century, in particular Saint-Simon and Comte, both of whom sought, in the words of Bury, 'a social law as valid as the physical law of gravitation'. [15]

Collectively the *Idéologues* offer a paradoxical picture of rigorous system and lively diversification, logical abstraction and detailed practicality. Unlike their predecessors before the Revolution, they bear witness to a remarkable unity of temperament; they enjoy close ties of friendship, particularly the *salon* of Mme Helvétius at Auteuil, as well as common interests of research within the Institut. Despite differences of emphasis and opinion, they formed a remarkably homogeneous group, and at the centre of that group - to turn to a specific point raised by Professor Lough - stands Volney. Although he did not provide a detailed account of *Idéologie,* despite being a member of the Institut and a teacher of the Ecole normale, Volney shared the common aims of the *Idéologues,* and in both temperament and outlook he is typical of these philosophers whom his biographer, Gaulmier, describes as follows:

> ... race si profondément française de mécontents sans aigreur, pour qui la Révolution ne consiste pas dans les élans spectaculaires de quelques grandes journées où flambe l'enthousiasme, mais dans une revendication patiente et jamais satisfaite; race de démocratie paysanne et petit-bourgeoise, race têtue, craignant toujours d'être dupe, peu sensible à la gloire militaire, indifférente aux pompes religieuses, douée d'un bon sens robuste, obstiné et un peu étroit.[16]

15. J.B. Bury, *The Idea of Progress,* New York, Dover Publications Inc., 1955, p. 284.
16. J. Gaulmier, *L'Idéologue Volney,* Beyrouth, Impr. catholique, 1951, Introduction.

THE ENLIGHTENMENT AND THE LANGUAGE
OF THE FRENCH NOBILITY IN 1789:
THE CASE OF ARRAS

N. Hampson

 OW far the ideas and vocabulary of the Enlightenment had penetrated French society before the Revolution is a question which has been more often asked than answered. Recent research into the content and diffusion of popular literature, however, has dug a trench across one end of the site and found virtually no traces of its occupation by the philosophes. Excavation at the other end, to see how far the nobility had adopted the new ideas or expressed the old ones in new terminology, is likely to turn up more positive evidence. Anyone who has glanced at the irate pamphlets of the parlementaires after the judical coup d'état of 8 May 1788 knows how much they owe to Montesquieu. He was quoted from Dauphiné to Roussillon, from Brittany to Lorraine and paraphrased everywhere. The enthusiastic *Patriote* who wrote 'On étale, on répète tout ce que Montesquieu et Rousseau ont si bien déduit contre le despotisme' was perhaps overdoing things so far as Rousseau was concerned but he was certainly right about Montesquieu. All this, however, was only to be expected from Montesquieu's fellow-parlementaires and it leaves open the question of how far the excitement was confined to the world of the basoche. The election of the noble deputies to the Estates General in the spring of 1789 offers an opportunity of extending the

investigation to a wider public.

At first sight the outlook is not very promising. One can see that Frenchmen of every class were convinced that the convocation of the Estates General involved some kind of a new start and there was keen competition to secure a place as one of the Founding Fathers of the new order. Nevertheless, where the Pays d'Etats were concerned, the immediate result was mainly to infuse a new passion into the trench warfare that competing vested interests had been waging against each other for a very long time. Everywhere the local Estates claimed the right to nominate representatives to the new national gathering. In Franche Comté, where they were revived in 1789, they admitted only those with a century of nobility or four quarterings, which excluded five-sixths of the nobles of the province. Provence insisted on the possession of a fief, which made a present of Mirabeau to the Third Estate. At Montpellier the Cour des Aides championed the local radicals in the hope of keeping the power to nominate out of the hands of its old enemy, the Estates of Languedoc. The Breton nobility were so incensed by the attitude of Versailles that they boycotted the Estates General altogether. All this sounds a very long way from *Du Contrat Social*. The advent in France of what the British understood by politics appeared to have done no more than to focus a new critical attention on hoary questions of precedence that had aroused less passion when they had been confined to local issues. An examination of what happened at Arras, however, suggests that things were not quite so simple as they seemed. The disputes of 1789 are quite well documented and the evidence of the Archives Nationales (B^a 15, C 12 and 14 and H 38) allows the debate to be followed in a fair amount of detail.

The Estates of Artois were convened on 29 December 1788 for the purpose of voting a don gratuit and aide extraordinaire of 400,000 livres. The Second Estate consisted of the noblesse entrante, men who possessed six generations of nobility and a seigneurie de clocher. Once admitted, such nobles sat for life, which meant that there was a brisk trade in seigneuries amongst those with the necessary quarterings. There were 117 entrants, which excluded about another 300 nobles. Whatever the non-entrants had thought about this in the past, they were now determined that their exclusion from local politics should not deprive them of a chance to sit in the Estates General. The first thing they needed was a forum where they could muster their supporters. This was conveniently provided by the local newspaper, the *Affiches d'Artois,* that was launched at the end of 1788. Quick to appreciate the possibilities of the media — or more accurately the medium, since the *Affiches* had no competitors — the non-entrants, in a letter to the editor published on 2 January 1789, appealed for signatures to a petition to the king to allow the deputies to the Estates General to be chosen by and from the local nobility as a whole. They eventually obtained 127 signatures, or slightly more than the number of the entrants, for those who believed in counting heads.

Strictly speaking, there was no precedent for either side to appeal to, since Artois had not been French when the last Estates General were elected in 1614. Within the province itself, however, prescription was on the side of the entrants, in the sense that conditions for membership of the local estates were traditional. Looking for a theoretical basis for their claim to a say in the elections to the Estates General, the non-entrants might have chosen to rest their case on the need for obedience to the royal will, as personified by Necker. The position they actually adopted was very different. They professed themselves ready to accept

> s'il le faut, les plus grands sacrifices pour régénérer la patrie, à la face de l'univers étonné; il sera renouvelé, ce pacte primitif qui a fait choisir à nos ancêtres la meilleure forme de gouvernement. Nous verrons donc la nation la plus libre délibérer avec liberté

> sur les clauses de son association politique, écarter de son
> contrat social les erreurs, les vices, les abus presque réduits en
> principes par les siècle d'ignorance, de superstition et de
> séduction...
>
> Tout homme a le droit personnel d'assister au pacte qui
> lui impose des obligations et lui assure des droits; sans cette
> assistance volontaire il n'y a plus de contrat. Ce principe est un
> des premiers du code de l'humanité; de la naît le droit
> individuel et imprescriptible qu'a tout Français d'aller partout
> où l'on doit discuter les droits et les obligations des Français.

If this meant what it said (and only time was to show that
it did not), it implied a good deal. The *patrie* was to be regener-
ated by a new social contract, which was certainly not what
Louis XVI had intended by the Estates General. 'Centuries of
ignorance and superstition' was the standard terminology of the
Enlightenment. The principle of no taxation without representation, dear to the American colonists, was asserted from the
start and if the petition stopped short of popular sovereignty it
at least insisted on the right of everyone to participate in the
acceptance of the social contract itself. Despite the radical
language, the duc de Guines, governor of the province, the
Intendant and the President of the Conseil d'Artois forwarded
it to Necker with no comment beyond a plea for a quick
decision. This was probably because they were much more
concerned by the noises being made on the other side, which
constituted a more immediate threat to royal authority.

On January 6 the entrants asserted bluntly that it was
impossible to distinguish between eligibility for the local estates
and the right to elect deputies to the Estates General. To change
the former would overturn the 'anciens usages de la province'.
There was therefore nothing that anyone could do. True to the
position they had adopted, their opponents rejected this appeal
to tradition, in the name of progress. 'On n'avait pas, il y a
trente ans, des idées aussi nettes des droits de l'homme,

considéré comme Homme et comme Citoyen. Depuis trente ans
la raison a fait du progrès. Sommes-nous Français? Sommes-
nous sujets de Louis XVI? ... Qu'importe d'être noble si l'on
n'est plus Citoyen? '

An anonymous report, dated January 8, allows us to
penetrate behind the grandiloquent professions of faith that
were coming from both sides. According to the writer, the
nobility were divided between 'un tiers de gens sages, gens d'âge
et d'expérience, deux-tiers de têtes ardentes parmi lesquelles il y
en a beaucoup de fort jeunes. Les gens sages... n'osent pas
s'exposer aux reproches et aux propos violents de l'autre parti.
[The extremists] s'étaient déjà arrangés entre eux pour envoyer
trois têtes sulphureuses qui ne seraient certainement pas élus si
les autres nobles participaient à l'élection.' This impression is
confirmed by a letter to the *Affiches* which supported the case
for the entrants with a quotation from Montesquieu to the
effect that the vote par ordre would be necessary in the Estates
General in order to keep royal influence in check.

The royal government had no illusions about the situation.
Puységur, on behalf of Necker, had already written to de Guines,
the Intendant and the President of the Conseil d'Artois to press
for the widest possible representation of the nobility. The
entrants could only hope to win by the successful defiance of
royal authority. They had the local estates securely under their
control but they knew as well as the writer of the anonymous
letter that 'Lorsque nous serons débarrassés de cette assemblée
il sera très facile de convoquer les trois ordres.' Time was on
Necker's side.

This perhaps explains why nothing much happened during
the next fortnight. The government was playing for time and the
estates of Artois could not prolong their meeting indefinitely.
On January 20 Madame Marchand, who must have been congratu-
lating herself on launching the *Affiches* just when so much free
copy was available, printed an arrêté of the nobility. Knowing

the end of their sessions to be at hand they were probably trying to forestall the royal offensive they expected as soon as they had gone home. 'La Noblesse n'a point de raison pour dire et pour croire que la Royaume *va adopter un nouveau régime* et quand le royaume l'adopterait, elle pense que les états d'Artois devraient réunir tous leurs efforts pour qu'il ne soit rien changé dans celui de la province. Elle ne peut imaginer, d'ailleurs, qu'il doive être question aux Etats Généraux du royaume, de *changer ou de donner une nouvelle Constitution à la Monarchie;* elle croit, au contraire, qu'il s'agit de l'affermir sur ses bases inébranlables, sans en altérer les principes.' This may have pleased some of Necker's more conservative colleagues but behind the appeal to tradition there was the first hint of local separatism.

On the following day the estates of Artois resigned themselves to voting the inevitable subsidy and consoled themselves for their future impotence by directing a few home truths at the government. 'Oublions, s'il est possible, cette commotion générale, qui s'est fait sentir dans tout le royaume par des lois, la plupart inconstitutionelles et incohérentes, que la précipitation fit naître et dont la force armée tenta de soutenir l'effrayant édifice.' After repeated references to the *nation,* they denounced 'les restes d'un système destructeur, né de l'anarchie féodale, qui rendait presque respectables ces préférences, ces privilèges pécuniaires qui faisaient retomber sur la classe laborieuse et souffrante des citoyens, le fardeau des impositions. Tout semble à cet égard se porter vers cette égalité si nécessaire dans un grand gouvernement où les membres de tous les ordres, trouvant la même protection, lui doivent, à ce titre, les mêmes secours et les mêmes contributions; sans nuire, toutefois, à ces distinctions légitimes que l'honneur du nom, l'éclat du rang et de la naissance doivent conserver à ceux qui ont reçu des prérogatives de leurs ancêtres ou qui les ont obtenus par leurs vertus ou leur état.'

This was having their cake and eating it, with a vengeance. When all the conditions had been met, the *égalité si nécessaire dans un grand gouvernement* would be purely fiscal, and even that was advanced without much enthusiasm. In fact, as time was to show, there was very little difference between the outlook of the entrants and that of their opponents. The fact that they sailed under very different colours was a product of the tactical requirements of their struggle to control the elections to the Estates General.

As soon as the local estates were out of the way the non-entrants sent off a second petition to Necker and the clergy read the Second Estate a rather smug lecture on political theory, that was duly printed in the *Affiches*. 'On leur dirait que les droits dont ils jouissent ont des bornes, que les usages, lors même qu'ils seraient constants, les examples, s'ils étaient parfaitement applicable aux circumstances actuelles, ne peuvent rien contre les lois immuables de l'ordre social; qu'ils ne représentent aux Etats tous les citoyens qu'en vertu d'une constitution antique qui fut dans le principe le résultat d'un vœu commun et que ce privilège est du nombre de ceux qu'ils peuvent faire valoir avec succès contre tous autres que leurs concitoyens.' This also was having it both ways: prescription was still valid as a guarantee of the privileges of the province as a whole, but not of the constitutional arrangements within it. At the local level at least, the clergy had taken a long step towards popular sovereignty, whether or not they were aware of it, and their argument about the representation of all the 'citizens' would be used to justify the abolition of the three orders, which was presumably no part of their intentions.

The interests of the entrants were now entrusted to the standing committee of the local estates and the estates' *députés à la Cour*. The latter proposed a compromise that would have allowed some of the non-entrants to take part in the elections to the Estates General, although not to be elected. This was

unlikely to satisfy anyone. Away from Versailles and exposed
to local pressure, the standing committee took a much tougher
line in a memoir they drafted on February 15. They began by
asserting that their right to *députer en Corps d'Etats* was an
integral part of their constitution since the province was a
single unit, 'de sorte que chaque individu de cette grande
Corporation a nécessairement le même intérêt. Que cet intérêt
particulier et l'intérêt de tous ne peuvent être stipulés et discutés
que dans une assemblée générale des ordres, tenue et convoquée
suivant les formes ordinaires.' Their position was traditional
enough but their language *sentait le fagot* and the shade of
Rousseau might well have murmured 'When me they fly, I am
the wings.' They went on to say that if the king was not satisfied
with the concessions they had offered, he should suggest others
and not 'anéantir la constitution, les privilèges et les formes d'un
pays qui ne s'est rendu qu'à la parole inviolable du monarque
de les lui conserver tous.' In case he had missed the hint, they
added bluntly that all cahiers would be illegal unless jointly
accepted by the three orders, the province could not be bound by
deputies who had been elected irregularly and taxation could
only be raised by the local estates.

If there was a hint of desperation behind these extreme
claims, it was due to a well-justified fear that the royal government was about to disregard the local estates altogether and
order the elections to be held by bailliages, as in the Pays
d'Election. This called the bluff of the entrants. Completely
isolated and vigorously opposed by the majority of their own
order, they had no alternative but to comply. When the nobility
were convened in April all were therefore invited and about
three-quarters attended, which gave the non-entrants a comfortable majority. In theory this was a unique gathering whose
business was concerned solely with the Estates General, but
the opportunity was too good to miss. Forty nobles signed a
petition to include in the cahier a demand for 'une représentation

plus parfaite des ordres dans les états d'Artois.' The entrants opposed this on the grounds of both practice and principle. Claiming, rather implausibly, that there were 7—800 nobles in the province and 1,600 clergy, they argued that the admission of all would bring up to 4,000 members into the local estates. A proposal so absurd would offer the royal government at Versailles a pretext for amending the constitution of Artois to suit its convenience. This was all the more to be deplored since 'La province d'Artois, quant à sa constitution, est absolument étrangère et indépendante des états généraux. C'est à la nation artésienne seule à prononcer sur ce point.' As the only legitimate spokesman of this 'nation' they then offered concessions: the extension of the franchise to all nobles with four generations of nobility (instead of six) and a *terre à clocher,* and the addition of an unspecified number of representatives of the non-entrants, who were to have full voting rights. Dubois de Fosseux, the secretary of the Arras Academy and a friend of Robespierre (at least, until the elections) persuaded his colleagues to reject this. 'L'universalité de la Noblesse Artésienne est ici assemblée; elle a donc le droit de traiter de sa constitution.' The spokesman of the entrants, the comte de Cunchy, then withdrew his offer. He said that the admission of the non-entrants to future meetings of the local estates would infringe not merely the general rights and privileges, but also the property rights of the entrants (presumably by devaluing *terres à clocher*). He repeated that the Estates General would have no power to tamper with the local constitution and that taxation could be authorized only by the local estates, meeting in accordance with their traditional constitution. In the end the conflict of principles had come right out into the open. The argument of de Fosseux implied popular sovereignty, at least where the actual drafting of a constitution was concerned. Cunchy replied by asserting the inviolability of prescription which meant that all change must be acceptable to those who held power under the traditional order. The entrants were out-voted 121 : 64, which suggests a good many abstentions, since nearly 300 nobles took part in the election of deputies. After this final defeat 56 of them walked out, leaving the field to their opponents.

The way was now clear for those who had called themselves citizens and spoken up for the rights of all Frenchmen, to inaugurate the Brave New World. They went about it in a curious way, for their cahier contained fourteen separate demands for the entrenchment of noble privileges, such as a monopoly of commissioned entry into the army and the preservation of their exclusive right of admission to noble chapters and military orders. Article IX explained what they had meant from the beginning. 'Les nobles doivent admettre entr'eux la plus parfaite égalité.' They had been taking the separate identity of the three orders for granted all the time.

Artois was therefore no exception to the pattern observed elsewhere. The elections of 1789 prised open cracks in the social fabric of the nobility that had existed for generations without seeming particularly important. From one point of view the issues involved belonged to a different world from that of the philosophes. As the nobility split, however, with results that both sides were eventually to regret, each looked for ideological ammunition. In the process, both factions showed how their modes of thought, if not their conception of their interests, had been influenced by the ideas of the Enlightenment. The entrants took their stand on the venerable principles of prescriptions and traditional rights, but they saw these as guaranteed by Montesquieu rather than by God. No one, in fact, was talking about God at all. The terms in which the clergy lectured the Second Estate suggested that no one had any more use for the kind of thinking that had once seemed so persuasive to Bossuet. One should perhaps say, none of the nobility and upper clergy, for the curé of Cogeuil did write to Louis XVI to complain about the activity of the Protestants 'qui ont gagné au diable des créatures de dieu par le feu de la concupiscence et plus encore ils font gloire de manger de la viande les vendredi et samedi'. There were still some people who got their priorities right!

It was all very well for the marquis de Croix, after the elections, to indulge in sardonic comments about 'Les grands mots de droit naturel, de droit imprescriptible, de premières notions des hommes; comme si ces mots viennent d'enrichir notre langue et n'eussent point été connus de nos pères.' That was the language that the nobility chose to speak. They admittedly construed it in a rather special way, in terms of their rights to what had formerly been monopolozed by others, rather than their obligation to renounce the privileges they themselves already enjoyed, but in this respect they were in numerous, if not necessarily good company, and there were plenty of people, like Robespierre in his *Ennemis de la Patrie démasqués,* to draw the appropriate conclusions. There is nothing new about political theories being pressed into the service of causes that would have surprized their authors. The language *was* new and it was the language of the philosophes.

NEO-CLASSICISM IN FRANCE:
A REASSESSMENT

W.D. Howarth

N spite of the considerable ambiguity that attaches to their use in this field, the terms 'neo-classical', 'neo-classicism' and their French counterparts appear to be gaining in currency in the vocabulary of literary history and literary criticism. It is the purpose of this article to identify the different ways in which the terms are commonly used, and to examine critically the most controversial of their possible meanings.

'Neo-classicism', itself a comparatively recent coining, has had an especially brief career in the field of literary criticism. It is absent in this sense from the nineteenth-century dictionaries and encyclopedias - indeed, it is entirely missing from Littré - and though it appears in a number of more recent reference works, it is still commonly treated as applying solely to the visual arts. For instance, it is not to be found in the Oxford *Companion to English Literature* (1932, fourth edition 1967), *Companion to French Literature* (1959), or *Companion to German Literature* (1976), even though the second of these glosses the much more esoteric *néo-romantisme* and *néo-Mallarmisme*. Whereas the eleventh edition of the *Britannica* ignored the word in 1910, its successor of 1970 devotes the whole of a lengthy article entirely to 'neo-classicism' as a term of art history; and the same is true of both the *Enciclopedia*

Italiana of 1949 and the *Brockhaus-Enzyklopädie* of 1966. Exceptions to this general neglect by lexicographers of the literary connotations of the word are Robert (vol. IV, 1959) and the 1961 Webster; while early testimony to its use in a literary context is to be found in the Spanish *Encyclopedia Universal Illustrada* (1928–30). In its most straightforward meaning, the term serves to remind us of the differences, while at the same time acknowledging the affinities, between the literary culture of Greece and Rome on the one hand, and that of post-Renaissance Western Europe on the other. In this first sense - a strictly neutral one, devoid of critical nuance - 'neo-classical' can be said to be interchangeable with 'classical', for which it offers a more precise alternative (Webster, for instance, cross-refers from one to the other); and it is not difficult to find examples of this usage. Thus A.O. Lovejoy, in an article entitled 'The Parallel of Deism and Classicism' *(Modern Philology,* 39 (1931), 281–99) has already, by the end of his first paragraph, substituted one term for the other, so that we find him referring to 'the parallel of deism and neo-classicism'. In R. Wellek and A. Warren's *Theory of Literature* (1949), the two terms are used interchangeably throughout; for example (p. 127):

> No doubt, we can show that there are some similarities in the theories and formulas behind the different arts, in the neo-classical or the romantic movements... But 'classicism' in music must mean something very different from its use in literature...

And Northrop Frye *(Anatomy of Criticism,* 1957, p. 83) even more explicitly links the two terms, when he writes of 'the literary standards generally called "classical" or "neo-classical", which prevailed in Western Europe from the sixteenth to the eighteenth centuries'. Among the most recent examples noted, G. Pocock, in *Corneille and Racine* (1973), uses 'neo-classicism' throughout in the sense of 'seventeenth-century classicism': Racine's tragedies, for instance, are seen (p. 305) as 'the logical

culmination of French neo-classicism'; a work by T. Burnley
Jones and B. de B. Nicol (1976) bears the title *Neo-classical
Dramatic Criticism 1560–1770;* and an American scholar,
H. Lindenberger, in his *Historical Drama* (1957), repeatedly
contrasts 'Shakespearean' with 'French neo-classical' drama
(e.g. p. 150). To give further examples would be otiose; though
it will no doubt be remarked that those quoted are all from
British or American sources. While perhaps not unknown, the use
of the French term as interchangeable with *le classicisme*
evidently remains extremely rare.

French (or perhaps one should say Continental) usage
appears to favour the application of the term not to the whole
of the 'classical' period, but to the eighteenth century in contra-
distinction to the seventeenth. J. Truchet, for instance, writes
in the Introduction to Volume I of the Pléiade anthology,
Théâtre du xviiie siècle (1972, pp. xxvi–xxvii):

> Il est d'usage de caractériser d'un mot la tragédie du xviiie
> siècle: *néo-classique...* Ce qu'on veut souligner..., c'est...
> l'impossibilité de s'arracher à certains archétypes issus de
> Corneille et de Racine...; la constante retombée dans un nombre
> restreint de situations connues; l'incessant retour, volontaire
> ou non, d'hémistiches, voire d'alexandrins tout faits.

When 'neo-classical' is used as a label for writers who took as
their models not the literature of antiquity itself, but that of
their own seventeenth-century predecessors, it goes without
saying that it is likely to carry a pejorative implication[1]. The
critical value of the epithet becomes quite explicit when, discussing De Belloy's *Siège de Calais,* Truchet writes:

> Dans sa médiocrité même, [cette pièce] présente un caractère
> exemplaire en tant que chef-d'œuvre de néo-classicisme.
> Crébillon père, La Motte, Voltaire étaient néo-classiques; mais il

---

1.   As applied to eighteenth-century *English* literature, on the other
      hand, the term 'neo-classical' has long been established with no
      pejorative implication. See D. Secretan, *Classicism,* 1973, p. 2; and
      I. Simon, *Neo-classical Criticism, 1660–1800,* 1971, *passim.*

n'appartenait qu'à de Belloy... de l'être à ce degré (II, 1439).
The same critical attitude informs the article "Neo-clasicismo'
in the *Encyclopedia Universal Illustrada,* whose author limits
its literary application to the (by implication) degenerate
classicism of 'the late seventeenth century and the whole of the
eighteenth', characterised by 'sometimes servile' imitation of
classical models. I should judge that there is also a critical
implication in the reference by H. Peyre (1942, quoted in
French Classicism, A Critical Miscellany, ed. J. Brody, 1966,
p. 113) to 'la littérature allemande, où le néo-classicisme du
début du xviiie siècle précéda le romantisme, lequel précéda
lui-même un prétendu classicisme'. Similarly, the following
quotation from R.S. Ridgeway, *Voltaire and Sensibility* (1973,
p. 14):

> [In the early nineteenth century] feeling became associated
> with piety and political conservatism, while the *philosophes*
> were identified with the losing cause of anemic neo-classicism

shows that this pejorative use of the term is also current
among Anglo-Saxon writers. Indeed, it is interesting to note
that where the original text of P. Hazard's *Crise de la conscience
européenne* (1935, p. 373) uses the term 'pseudo-classicisme'
to characterise 'ce fatras de fables sans fraîcheur, de tragédies
sans vérité, de vers sans poésie' which the author sees as 'la
rançon des bienfaits que le classicisme avait apportés au monde',
the English translation by J.L. May *(The European Mind,
1964, p. 356) replaces 'le pseudo-classicisme' by 'the neo-
classical period.'
   The semantic problem posed by the need to distinguish
the classicism of the seventeenth century from the work of
eighteenth-century continuators or imitators has inspired a
sustained attempt by P. Brady to justify the use of 'neo-
classical' in a more limited sense, and not necessarily with a
pejorative nuance. In three articles: 'Rococo and Neo-classicism'
(Studi francesi, 22 (1964), 34–39), 'The *Lettres persanes:*

rococo or neo-classical? ' *(Studies on Voltaire and the Eighteenth Century,* 53(1967), 47–77) and *'Manon Lescaut:* classical, romantic or rococo? ' *(ibid.,* 339–60), this critic develops the thesis, to which he had already given expression in his review *(Studi francesi,* 21 (1963), 511–14) of R. Laufer's *Style rococo, style des 'lumières'* (1963) - namely, that 'rococo' is an imprecise and misleading term when applied to the literary style of the Enlightenment, and that a more discriminating critical terminology is needed. Brady's own contribution is at first expressed fairly simply in the 1964 article, where he establishes a detailed parallel between the visual arts and the literature of the rococo and neo-classical periods respectively - and where the contrasting analysis of the two styles is reinforced by the notion of a chronological evolution from one generation to another.

> If it is possible and useful to apply the concept of rococo to literature, it may well be just as possible and just as useful to apply to literature the concept of a neo-classical style developing (or at least coming to pre-eminence) late in the century, analogous in many ways with the furnishing of the period and providing by comparison a most valuable aid to the definition of rococo (p. 43).

This criterion once established, he is able to refer in conclusion (p. 49) to 'the neo-classical style of Voltaire and the rococo style of Marivaux'.

However, in the two articles published in 1967, Brady has moved away from this contrast between two styles with a clear-cut chronological basis, and now attempts to develop a subtler distinction between works, or aspects of the same work, co-existing in a single period (roughly, the 1720s to the 1750s):

> With regard to eighteenth-century modes of classicism, we propose to distinguish between works preserving from classicism both the letter and the spirit (post-classicism: *Manon Lescaut*), only the letter (pseudo-classicism: Voltaire's epic and theatre), or only the spirit (neo-classicism: Voltaire's novels) (p. 49)[2].

2.   Brady's suggestion is not entirely novel; cf. W.H. McCabe's definition:

However praiseworthy this attempt to discriminate between the various legacies of seventeenth-century classicism in the conservatively-orientated literature of the following century may be, there is inevitably something very arbitrary about such a proliferation of categories. Brady's own application at the end of the *Lettres persanes* article is commendably flexible and undogmatic:

> The main characteristics of the work - the predominance of analysis and antithesis in the form (style and situation) and of criticism and didacticism in the content (subject, themes, meaning, philosophy) - together with the presence of some elements of violence and tragedy, suggest that the work tends most towards post-classicism or neo-classicism; and this accords with what we know of Montesquieu's professed tastes (p. 77).

On the other hand, the conclusion of the article devoted to *Manon Lescaut* already exhibits a greater degree of systematic abstraction:

> Apart from the... elements [which] may perhaps be considered rococo, we find the work a mixture of baroque (themes, meaning, philosophy), romanticism (point of view, atmosphere) naturalism (setting) and classicism (structure and style). It is apparent that the classicism is to be found in the form, the baroque elements in the content (p. 359)

- a danger inherent in all criticism that places too much reliance on labels[3].

2. 'Strictly speaking, only the modern work which succeeds in re-
cont. capturing the spirit of the ancients is properly called neo-classical; work that fails to recapture that spirit is pseudo-classical' (art. 'Neo-classicism', *Dictionary of World Literatures*, ed. J. Shipley, 1943).

3. This kind of approach is more successful in Laufer's analysis of *Les Liaisons dangereuses:* 'Pour apercevoir le caractère vraiment rococo des *Liaisons,* il faut d'abord distinguer entre le néo-classicisme un peu grêle de leur maniérisme et le classicisme puissant de leur contrepoint, entre les maximes du libertinage et les alternances du coeur. Alors seulement apparaît la merveilleuse imbrication du plan classique de la liberté humaine et du plan baroque de la nécessité inhumaine' (*op. cit.,* p. 135).

A different sort of danger attends the use of the term
'neo-classicism' in the last of the senses that I propose to
examine [4]. The most specific and limited of these related
meanings, it is based on the supposed affinity between the late
eighteenth-century art movement to which the label 'neo-
classicism' is generally applied, and the literary productions of
the same period - an affinity which, as has been seen, the first
Brady article was quite ready to recognise. The danger here is
of course that which accompanies any attempt to interpret
one art-form in terms of criteria derived from another; and the
closer the analogy is pressed, the greater is the temptation to
distort the evidence: the history of the term 'baroque' in a
literary context illustrates this only too well. It is one thing to
note, as Brady does, the evolution of a literary style 'developing,
or at least coming to pre-eminence, late in the century', which
exhibits, *mutatis mutandis,* some of the same features as neo-
classical painting, architecture and decorative arts. It is something quite different to characterise the literature of the closing
decades of the eighteenth century, as does H. Hatzfeld in
Literature through Art (1952), as 'romantic neo-classicism,
fundamentally different from the baroque classicism of the
seventeenth century' (p. 121), and to attribute to this literature,
almost without qualification, the distinctive features of the
visual arts of the period.

Hatzfeld's epithet 'romantic' is something of a red herring:
let us leave the art historians to debate whether the neo-classical
painting of the late eighteenth century can properly be seen as

4.   I am deliberately leaving out of consideration the twentieth-century
      connotations of the term, which is sometimes applied to the poetic
      movement inspired by Charles Morice, originating c. 1910 and
      following on from Moréas's 'Ecole romane'. See *Dictionnaire des
      littératures,* ed. p. van Tieghem, 1968; and H. Peyre, *Qu'est-ce que
      le classicisme?,* 1942 (ch. viii, 'Classicisme et néo-classicisme'),
      who also applies the term to T.S. Eliot.

an early manifestation of romanticism - as is claimed, for instance, in a recent book by F.G. Pariset:

> Néo-classicisme et préromantisme se rapprochent par un élan, des thèmes et des sentiments analogues. Le néo-classicisme interprète des tendances préromantiques avec une coloration antiquisante (L'Art néo-classique, 1974, p. 3).

Elsewhere, however, the same writer makes it quite clear that for him 'le néo-classicisme' is not confined to the fine arts, and is to be taken in the widest possible cultural sense:

> Le néo-classicisme est l'objet de la plus grande enquête de notre époque. Sa résurrection et l'admiration qu'il suscite sont des phénomènes dont on saura plus tard la portée (p. 180).

If he is right, it is all the more important to set appropriate limits to such an enquête, and to ensure that the term 'neo-classicism' is used with clarity and critical rigour.

Whether one views the so-called 'retour à l'antique' in the French literature of the closing decades of the eighteenth century as a second Renaissance (with or without a distinctively pre-romantic flavour), or as the final phase of a single cultural movement begun by the Italian humanists of the fifteenth century, is very much a question of perspective. Nevertheless, it is difficult not to believe that those who speak in terms of a late eighteenth-century 'renaissance' have chosen to adopt a perspective which more properly belongs to the history of the fine arts - or to a Geistesgeschichte which, for all its cosmopolitan characteristics, seems too often to have been coloured by the German experience. It may be true that, as P. Francastel puts it, a key cultural event of the 1770s was 'le transfert du cosmopolitisme de Paris à Rome'; but it is also true that in France, as the same critic says, 'toute la culture du xviiie siècle reste fondée sur les prémisses de la Renaissance' ('L'Esthétique des Lumières', Utopies et institutions au xviiie siècle, ed. Francastel, 1963, p. 354). When painters like Vien, David and Girodet made the pilgrimage to Rome, this was very much in the tradition of Poussin and others before them; and so faithful had French culture remained to the inspiration of Greece and Rome, that one can hardly conceive a French writer, or even a French painter, experiencing the sort of cultural awakening that was to revolutionise the lives of a Winckelmann or a Goethe. Although Winckelmann's writings were translated into French quite early (and although they were much admired by Diderot and others), their impact in France was necessarily limited, since there they merely helped to feed a copious stream of works written by travellers to the sites of the ancient cultures, from Spon and Wheler, *Voyages d'Italie, de Dalmatie, de Grèce et du Levant* (1678), through Monfaucon, *L'Antiquité expliquée* (1719—24), L. Bos. *Antiquités de la Grèce* (1769), Le Roy, *Les Ruines des plus beaux monuments de la Grèce* (1770) and Guys, *Voyage littéraire de la Grèce* (1776) to Barthélemy's best-selling *Voyage du jeune Anarcharsis en Grèce* (1788)[5].

Writers in France at the end of the eighteenth century were inspired, like their predecessors, by a well-established classical tradition that was overwhelmingly literary, rather than visual, in character; and it would be wrong to underestimate the importance, for David and the other painters of the time as well, of this strong literary tradition[6]. To take as examples three of David's most celebrated paintings: the *Oath of the Horatii*

5.   Similarly, P. Dimoff writes: 'Sans doute l'influence de Winckelmann sur les théories littéraires et artistiques d'André Chénier... est-elle moins nette et moins importante que ne l'ont été celles de Montesquieu, de Rousseau, de Louis Racine ou d'Edward Young. Elle s'est d'ailleurs probablement confondue avec telle ou telle de celles-ci, qu'elle n'aurait fait que renforcer ou compléter'. ('Winckelmann et André Chénier', *Revue de Littérature comparée*, 21 (1947), 321—33 (p. 333)).

6.   Cf. David's observation on the limited effect of the study of works of the past in museums: 'La vue de ces chefs-d'œuvre formera peut-être des savants, des Winckelmann, mais des artistes, non!' (quoted by T.M. Mustoxidi, *Histoire de l'esthétique française, 1700 1900*, 1920, p. 97).

has an obvious debt, as regards theme and spirit, to Corneille's play; his *Brutus* stands in a similar relationship to Voltaire's tragedy of the same name; and though it is impossible to point to a similar 'source' for his *Marat* (whose deliberately chastened manner certainly marks a move away from the style of history paintings in vogue for over a hundred years, towards the more distinctively 'linear' style we associate with the turn of the century), the didactic force of this work, and the moral values it expresses, are those which French writers had been accustomed to find in Plutarch and the Roman historians for two centuries or more.

The 'edle Einfalt und stille Grösse' that Winckelmann declared to be the distinctive characteristics of Greek art, and which he saw as necessary to the emancipation of German culture from the nefarious influence of the French tradition, gave a unifying moral inspiration to Weimar classicism; and Goethe's *Iphigenie* represents, in its spiritual message as well as in its form, the consummate expression of this hellenistic ideal. One would search in vain for any reflection of a similar ideal in the most representative 'classical' works of the period in France. In contrast, the 'retour à l'antique' which marked so many aspects of the Revolution - its oratory, its 'fêtes populaires,' its iconography, as well as the imaginative literature produced at this time - was almost exclusively Roman in character. And in spite of the naivety with which it was often expressed, and despite a certain shift of emphasis with regard to the models chosen as objects of admiration (emperors like Augustus giving way to republican heroes such as Lucius Junius Brutus or Caius Gracchus), this attempt to identify the revolutionary spirit with the patriotic and civic virtues of ancient Rome[7] can be shown to have been much less a 'revival' than

7.   '... Seront représentées trois fois la semaine, sur les théâtres de Paris qui seront désignés par la municipalité, les tragédies de *Brutus, Guillaume Tell, Caius Gracchus*, et autres pièces dramatique, qui retracent les glorieux événements de la Révolution, et les vertus des défenseurs de la liberté' ('Décret relatif à la représentation des pièces propres à former l'esprit public', August 1793).

the continuation of a long-standing tradition. M.—J. Chénier, the foremost writer of tragedy of the revolutionary years, prided himself on his ability to 'concevoir et exécuter des choses nouvelles', but his *Caius Gracchus* (1792), for all its topicality as a vehicle for revolutionary sentiment, was thoroughly backward-looking - towards Voltaire, and beyond him Corneille - as regards manner. Moreover, it is well known that the tragedy which enjoyed by far the greatest prestige throughout this period was Voltaire's *Brutus,* first performed in 1730; the complex interrelationships between Voltaire's play, David's painting, and the contemporary cult of Brutus and other Roman heroes have been most interestingly explored by R.L. Herbert *(David, Voltaire, Brutus and the French Revolution,* 1972).

'Il faut avouer', writes J. Haraszti, 'que Rome, malgré tout leur hellénisme prétendu, restait toujours mieux connue, mieux goûtée par les Gaulois latinisés' *(La Poésie d'André Chénier,* 1892, p. 27). On the other hand, even if it may be correct to think of the classical culture of the end of the eighteenth century primarily in Roman terms, it cannot be denied that it was also a period of reverence for Greece; and it is in this sense - especially if one has the figure of André Chénier in mind - that the notion of a neo-classical 'renaissance' must present a certain attraction. There have been those, indeed, who have seen Chénier's works as a one-man renaissance: Saint-Marc Girardin wrote of them as if they had been 'retrouvées dans les cendres de Pompéï ou dans un manuscrit palimpseste', while Nisard declared:

> Les Muses ont endormi Chénier d'un sommeil de deux mille ans; il s'est réveillé parmi nous sans avoir traversé l'église mystique; tout est grec, tout est païen, tout est antique dans A. Chénier (quoted by Haraszti, *op. cit.,* p. 14).

And it would be quite impossible to read the *Bucoliques* without being profoundly impressed by the author's debt to

Greek culture (even though much that may appear 'Greek' has been filtered through the Latin poets: Ovid and Virgil, Catullus, Tibullus and Propertius). There has been much argument as to the nature of Chénier's hellenism: whether it was essentially plastic in character - as those who stress the affinity of his art with that of Prud'hon or Canova would maintain, and as Heredia suggested in editing the *Bucoliques* - or dynamic. No doubt the former view could best be illustrated by selective reference to 'La Jeune Tarentine' or to a fragment like 'Aglaé', the latter by citing, for instance, the battle of the Centaurs in 'L'Aveugle'. But as Francis Scarfe insists, Chénier's poems give evidence of 'both dramatic and a plastic inspiration' *(André Chénier, his Life and Work,* 1965, p. 216) - and both of these were almost wholly literary in origin. The role of heredity and of parental influence in shaping Chénier as a poet has often been debated; but despite his mother's Greek birth, the poet himself never visited Greece, and had left the Levant before he was three years old. In any case, it hardly seems necessary to invoke such a romantic notion of causation in order to account for the particular effect of French classical culture - the imaginative writing of two centuries, reinforcing an educational system firmly based on the literature of antiquity - on the individual sensibility of a poet of genius.

   Chénier's own estimate of his relationship to the culture of the ancient world is best expressed in these lines from 'L'Invention':

> O terre de Pélops! avec le monde entier
> Allons voir d'Epidaure un agile coursier
> Couronné dans les champs de Némée et d'Elide;
> Allons voir au théâtre, aux accents d'Euripide,
> D'une sainte folie un peuple furieux
> Chanter: *Amour, tyran des hommes et des Dieux.*
> Puis, ivres des transports qui nous viennent surprendre,
> Parmi nous, dans nos vers, revenons les répandre;
> Changeons en notre miel leurs plus antiques fleurs;

> Pour peindre notre idée, empruntons leurs couleurs;
> Allumons nos flambeaux à leurs feux poétiques;
> Sur des pensers nouveaux faisons des vers antiques.

Indeed, he illustrates the paradox of a late eighteenth-century artist using the example of the ancients in order to attack the eighteenth century's aesthetic based on excessive (if unadventurous) respect for the ancients. To quote Scarfe again, Chénier was:

> not the kind of poet whose work or ideas would have brought about a complete revolution in poetry. Rather, he had gifts which were enabling him to fulfil, in his practice, a neo-classical theory of poetry which was little more than wishful thinking and, until he appeared, a pretentious mask behind which third-rate minds could easily masquerade as poets (ibid., p. 92).

In one sense, then - as regards his intellectual formation - a product of his age, Chénier was at the same time unique as a poet of genius, equipped to make striking individual use of that intellectual formation. And if he did succeed in translating the sterile neo-classicism of his century into something genuinely creative, he should not be seen on that account as representing a spontaneous and uniquely personal 'retour à l'antique', any more than did David in the visual arts[8]. For other writers among Chénier's contemporaries also turned to Greek sources, and they too were merely following the footsteps well-trodden by previous generations. In the theatre, it may well be that the vogue for translations and close adaptations of the originals (M.−J. Chénier's Œdipe-Roi and Œdipe mourant, Ducis's

8.   Jean Seznec writes of David in relation to the neo-classicism of the preceding generation: 'Le malheur, c'est que l'art français, jusqu'à la veille de la Révolution, est resté incapable d'exprimer le vrai caractère de l'Antiquité, de retrouver son langage et son accent. Les artistes voulaient transmettre son exemple et ses leçons; mais l'exécution a démenti leurs intentions. Pour que l'Antiquité devînt une influence active, il fallait David' (Studies on Voltaire and the Eighteenth Century, 154−5 (1976), 2033−47 (p. 2043)).

Œdipe à Colone) was stimulated by the publication of a much enlarged edition of Brumoy's *Théâtre des Grecs* in 1785–9 (though La Harpe's *Philoctète* had led the way as early as 1781); but if we take the case of Népomucène Lemercier's *Agamemnon* (1797), for instance, which was one of the biggest successes at the Théâtre-Français in the revolutionary decade, we have a play that was not only highly derivative as regards its dramaturgy and style, but was also very much in the main line of eighteenth-century tradition as regards subject-matter. Quite apart from the examples of Crébillon and Voltaire, there were few writers of tragedy throughout the century who did not contribute to the maintaining of this particular tradition by the choice of subjects from Greek legend or mythology; and if we look at the period around 1760, plays like Guimond de la Touche's *Iphigénie en Tauride* (1757), Lemierre's *Hypermnestre* (1759) and *Idoménée* (1764), Poinsinet's *Briséis* (1759) and *Ajax* (1764), or the four plays by Chateaubrun, illustrate such a degree of interest in Greek subject-matter on the part of one generation of playwrights and their audiences, that this phenomenon has been presented in its turn by one literary historian as a mid-century 'neo-classical revival'[9].

It is surely the case, however, that viewed from a twentieth-century standpoint, the continuity of the classical influence on French literature for well over two hundred years remains more impressive than the variation in emphasis and interpretation from one generation to another within that period. The protracted controversy between the Ancients and the Moderns certainly affected the way in which various groups of writers, during the seventeenth and eighteenth centuries,

9.   L. Breitholtz, 'Nyklassicism på franska scener vid mitten av 1700–talet', *Studier tillägnade A. Blanck*, 1946, pp. 121–38. See also H.C. Lancaster, *French Tragedy in the Time of Louis XV and Voltaire*, 1950, II, 383 *et seq.*

reacted to the classical example; but even the irreverent attitudes shown on the one hand by the burlesque poets of 1650
with their *Virgile travesti* or *Ovide bouffon,* and on the other
in Marivaux's *Télémaque travesti,* or in *Arlequin Enée, ou la
Prise de Troie* and many another trifle typical of the rococo age,
are not to be entirely disregarded as evidence of the tenacious
appeal of classical culture for the French throughout the period
from 1549 to 1789 and beyond.

If this is true, there would seem to be a strong case for
continuing to use the term 'neo-classical' in the first of the
senses here examined (i.e. referring to the whole of this
period), as a reminder of the continuity of the cultural influences we have been discussing. (This would in fact match the
common usage in the context of *English* literature, where the
term, applied to the eighteenth century, likewise covers the
whole of the period during which such influences were active
on this side of the Channel). Within this time-span, it seems
likely that the secondary meaning (referring to the imitative,
derivative French classicism of the eighteenth century) is too
well established to be easily dislodged; it is also probable that
the particular connotations, and the pejorative implications,
will be sufficiently apparent from the context to avoid
ambiguity. For the rest, however, attempts to pin the label
'neo-classical' on to more restricted, ephemeral, or partial
manifestations of the classical influence should be treated with
caution. These will at best - as in Brady's case - produce
categories that are too subjective and arbitrary to be generally
acceptable; while more specifically, in the case of Hatzfeld
and others, the pursuit of too close a parallel between the
'retour à l'antique' in the visual arts at the end of the eighteenth century and contemporary developments in French

literature, can only lead to a distortion of the historical perspective[10].

10. I am grateful to my colleague Mr. M.J. O'Regan for kindly reading my typescript, and for allowing me to see the typescript of his own paper 'André Chénier and English Neo-classical Art.' As the title suggests, this paper explores precise affinities between Chénier's poetry and the visual arts, whilst I have sought to situate Chénier in the wider context of eighteenth-century cultural history, looked at more generally. Our approaches are complementary rather than contradictory.

VOTAIRE'S POEMS ON LUXURY

H.T. Mason

BOUT *Le Mondain* not a word is heard until Mme du Châtelet's letter to Cideville of 18 July 1736 (Best. D1116), in which she speaks of Voltaire's writing the poem 'dans sa chaise de poste en revenant icy'. There seems no good reason to doubt her word, even though, as so often with Voltaire's work, the history of the poem's creation is likely to be more complex than this.

Certainly conditions had lent themselves to completing the poem at this dramatic juncture. Voltaire had left for Paris some time between 16 and 20 April (cf. Best. D1061, 1065), most probably on 18 or 19 April.[1] Already by 6 May he was speaking of his stay as being an exile and announcing an early return home (Best. D1072). But the distractions of his wearisome quarrels with the printer Jore over the *Lettres philosophiques,* which had prompted his sudden departure to Paris, kept him in the capital for many more weeks, despite his frequent expressions of unhappiness at his stay and impatience to return. Jore attempted to blackmail Voltaire into paying

1. On 6 May Voltaire wrote to Cideville that he had been in Paris for 12 days (Best. D1072). The editor's textual Note 6 reports that Clogenson considered the original copy of the letter to have said 21 days. If so, that is an exaggeration; whereas 12 days can be right if Voltaire took several days *en route.*

him a thousand *écus,* in return for which Jore would not reveal the evidence he held of Voltaire's authorship of the *Lettres philosophiques.* When Voltaire refused, Jore published a faction denouncing him (D. app. 39). The affair dragged on through May and June, Voltaire appealing to Hérault, the chief of police in Paris, and eventually obtaining his support so that Jore was obliged to withdraw his suit. But it was a Pyrrhic victory only. Voltaire was obliged to give 500 *livres* to the poor, which left him, as he recognised, technically at fault and therefore 'déshonoré' (Best. D1107). Besides, the squabble had done much harm to his prestige, if we are to accept Jean Le Blanc's report on the matter to Bouhier written around mid-June: '*Voltaire* est bien misérable, bien bas... dut-il gagner son Procès, il n'y a qu'un cri d'indignation publique contre lui... la vanité, les airs de bienfaicteur qu'il y affecte, un certain ton d'impudence qui s'y fait sentir partout, surtout les Mensonges qu'il y avance avec tant d'éffronterie sur sa pauvreté & sa Générosité, tout cela fait crier contre lui' (Best. D1089). Le Blanc, never one of Voltaire's greatest admirers, was no doubt exaggerating with characteristic *Schadenfreude* the degree of Voltaire's unpopularity, but he had made a fair assessment of the *philosophe*'s state of mind. As the latter wrote feelingly to Cideville just before leaving Paris for Cirey: 'L'accablement des affaires a tué mon esprit pendant mon séjour à Paris. J'ai eu à essuier des banqueroutes et des calomnies' (Best. D1108).

So Voltaire withdrew to Cirey under a cloud. Le Blanc had correctly predicted in his letter to Bouhier that all hopes the author held of aspiring to the Académie Française had retreated into the distance (he was not to be elected until 1746, succeeding to Bouhier's own chair). One could easily imagine Voltaire's relief at shaking the dust of Paris off his feet as he returned to the idyllic peace of the countryside and the charms of Mme du Châtelet. But the author's complex personality, as usual, does not admit of such easy answers.

Le Mondain, as is obvious on the first reading, is a hymn to hedonism - to the point where Voltaire, that indefatigable worker, pens one of his most surprising lines:

> J'aime le luxe, *et même la mollesse* (l. 9).[2]

This scarcely sounds like the *philosophe* who during the years 1734—40 was, to quote W.H. Barber's trenchant summation,

> engaged upon the composition or revision of one serious and one burlesque epic, five tragedies, four comedies, two operas, two major poems of moral and philosophical reflexion, two *contes philosophiques;* two works on metaphysics, a handbook on Newtonian science, a prize essay based on original research into a contemporary scientific problem; a major contribution to French historical literature, a literary biography, an essay on contemporary economic theories and the editing of Frederick of Prussia's attack on the politics of Machiavelli.[3]

Yet *Le Mondain* speaks of work only in so far as luxury creates employment for others. The *honnête homme* expends his energy on naught but the frenetic pursuit of enjoyment:

> Il court au bain ...
> Le plaisir presse: il vole au rendez-vous (ll. 88—90).

Where then is all this taking place? Voltaire's answer is explicit:

> Soit à Paris, soit dans Londre ou dans Rome (l. 62).

This is reminiscent of the sixth *Remarque sur Pascal* in the *Lettres philosophiques,* where Voltaire links Paris with London as examples of flourishing, happy cities. But in *Le Mondain,* it is clear, he essentially has only Paris in mind. Illustrative details such as the dancer Camargo and the actress Gaussin are

2.   My italics. All references to the poem will be based on the text established by André Morize in his *L'Apologie du luxe au XVIIIe siècle et 'Le Mondain' de Voltaire,* Paris, 1909.
3.   'Voltaire at Cirey : Art and Thought', *Studies in Eighteenth-Century French Literature presented to Robert Niklaus,* edited by J.H. Fox, M.H. Waddicor and D.A. Watts, University of Exeter, 1975, p. 1.

all drawn from Paris. Besides, Voltaire was well aware that London offered far fewer luxuries than Paris, as he makes clear in a letter to Machault in 1749: 'Je ne craindrai de me tromper en assurant qu'il y a cinq cents fois plus d'argenterie chez les bourgeois de Paris que chez les bourgeois de Londres... Il se mange en un soir, à Paris, plus de volailles et de gibier que dans Londres en une semaine' (Best. D3927). As for all other capital cities, he goes on to indicate that they are far worse (Rome for example, 'n'est guère plus peuplée que Lyon, et je doute fort qu'elle soit aussi riche').

It was the Paris whose brilliant society he had known so well, especially as a young man. Rabutin, the comte de Bussy, who received one of the manuscript copies of the poem, had been a fellow-member of the *bons viveurs* of the Société du Temple (it was in fact this very copy which, discovered after Bussy's death in November 1736 and duplicated many times over for distribution across Paris, led to the scandal over *Le Mondain* when it became public knowledge). The Paris of *Le Mondain* is a city in which Voltaire has not lived (apart from brief visits) since his precipitate flight after the publication of the *Lettres philosophiques* in 1734. As he complains bitterly to Chauvelin, the Garde des Sceaux, just before his return to Cirey in July 1736: 'Je me trouve enfin déshonoré après avoir essuié deux années entières d'exil...' (Best. D1109). Paris is the homeland, Cirey the place of banishment.

Now can one really imagine a *mondain* leading his life to its fullest extent in a château buried in the depths of Champagne? Voltaire appears to use the word only once during the years between the flight to Cirey and the poem's appearance, and the reference is unambiguously to rich, sophisticated Paris society and its fleshpots: 'Ah! vous savez sans doute que M. de Brancas est plus mondain que jamais; il va se damner pour le c .. de madame de Parabès et pour avoir 50 mille livres' (Best. D930, [c. 15 October 1735]).[4]

Le Mondain concludes with the famous line, outwardly redolent of self-contentment:

Le Paradis terrestre est où je suis.

But it is significant to note that this was not how the verse appeared in the first printed edition. There the verse is balder:

Le Paradis Terrestre est à Paris.[5]

In his valuable commentary on *Le Mondain*, Georges Ascoli speculated that Voltaire made the change out of gallantry to Mme du Châtelet.[6] Plausible though that motive is, it does not exclude other interpretations. True, Voltaire's attachment to his Emilie and gratitude for the sanctuary she provided at a critical time must not be under-estimated. His interest in Cirey is well attested by the contributions he made to the upkeep and improvements in the château. The correspondence reveals from time to time an apparently blissful absorption in his rustic life. To Thieriot for instance, he writes: 'et moy quand je vous auray dit que je suis heureux loin du monde, occupé sans tumulte philosophe pour moy tout seul, tendre pour vous et pour une ou deux personnes, j'auray tout dit' (Best. D928, 13 October 1735). A few weeks later, once again to Thieriot, he elaborates the picture in pleasing terms:

Nous [he, Mme du Châtelet and Algarotti] lisons quelques chants de Jeanne la pucelle, ou une tragédie de ma façon, ou un chapitre du siècle de Louis i4. De là nous revenons à Neuton et à Loke, non sans vin de champagne, et sans excellente chère, car nous sommes des philosophes très voluptueux...

4.   From Voltaire's part of a joint letter addressed by him and Mme du Châtelet to the duc de Richelieu.
5.   Morize ed., p. 139. It is interesting to discover the same line in the early edition unknown to Morize, also based on a manuscript copy of 1736 and conceivably the original version of the poem; cf. C. Dédéyan, 'Une version inconnue du "Mondain",' RHLF 49, 1949, pp. 67–74.
6.   *Voltaire: Poèmes philosophiques*, Paris, n.d., p. 41.

Buvez ma santé tout les deux
Avec ce champagne mousseux
Qui brille ainsi que son génie.
Moy chez la sublime Emilie
Dans nos soupers délicieux
Je bois à vous en ambroisie.

(Best. D935, 3 November [1735])

The reference to champagne somewhat prefigures the Bacchic evocation of *soupers fins* and the 'Vin d'Aï' in *Le Mondain*. Indeed, Ira Wade feels the *train du jour* described in this letter to be sufficiently like that of the poem for him to postulate the most likely time of its creation as around the same date; and he is in any case right to point out that Voltaire's letters of 1735 reveal a happiness that is never so enthusiastic in the following year.[7]

Indeed, as 1735 progresses, the expressions of simple contentment appear to diminish or become more muted. The first letter to Thieriot cited above already testifies to a more mixed reaction. Voltaire's satisfaction with his immediate surroundings is balanced by a longing for news from outside. Set in its context, the passage quoted can even be read as a rather wistful sigh of resignation to the fact that a virtue must be made out of the necessity of exile. Emilie is adorable, he says; but he is starved for information and calls on Thieriot to 'm'inonder de nouvelles'. When at the end of 1736 he flees to Holland because of the scandal provoked by *Le Mondain*, it seems likely for a while that he will never return to Cirey, while his ardour for his mistress appears to have modulated into simple affection. Mme du Châtelet is herself deeply apprehensive on both scores (cf. e.g., Best. D1274, January 1737).

The term 'paradis terrestre' applied to Cirey appears in Voltaire's correspondence in 1734, but it is used conditionally

7.   *Studies on Voltaire*, Princeton, 1947, pp. 37—38.

and has little positive value. Writing to Mme de Champbonin, he expresses his regret that he cannot find himself in her company along with that of the comtesse de La Neuville and Mme du Châtelet all at the same time: 'Quand vous serez toutes trois ensemble, la compagnie sera la paradis terrestre' (Best. D805). Voltaire comes nearer to a committed statement in his letter to Thieriot of 3 November 1735:

> Ah croyez moy, j'habite au haut des cieux.

But here again he at least envisages the possibility of leaving Paradise, for the verse continues:

> J'y resteray, j'ose au moins le prétendre,
> Mais si d'un ciel et si pur, et si doux,
> Chez les humains il me falloit descendre
> Ce ne seroit que pour vivre avec vous (Best. D935).

One must allow for the *politesses* of epistolary convention in such remarks and not attempt to place a heavier interpretation on these perhaps casual words than they will bear. It is however possible to argue that, whatever the reason, Voltaire's attitude to Cirey seems increasingly attenuated by the knowledge that other, equally desirable worlds and situations exist.

That view, however, tends to be less hesitant once *Le Mondain* has been written. Voltaire thereafter tells Thieriot of the 'entresoles vernies, d'orées, tapissez de porcelaine, où il est bien doux de philosopher' (Best. D1141, 5 September 1736). About the same time he assures Berger that he has no need of consolation when he has 'une retraite comme Cirey' (Best. D1142). He even turns the Paris of *Le Mondain* into Cirey, promising La Faye that if he comes to pay a visit he will enjoy the same exquisite champagne, quoting the relevant lines from the poem to make the point (Best. D1178, [c. 20 October 1736]). Newton is the God of this place, he tells Cideville, and life is so much better than in Paris as his poem narrates it - or at least it would be if he were in better health and could see his friend (Best. D1154, 25 September 1736). A year later he describes the château in uncompromisingly Edenic terms to Formont: 'Pour moi, sans parti, sans intrigue, retiré dans le paradis terrestre de Cirey, je suis si peu attaché à tout ce qui se passe à Paris...' (Best. D1410, 23 December [1737]). But by then he has undergone the further misery of flight from persecution into Holland for a period, so the attractiveness of Cirey as a haven may well have been enhanced once he had returned and settled down there again.

In brief, we witness in Voltaire's letters before and after *Le Mondain* the same shifting, ambivalent attitudes to his isolated home, offering many intrinsic joys but unalterably removed from the brilliance and stimulation of the capital, as his correspondence will show during the years surrounding *Candide*.[8] Happiness shot through with loneliness; there is no way to resolve the dilemma for long. At times he will, particularly in verse, sing the praises of his rustic retreats, as in *L'Auteur arrivant dans sa terre, près du lac de Genève* (1755), where he apostrophises liberty, equating it with simple dwelling - places:

> Embellis ma retraite, où l'Amitié t'appelle;
> Sur de simples gazons viens t'asseoir avec elle.
> Elle fuit comme toi les vanités des cours,
> Les cabales du monde et son règne frivole.

> (Moland ed., X, pp. 362–6)

And yet there is no gainsaying the magnetism of the great city: 'Paris sera toujours le paradis terrestre. Musique, soupers, bals, téâtres, amours, sciences, société...' (Best. D2931, 10 February [1744]).

8.   Cf. G. Murray, *Voltaire's 'Candide': the Protean gardner, 1755 – 1762*, Studies on Voltaire and the Eighteenth Century LXIX, 1970; P. Ilie, 'The Voices in Candide's garden 1755–1759,' *Studies on Voltaire*, CXLVIII, 1976, pp. 37–113.

Let us return to the question of when *Le Mondain* was written. Morize attributed it to September 1736 (p. 8), a date which has been proved wrong by the discovery of Mme du Châtelet's letter of 18 July 1736 that provides a *terminus ad quem*. Wade also thinks it was written at Cirey, attributing it as we have seen to late 1735, largely on the basis of Voltaire's letter to Thieriot of 3 November. But the similarities are not particularly profound or compelling (as Wade himself admits), and no other evidence from that time supports this thesis, though it is quite possible to see this as the seminal moment of the poem. A paradox still remains; that Voltaire, at Cirey, wrote a poem about life in Paris. But the paradox appears so easily disposed of that it has not ever been seen as such. Morize builds a persuasive picture based on details of the appointments at Cirey as gleaned from the invaluable gossipings of Mme de Graffigny when she stayed there in 1738—39 (pp. 31—32). All that is needed is to construct around this framework a way of life recollected in tranquillity and the poem is complete. Even so, our question abides: if, as Morize rightly says, *Le Mondain* is 'la profession de foi, spirituelle et épicurienne, d'un Parisien libertin' (p. 34), why write it at all at Cirey?

Réne Pomeau takes a different line. Seeing the poem as 'l'ouvrage d'un temps d'ivresse', written in the euphoria consequent upon the success of *Alzire* in January 1736, he argues that it was composed during Voltaire's stay in Paris between April and July and is essentially a celebration of the poet's joy at rediscovering the city after the austerity of provincial Cirey.[9] But this view runs wholly counter to the evidence of Voltaire's letters extant from his stay in Paris. It is difficult to find a single expression of contentment, let alone joy. Quite the contrary: the correspondance is a long, doleful tale of Voltaire's failures and humiliations. All his hopes of defeating

9.   *La Religion de Voltaire*, Paris, 2nd ed., 1969, p. 238.

Jore, rehabilitating his reputation, gaining election to the Académie Française turn to ashes. The final letter from Paris in the Besterman edition shows him attempting to treat with Hérault over the sum he has to pay; the posture is pathetic. This particular departure was crowned with failure, as indeed the whole stay had been. Wretchedly, he announces to Cideville his impending journey, adding that at Cirey 'mon coeur parlera au vôtre, et... je reprendray ma forme naturelle' (Best. D1108, 2 July 1736).

Why not, then, accept Mme du Châtelet's remark at its face value ? Is there any inherent reason why Voltaire should not have composed *Le Mondain* in the postchaise carrying him back to Cirey ? The journey would probably have taken three or four days[10], giving ample time for poetic composition, nor are there any esoteric references in the poem indicating the need for bookish knowledge. Material difficulties do not appear to be insuperable. What however about the psychological circumstances?

At first sight, no time might seem less propitious. One can easily conjure up a despairing figure sunk in gloom. But such a picture does no justice to Voltaire's volatile temperament. A phase of his life has ended; even so, Cirey awaits. In a few days he will be restored to his studies alongside Emilie. For a moment he is suspended between two worlds. Despite his tribulations in Paris he must have participated too in its *douceurs* (Le Blanc speaks of a dinner he had with Voltaire at which they talked much of theatre, Best. D1068; and the poet arranges to meet Baculard d'Arnaud at the Procope, Best. D1090). Nor is the recollection of these pleasures incompatible with the squalid lawsuit pressed by Jore upon him, which exists in a different realm from the elegance of Correggio and the enchantments of the Opéra. What better moment, then,

10.   T. Besterman, *Voltaire*, London, 1969, p. 224.

while the memories of these delights are fresh yet removed from all the late *tracasseries*?

Even so, the ambivalences remain. Neither Paris nor Cirey is totally deserving of the title 'le paradis terrestre'. The hedonist attitudes outlined in *Le Mondain* are bolder than anywhere else in Voltaire's work and do not genuinely represent his position. Nor indeed is it Voltaire who follows the programme of *divertissement*, but the 'honnête homme' (l. 63), at whom the authorial 'je' looks on (ll. 77, 79, 80, 85)-with sympathy, it is true, but at a remove. In the end, the ideal place is not to be located on the map, but rather in that more diverse mental universe 'où je suis'. It is perhaps not too fanciful to imagine that world temporarily removed from the world of everyday reality, in transit between the two poles of Voltaire's existence.

All this helps to confirm the point first made clear by Wade, that *Le Mondain* is not, as Morize had suggested, a treatise on economics.[11] It is rather a 'défense du Mondain', apologising for the worldly way of life in opposition to the theologians and moralists: explicitly, it is an *anti-Télémaque*[12]. The most famous line of the poem, 'Le superflu, chose très nécessaire' (l. 22), is probably derived, not from Marivaux as Morize speculates (Marivaux and Voltaire seem to have derived virtually nothing from each other), but from Fénelon's remark discussing luxury that 'Toute une nation s'accoutume à regarder comme les nécessités de la vie les choses les plus superflues'

---

11. *Studies on Voltaire*, p. 51.
12. J. Ehrard, *L'Idée de nature en France dans la première moitié du XVIIIe siècle*, Paris, 1963, p. 593.

(*Télémaque*, Bk. XVII)[13]. In defiance of the Fénelons, Voltaire permits himself an unusually adventurous response. Even so, the basic intention is as elsewhere: to assert the pleasure principle only if and where it is useful to society. Ehrard points out that the eighteenth century is not defending enjoyment as such but action (op. cit., p. 383). The statement is particularly applicable to Voltaire, for whom happiness finds its source in action, following a universal law that makes sense of human nature: 'L'homme est né pour l'action, comme le feu tend en haut et la pierre en bas' (*Remarques sur Pascal*, XXIII). In this context hedonism had a place, denoting as it did that awakening to consciousness via sense-experience which is the topic of the thirteenth *Lettre philosophique*.

Le Mondain, then, sees the poet somewhat distanced from that whereof he speaks, enjoying the writing of what he was to call a 'badinage si innocent' (Best. D1210, to Thieriot, 27 November 1736). Much of the glee is expended upon the condescending and iconoclastic portrait of Adam and Eve, a rare example from the 1730's of Biblical criticism appearing (unintentionally) in print under Voltaire's name. Such audacity could hardly fail to draw down the wrath of authority upon his head once his manuscript *badinage* was made public in November 1736, making his flight to Holland in December a measure of necessary prudence. In reaction to that scandal the *Défense du Mondain* was written. Voltaire sent a copy to

---

13. It must however be added that the juxtaposition of *superflu* and *nécessaire* also occurs elsewhere, notably in La Bruyère's *Les Caractères* where he approves of Parisians' frugality in times past: 'Ils ne savaient point se priver du nécessaire pour avoir le superflu' ('De la ville', 22). Voltaire attacks this passage in 1738 *(Observations sur MM. Lass...)*, and Wade speculates that *Le Mondain* may have been a reply to it *(Studies on Voltaire*, pp. 53–54). This thesis, though quite plausible, seems to lack any other supporting evidence. Besides, the space devoted to La Bruyère in the *Observations* is brief. One gains the impression that, philosophically speaking, Fénelon offered a larger target.

Frederick from Leyden in early January 1737; presumably it
was completed (perhaps wholly composed) in exile.

The *Défense* was therefore written under quite different
circumstances from *Le Mondain*. Though the manner is just as
light and the shafts directed against 'maîtres cafards' even
sharper, Voltaire this time has a thesis to defend. The mis-
anthropic ascetic who is seated near him at dinner is overwhelmed in argument by the poet's proofs that luxury is
socially and economically beneficial. Such ideas are not wholly
absent from *Le Mondain* (esp. ll. 14—29), so it would be unwise
to see the two poems as antithetical. But in the *Défense* this
apology becomes paramount, and now Voltaire invokes the
Bible not to mock but to praise, selecting Solomon as a
roi philosophe (as he had already done in a poem addressed to
Frederick around 30 September 1736, Best. D1157) who knew
how to make luxurious appurtenances work for the common
good.

This shift of emphasis from the moral to the economic
arguments in favour of luxury is in line with the thinking of
the age as affluence increases. Trade with the East Indies
(referred to in *Le Mondain*) became particularly active after the
East Indies Company abandoned Louisiana in 1731 (Morize,
p. 142, n. 12). Between 1715 and 1750 French foreign trade
almost tripled[14]; it almost quadrupled by 1788[15]. Luxury
ceases to be a sign of status, becomes a matter for debate as
eighteenth-century France gradually moves away from a
subsistence economy. From public ostentation a transfer of
emphasis occurs to private enjoyment of the comfortable.[16]

14.   P. Sagnac, *La Formation de la société française moderne*, Paris,
      1945—6, 2 vols., II, p. 12.
15.   J. Lough, *An Introduction to Eighteenth Century France*, London
      1960, pp. 71—72.
16.   Cf. the excellent chapter on the subject by G. Gusdorf, *Les Principes
      de la pensée au siècle des lumières*, Paris, 1971, pp. 444—461.

With the general economic boom in agricultural prices that begins around 1730 and will go on for a half-century landed proprietors can indulge their new—found wealth in wider consumption, as *Le Mondain* and the *Défense* show. Melon's *Essai politique sur le commerce* (1734) and Cartaud de la Villate's *Essai historique et philosophique sur le goût* (1736) move the argument away from a defence of frugality for its own sake into a wider discussion on the uses and abuses of luxury. In this complex debate,, the charting of which still awaits its historian, Voltaire's two poems play their part. 'Le superflu, chose très nécessaire' becomes a common catch-phrase through the incisiveness of its paradox; one finds it turning up, for instance, in Fréron's *Année littéraire* in 1764 when he is discussing luxury (VIII, pp. 164—168) or as the epigraph to Butel-Dumont's *Théorie du luxe* (1771). In his *Considérations sur les richesses et le luxe* (1787) Sénac de Meilhan quotes (without stating the author) Voltaire's almost equally famous remark in the *Défense,* that 'Le Luxe enrichit/Un grand Etat' (ll. 53—54), and then goes on to refute it (p. 123). As late as 1800, one finds Mme de Staël arguing in the Préface to *De la littérature* against an anonymous 'littérateur de nos jours' that *Le Mondain* did not provide the seminal inspiration for the concept of human perfectibility: the very refutation is itself remarkable testimony to the attention which the poem still continued to attract.

Voltaire's economic views on luxury do not basically change after the *Défense du Mondain*. However, the moral problems posed will go on troubling Voltaire for the rest of his life, bound up as they are with his evaluation of sophisticated society. In *Le Monde comme il va* (1748), he remains fairly indulgent, and Persépolis (Paris) is saved from destruction on the grounds that 'Si tout n'est pas bien, tout est passable'. *Candide* is more complex. Does luxury exist in Eldorado ? No one is interested in the precious stones lying around, which are seen as irrelevant. There appears to be little sign of that surplus of resources available to only one group at the expense of the rest which is one of the usual hallmarks of luxury. Yet the country is undeniably prosperous and the *roi philosophe* puts the bounties to good use in a manner reminiscent of Solomon in the *Défense*. In this respect as in many others a certain unreality attaches to Eldorado. Candide himself learns that untold wealth brings no happiness and he eventually rejects the pleasure palaces of Europe for a new world on the continent's periphery. But though the principle of his community is self-sufficiency through work, they have the old Turk as model and inspiration, leading a life which while simple is most decorous and comfortable, elegant, clean, civilised - and not in the least like the Garden of Eden. *L'Ingénu* bears out the same conclusions: civilisation may have many miseries, but the primitive life has no pleasures. Besides, the cornerstones of Voltaire's morality, pity and justice, are possible only in a civilised community.

Voltaire's intervention in the debate on luxury may well have had a decisive effect upon the argument. Few will after 1736 go on supporting limitations upon production as a good thing in itself. Even a Rousseau does not feel that the answer lies in that direction. At the same time, the endorsement of total enjoyment regardless of the consequences also seems outmoded; Voltaire's hardening resistance to this between *Le Mondain* and the *Défense* also foreshadows the turn in the debate. For Diderot, Beccaria, Montesquieu, Helvétius, Condillac, Saint-Lambert it will be a matter of distinguishing between the good and evil uses of luxury and of harnessing the former for the public welfare. In two poems of just 128 lines each, Voltaire had encapsulated so much that prevailed in the climate of his age: a *badinage* and its subsequent defence, which count amongst the most important poems of the French Enlightenment.

LE DISCOURS DE MIRABEAU SUR LA 'CONTRIBUTION DU QUART' A-T-IL ÉTÉ RÉCRIT?

R. Mortier

 ANS l'histoire de l'éloquence parlementaire, le discours prononcé par Mirabeau, le 26 septembre 1789, devant l'Assemblée Nationale, est resté une manière de classique, abondamment reproduit par les manuels et analysé comme un modèle devant plusieurs générations d'élèves. Mirabeau y défendait avec chaleur un projet d'emprunt imaginé par le ministre des finances Necker, et qui visait à décréter un *secours* extraordinaire du quart des revenus de chaque citoyen français. Combattu par les uns, renvoyé insidieusement en commission par les autres, le projet était sur le point de s'enliser, et le sauvetage des finances de l'Etat avec lui, lorsque Mirabeau reprit la parole, pour lancer une admonestation pathétique et pressante à une assemblée stupéfaite et médusée:

> Messieurs, au milieu de tant de débats tumultueux, ne pourrai-je donc pas ramener à la délibération du jour par un petit nombre de questions bien simples? Daignez, messieurs, daignez me répondre... *(OEuvres de Mirabeau,* Paris, Brissot-Thivars et Dupont, 1825, t. VII, p. 296 à 301).

Un des traits les plus admirés de cette prouesse d'éloquence était la réponse improvisée, tout au début du discours, à l'intervention d'un contradicteur anonyme:

> Avons-nous un plan à substituer à celui qu'il nous propose? *Oui,* a crié quelqu'un dans l'assemblée. Je conjure celui qui répond *oui* de considérer que son plan n'est pas connu, qu'il faut du temps

pour le développer, l'examiner, le démontrer; que, fût-il immédiatement soumis à notre délibération, son auteur a pu se tromper;
que, fût-il exempt de toute erreur, on peut croire qu'il s'est
trompé; que, quand tout le monde a tort, tout le monde a raison;
qu'il se pourrait donc que l'auteur de cet autre projet, même en
ayant raison, eût tort contre tout le monde, puisque, sans
l'assentiment de l'opinion publique, le plus grand talent ne saurait
triompher des circonstances... [points de suspension dans le texte
imprimé]. Et moi aussi je ne crois pas les moyens de M. Necker
les meilleurs possibles, etc., etc.

Que, dans la chaleur du débat, Mirabeau ait su improviser
une riposte aussi savamment graduée, aussi habilement balancée,
pouvait apparaître à bon droit comme le sommet de l'art
oratoire et la marque d'une exceptionnelle maîtrise de la pensée
et de l'expression. Plus que l'exhortation pathétique de la péroraï-
son, trop directement inspirée de Démosthène ('la banqueroute,
la hideuse banqueroute est là..., et vous délibérez!'), cette réfutation lancée à brûle-pourpoint établissait, ou confirmait, le génie
littéraire d'un des orateurs les plus éloquents de la Révolution.
Mais si, au contraire, il s'agissait seulement d'une performance
littéraire, forgée, la plume à la main, au lendemain de la joute?
Il est permis de se poser la question à la lumière d'un témoignage
d'époque.

Les historiens de la Révolution ne se sont guère intéressés
au vieux *Journal Encyclopédique,* fondé à Liège en 1756 par
Pierre Rousseau (de Toulouse) avec la bénédiction de Voltaire,
et poursuivi à Bouillon jusqu'en 1793 par son gendre Weissen-
bruch. Cet organe des modérés du parti 'philosophique' suivait
pourtant très attentivement les événements de Paris, où il
entretenait plusieurs correspondants fort bien informés. C'est
ainsi que le numéro du 1er novembre 1789 (VII, 3, 532–534)
faisait très amplement écho au discours du 26 septembre. Le
journaliste rappelait l'objet du débat, l'affrontement entre
Mirabeau et Lally-Tollendal, les manœuvres dilatoires de certains
membres partisans d'un 'encommissionnement', et il enchaînait
ensuite:

C'étoit à M. de Mirabeau qu'il appartenoit de préparer, de retarder et de déterminer les résolutions, les destinées en quelque sorte de ce jour, qui va ouvrir de nouvelles destinées et de nouveaux jours à la France. Lorsque tous les esprits, et ceux même qui n'avoient fait que prêter leur attention, étoient épuisés de fatigue, après une séance de près de huit heures, le sien se relevant avec des forces qu'il n'a jamais eues au même degré, mettant à quartier cette fois, avec sincérité, et les petites vanités d'une rédaction et des inimitiés adoptées pour la gloire plutôt qu'inspirées par la haine, a gourmandé avec une éloquence sublime les incertitudes et les hésitations de l'Assemblée.

Suit alors la substance du fameux discours, rapportée en style direct:

"Vous balancez, a-t-il dit, à adopter ce plan? Est-il parmi nous quelqu'un qui en ait un meilleur à proposer? Vous doutez du succès, et moi aussi; mais ce dont vous et moi, et personne au monde ne peut douter, c'est que tous les malheurs nous menacent de toutes parts, et nous atteignent tout-à-l'heure, si nous n'essayons pas des moyens qui nous sont offerts pour les écarter. Vous voudriez pénétrer dans l'avenir, regardez-le, il est près de vous; c'est la banqueroute. Ce gouffre du déficit, sans cesse ouvert devant vous, vous épouvante. Si quelqu'un de ces mauvais génies qu'on a cru longtemps présider aux choses humaines apparoissoit dans cette Assemblée, et vous disoit: "Jettez dans ce gouffre tous les créanciers de l'Etat, le gouffre va les dévorer, et il se refermera", vous frémiriez d'horreur. Eh bien! le sort que vous leur prépareriez par la banqueroute seroit cent fois plus cruel et plus affreux que cette mort prompte: elle les délivreroit dans un instant de tous les maux sur lesquels la banqueroute va leur faire traîner leur misérable vie. Vous redoutez des sacrifices: sont-ils plus redoutables que l'infamie, sont-ils plus redoutables qu'une ruine entière? Qu'aurez-vous conservé à ce peuple lorsque ce peuple lui-même sera perdu? Eh! quoi, dans un moment où le danger étoit plus dans nos imaginations que dans les événemens, j'ai entendu dire ici ces paroles: Catilina est aux portes de Rome, et nous délibérons! Catilina n'a jamais existé pour nous; il n'a jamais existé de Catilina aux portes de Paris; mais vous délibérez! et l'infâme banqueroute est aux portes de votre honneur et de vos biens: vous demandez du temps, le malheur n'en accorde jamais, et la nation est perdue si les représentans ne décrètent pas toutes les propositions du ministre avant de sortir de cette Assemblée."

Et le journaliste anonyme conclut ce résumé par une appréciation enthousiaste qui reflète aussi la réaction de l'Assemblée:

> Non, jamais en France l'éloquence du moment, jamais
> l'éloquence improvisée ne s'est élevée à cette hauteur, et n'a
> exercé une telle puissance sur des milliers d'âmes remplies
> d'opinions et de passions contraires. Un seul député s'est levé, et
> a dit: "Je demande à répondre à M. de Mirabeau", mais il est
> resté le bras tendu, immobile et muet, comme si son entreprise
> l'avoit glacé d'épouvante. Tous les autres n'ont interrompu leurs
> applaudissemens que pour demander qu'on allât aux voix, et le
> décret qui a adopté tout le plan de M. Necker a passé à la
> majorité de 473 voix contre 151 ou 152.

En passant de ce que le journaliste appelait 'l'éloquence du moment' à une éloquence écrite, et donc plus élaborée, la substance du discours ne s'est pas radicalement transformée, et certains passages du résumé se retrouvent presque mot à mot dans le compte rendu de l'Assemblée (qui parle d' 'applaudissements presque convulsifs').

Sur un point seulement, mais sur un point important, la disparité éclate. Il s'agit précisément de la riposte improvisée par Mirabeau contre son interrupteur anonyme, tout au début de son intervention. Aucune mention n'est est faite dans le *Journal Encyclopédique,* qui n'aurait certes pas manqué de noter pareille prouesse. Mieux encore: le journaliste a pris soin de signaler l'interpellation finale et d'en souligner la pathétique inutilité. L'image de l'opposant figé dans son refus, mais aussi dans son silence, est comme le symbole du triomphe de l'orateur dont le verbe éclatant a étouffé d'avance la voix de la contestation.

Si on en croit le correspondant du *Journal Encyclopédique,* personne ne s'est levé pour répondre à la question 'Est-il parmi nous quelqu'un qui ait un meilleur plan à proposer? ' , et Mirabeau n'a pas eu à improviser la réfutation dont le texte écrit immortalisera la structure admirablement ascendante. Or la *confutatio* était, depuis Cicéron et Quintilien, une des pièces maîtresses du discours, qui était supposée faire suite immédiatement à (ou même précéder) la *confirmatio,* ou énoncé du thème général.

S'il est permis de formuler une hypothèse dans l'état actuel du problème, c'est que Mirabeau, en récrivant son texte 'parlé ', a jugé opportun de déplacer l'intervention de son contradicteur à la seule fin de conformer plus strictement l'ordonnance de son discours aux préceptes de la rhétorique classique. Il y gagnait un avantage supplémentaire, celui de rédiger à tête reposée un des plus beaux échantillons de la réfutation oratoire dans notre prose française. Qu'importe, après tout, que ce morceau brillant ait été composé à froid, dans le silence du cabinet de travail: tel quel, il complète merveilleusement un ensemble où l'on a pu voir, pendant plus d'un siècle, un des sommets de l'éloquence politique française.

RE-EDITIONS AS A GUIDE TO THE
ASSESSMENT OF PUBLIC TASTE IN FICTION
V. Mylne

ASICALLY some of the works of fiction published in French in the eighteenth century are so weak and meretricious as to justify the conclusion that practically any new novel or tale could find a publisher. This in itself bears witness to the popularity of fiction as a type of reading-matter, since the printers and booksellers were, one must suppose, convinced that there was a ready market for the fiction they put on sale. The statistics of re-editions reinforce this supposition: in the period 1751–1800, for each new fictional work which appeared in book-form, there were roughly two re-editions of previously published works.[1] Some idea of the scale of production, including translations into French, can be gained from the figures which follow.

	New Works	Re-editions
1751–60	293	599
1761–70	465	878
1771–80	385	961
1781–90	601	1215
1791–1800	705	1207
Total:	2449	4860

1.   Statistics in this article are based on material from: A. Martin, V.G. Mylne, R.L. Frautschi, *Bibliographie du genre romanesque français, 1751–1800*, London, Mansell, 1977.

The second column, it should be emphasized, indicates how many re-editions were produced, not how many works were re-edited. Out of the total of 2449 new titles, 1234 were never re-edited, as far as we know. There remains the figure of 1215 works which had one or more re-editions, plus the 349 pre-1751 works which were re-edited during the second half of the century. This gives a total of 1564 re-edition titles.

I have offered these statistics as though they were simple and definitive, but this of course is not the case. The compilation of re-edition lists raises a number of problems which affect the way in which we should accept and interpret the figures.

In the case of a literary genre such as narrative fiction, there may be at the outset some uncertainty as to whether certain works should properly be classified as fictional — or narrative. The most obvious type of borderline case is the romanced biography, but there are others. There is room for disagreement, therefore, over the initial selection of the corpus of material.

Once this choice has been made, and the quest for re-editions is under way, we are faced with an awkward fact: one can never be entirely sure that the list of re-editions of a given work is complete. On a bookshelf in Russia or Peru, in New South Wales or North Dakota, there may be, all unknown to the searcher, a copy from a hitherto unrecorded edition. Or else the researcher may know that a copy of a certain work is available in such-and-such a library; but the details given by the library-catalogue correspond with those of a recorded edition, and thus conceal the fact that this copy belongs in reality to a pirated edition, not known to bibliographers. (It goes without saying that in this kind of quest, involving hundreds of works, one cannot usually hope to take into account such fine details as, say, different states of the same issue.)

On the one hand, then, any list of a work's re-editions, however carefully it has been compiled, may be incomplete. Conversely, it may well contain spurious items which should

not be there. Misreadings and errors of transcription, once
committed, tend to be perpetuated by subsequent bibliographers: the 1753 edition which is noted as '1755' can create a
phantom 1755 edition for ever after. Erroneous or misleading
entries may also depend not so much on mistakes as on certain
practices in the book-trade. What appear to be two separate
editions published in the same year, bearing the names of two
different booksellers on the title-pages, may be a single printing
which the two booksellers divided between them, with each
Libraire having his own version of the title-page in the copies
he undertook to sell.

Similar complications can arise in the case of a book which
did not sell well. If, after a certain lapse of time, the bookseller
had a fair number of copies left, he might substitute a fresh
title-page bearing the new date — and sometimes even a new
title — to tempt buyers with an apparently new work. In such
cases the 're-editions' which might be considered as evidence of
the book's appeal are actually an indication of its failure to sell.
Thus Pierre Duplessis's novel, *Histoire du marquis de Séligni et
de madame de Luzal,* first published in 1789, came out again
in a 1790 're-edition' which was merely the first edition with a
fresh title-page tipped in. What remained of the first edition
was then presumably sold to another bookseller, since a further
(undated) 're-edition' appeared, still using the sheets of the
original printing, but carrying the name of a different bookseller and a new title, *Les Contre-tems ou la femme crue veuve.*

This brief outline has suggested some, though by no means
all, of the problems involved in the collection, on a broad scale,
of data about re-editions. The inevitable imperfections of re-
edition lists need not make us wholly sceptical as to their uses,
but we should be careful not to consider them as definitive
statistics, and any conclusions we try to base upon them must
be flexible enough to allow for a certain margin of error.

When the researcher decides that he cannot devote any

more time to the unending task of compilation, he can begin to consider the implications of the figures he has collected. The business of evaluating a work's popularity by the number of times it was re-edited immediately raises one type of problem: how are we to judge a given work when it is repeatedly published in the same volume or set of volumes as other works ? For instance, if we count all the re-editions of *La Princesse de Clèves* between 1751 and 1800, we obtain a total of fifteen. But seven of these appeared in successive editions of the *Bibliothèque de campagne,* a twelve-volume collection of fiction, verse and essays, which began to come out in 1735. Since *La Princesse de Clèves* is only one of the numerous *nouvelles* in this collection, we can hardly accept the re-editions of the *Bibliothèque de campagne* as straightforward evidence of the popularity of Mme de La Fayette's story.

The form in which this problem most frequently occurs is the case of a single piece of fiction which is reprinted along with other works by the same author. How far do editions of Montesquieu's *Œuvres* bear testimony to the public's liking for the *Lettres persanes?* Or could any one of Voltaire's philosophic tales, even *Candide,* be considered as the main motive for buying a set of his *Œuvres?* Re-edition lists must obviously include those sets of *Œuvres* in which the relevant piece of fiction appeared, but we need to distinguish, when assessing public taste, between occasions when a work figures in such sets, and those when it is published on its own.

A clear case for comparison along these lines is provided by *La Nouvelle Héloïse* and Marmontel's *Contes moraux,* both of which first appeared in 1761. Between this date and 1780, the *Contes* had thirty-nine re-editions, and were also included in an edition of Marmontel's *Œuvres* (1777). Rousseau's novel had, over the same period, a total of some forty-one editions, but twelve of these were in editions of *Œuvres,* leaving only twenty-nine separate editions of the novel. One is therefore justified in saying that, as far as the evidence of re-editions goes, *La Nouvelle Héloïse* appears to have been less popular, in the two decades following its publication, than were the *Contes moraux.* (A further factor which should ideally be taken into account, the number of copies in each edition, is available for eighteenth-century works in only a few exceptional cases; the average number of copies in an edition is thought to have been in the region of two thousand.)

This approach, a comparison of the number of re-editions of various specific works, can give us some indications of the relative popularity of certain authors or works over an extended span of years. The method has been effectively demonstrated by Angus Martin for some eighteenth-century best-sellers.[2] Should we wish however to diagnose public taste at a given moment, we need to uşe a different method and a fresh set of criteria.

The first point to be decided is the length of our 'given moment'. A single year is probably not long enough. Among other reasons is the fact that one best-seller may provide an important proportion of a certain year's total of re-editions. In 1777, for instance, Marmontel's *Les Incas* had fifteen re-editions; while five years later *Les Liaisons dangereuses,* a vastly different type of work, also had fifteen re-editions. In both cases this number can be accepted as a significant indication of the taste of a certain section of the reading public. But to take either of these years in isolation would be to distort the overall picture of public taste at the time. I have therefore chosen a five-year period as a 'moment' of reasonable length; and in the hope of illustrating some changes in taste, I have concentrated on two such moments, 1776—1780 and 1796—1800. The total numbers

2.   'Romans et romanciers à succès de 1751 à la Révolution d'après les rééditions', *Revue des Sciences Humaines,* fascicule 139 (juillet-sept. 1971), pp. 383—89.

of re-editions listed for these two periods are 467 and 673 respectively.

The next stage is to ask which aspects of the re-edited works we should select as criteria for the purpose of classification. One can establish a kind of scale, running from the characteristics which can be objectively determined — for example, the length of individual works — to those elements whose evaluation is much more subjective, such as the predominant tone, grave or gay, of a given work.

Unfortunately the objective data are not as easy to gather as one might at first suppose. In the case of length, for instance, any attempt to achieve accurate figures would require one to make a word-count of each work; a page-count alone would give only the roughest of guides, since the number of words per page can vary so widely. Even supposing there were time enough for this laborious exercise, the results would not, I suspect, be particularly illuminating.

An aspect of fiction which seems more significant, and which has received considerable attention from modern critics is that of the narrative mode: first-person or third, letter-novels or *contes dialogués*. In the majority of cases, novels and tales can be classified without much trouble as falling into one of these four categories. A significant minority of works, however, combine two or more narrative modes; the commonest type is the third-person story containing long intercalated first-person *récits*. One can either multiply one's range of categories to allow for such variants, or else keep to the four main categories and classify each work according to the mode which seems to be predominant. In the table which follows, I have adopted the latter course. In order to facilitate comparison between the two periods, I have converted the actual numbers of re-editions into a percentage of the relevant total.

	1776–1780	1796–1800
First-person	25.6	26.9
Third-person	44.4	50.1
Letters	15.7	11.1
Dialogue	4.3	2.3
Unclassifiable	10.0	9.6

The final, Unclassifiable, category contains those sets of *Œuvres,* and multi-volume collections, whose doubtful status I have already discussed. (If the fictional works in these sets and collections were to be added to their relevant categories, the effect would be, for both periods, to increase the percentages slightly without significantly changing their relative proportions.) Also included under the Unclassifiable heading is a small number of works consisting of volumes of short stories whose narrative modes are too heterogeneous to be classified.

A final element in the category, affecting only the 1796–1800 total, is a figure of about 1.8% for works not seen. When one chooses to classify books by some characteristic of their contents, one is faced by the problem of those works of which one cannot locate a copy, even though their publication may be well attested by *annonces* and reviews in contemporary journals. In the case of narrative modes, a title or sub-title may of course provide the information we need: the common eighteenth-century practice of qualifying a novel as *Mémoires de...* or *Lettres de...* is a safe enough guide. By the end of the century, however, many novelists were adopting the habit which now prevails, of using titles that refer to the subject-matter without suggesting the type of narrative employed.

The numbers shown under Dialogue reflect the fact that the minor vogue for *contes dialogués,* which had been in force during the 1770s, was declining in the 1790s.[3] As for First-person narrative, we cannot safely attach any importance to the slender difference between the figures for the two periods.

The only differences which do seem worthy of note are the real decline in re-editions of letter-novels, and the increase in third-person narratives. This increase depends to a considerable extent on the vogue of the Gothic novel, which in most cases is narrated in the third person.

Before pursuing the question of the Gothic novel, we should however pause and ask what general conclusions we may justifiably draw from the statistics concerning narrative modes. These figures certainly provide us with a rough guide as to the relative prevalence of certain types of work. And were we to equate prevalence with popularity, we might conclude, for instance, that third-person novels were becoming more popular towards the end of the century. Since however we are trying to diagnose the taste of the reading public, we must surely look for some positive preferences which motivated the readers' choice of books (and thus influenced the printers' decisions about re-publishing certain kinds of works). Can we assume that the narrative mode was an important factor in such choices ? I would not rule out the possibility that some readers enjoyed memoir-novels or letter-novels as such, and might thus select their reading-matter largely on the grounds of literary form. Nevertheless it seems to me more probable — and in this domain we cannot go beyond impressions — that eighteenth-century readers, like the twentieth-century public, based their choices on content rather than form; what is the novel about, what kind of actions and events, feelings and ideas, does it deal with ? The supposition that this is what people want to know when choosing a novel is born out by the practice nowadays, in some public libraries, of classifying and shelving fiction under rubrics

3. For details of this vogue, see my article, 'Dialogue as narrative in eighteenth-century French fiction', in *Studies in Eighteenth-century French Literature presented to Robert Niklaus*, edited by J.H. Fox, M.H. Waddicor and D.A. Watts, Exeter, 1975, pp. 173—192.

such as 'Historical novels.' 'Westerns,' 'Detective stories',
'Science fiction,' etc. To discover what the eighteenth-century
reading public liked, we should therefore go beyond purely
formal characteristics when classifying our material.

It would probably be boring, and certainly take up too
much space, if I were to discuss in detail the difficulties of this
task. Some brief comments are however in order.

In the devising of our categories, we may have to take
into account various factors over and above the ostensible
subject-matter or story-line: while *Candide* is, in some sense,
a love-story, this is clearly not what the tale is chiefly 'about'.
We thus need to use themes, as well as plots, as a type of
criterion. And apart from *romans à thèse,* which are meant to
persuade the reader, we must allow too for the overtly didactic
and pedagogic approach. So our categories will cover a
spectrum of plot, theme and purpose.

Even when a relatively satisfactory range of categories has
been worked out, one still finds works which seem to belong to
two or more categories. Louvet de Couvray's long novel about
the Chevalier de Faublas provides a case in point: the early
episodes are in a vein of cheerful *galanterie,* but as the adven-
tures proceed they take on a more sombre tone, with the hero
eventually falling prey to a melancholy madness. If one wishes,
for statistical purposes, to classify each work as a unit, one
must decide in cases like this which aspect of the book is more
important and/or better known to the public. Some of these
decisions are open to debate and might differ from one reader to
the next. A certain proportion of our statistical data, though not
a large one, will therefore be dependent on personal judgements.

In the first of the tables which follow — presented again
in percentages — I have listed the seven categories which emerged
as being of the least importance numerically, together with the
group of unclassifiable works. (This group constitutes a lower
percentage than in the previous table because certain collections

of works are sufficiently homogeneous in content to be classified here, e.g. the Œuvres of Mme Riccoboni, sets of Voltaire's Romans et contes, etc.)

	1776-1780	1796-1800
Edifying stories, religious instruction	2.1	0
Fairy-tales, the supernatural, Biblical tales	2.1	2.2
Allegory	1.1	0.3
Historical and pseudo-historical stories	1.5	2.6
Tales of chivalry, genre troubadour	4.1	1.8
Political and court intrigue; war	0	1.8
Travels	1.9	2.1
Unclassifiable	8.6	8.6

With figures which are so small, it is perhaps unwise to draw any general conclusions except to note that these are apparently the least popular kinds of fiction. It may also be worth pointing out that the period 1796–1800 was not entirely devoid of fiction meant for religious instruction and edification: about forty new works of this type were published during these years — but none of them seems to have achieved any re-editions at this time. After 1800, on the other hand, we find fresh re-editions of various works of piety, including earlier stories such as Marin's Théodule ou l'enfant de la bénédiction (1762). Napoleon's official support of the Church presumably encouraged such developments. Variations in the political-cum-religious climate can thus be reflected in the re-edition figures, though these variations are not necessarily identical with changes in the reading public's taste.

This first table account for roughly one-fifth of the total output of re-editions, so that the remaining seven categories, listed below, cover the main bulk of the material classified.

	1776-1780	*1796-1800*
Sentimental and pastoral love-stories	23.6	22.9
Sexual intrigue, *galanterie*	19.5	10.1
Scabrous and pornographic tales	6.6	6.2
Stories of adventure, mystery, horror	4.9	13.7
Novels of manners, social criticism	13.1	11.4
Philosophic themes and ideas, utopias	5.1	5.9
Didactic and pedagogic works	5.8	10.4

In two cases at least, these figures conceal some problems or traps. The first of these chiefly concerns those works I have classified as scabrous or pornographic, but can also involve other works which are officially banned. If the powers-that-be have made it illegal for a certain work or kind of work to be put on sale, then printers and booksellers will have to wrestle with the conflicting factors of public demand for such works and the risks attendant on publication. In 1776, for instance, there seems to have been a marked rise in the number of re-editions of erotic and pornographic books. The only event I know of which might be connected with this phenomenon was a change in the administration of the book-trade in Paris. Between 1763 and 1776, the two men who successively held the post of Lieutenant de Police, Sartine and Albert, were also appointed to be Directeur de la Librairie. In 1776 this dual responsibility was divided, so that the new Directeur, Le Camus de Neville, no longer controlled the policing of Paris. Perhaps this fresh arrangement encouraged some printers to believe that there was now less danger of being caught and punished if they brought out forbidden works ? If so, the rise in the number of pornographic works in 1776 is a reflexion not of a swing in public taste, but of the fact that in preceding years fear or caution had prevented the printers and booksellers from catering for the preferences of a certain section of the public.

A second set of problems has to do with the apparent

rise in the popularity of didactic works. The difference between
the figures for the two periods can be accounted for largely by
re-editions of one work: Fénelon's *Les Aventures de Télémaque*.
In the latter period, this was published twenty-nine times
separately, and once in a set of *Œuvres*. However, these re-
editions raise three complicating factors. Firstly, the popularity
of *Télémaque* may have depended, in some quarters, less on its
didactic import than on its Neo-classical associations. (Beginning
in the visual arts, the Neo-classical movement later extended to
fiction, though in ways which are not always easy to define.)
This reminds us that different aspects of a book may assume
importance at different periods — an illustration of yet another
problem inherent in the business of classification. Secondly, as
an improving work which had attained the status of a classic,
Télémaque was liable to be awarded as a school prize or given
to young people as an edifying present; and such a function is
no guarantee of the book's popularity with those who received
it. Thirdly, some of the re-editions of *Télémaque* were produced
in Germany and Switzerland, in England, Ireland and America,
for home consumption. To what extent, therefore, can they
bear witness to the taste of the *French* reading public ?
Considerations of this kind emphasize the fact that we must
never allow our statistics to mask the special characteristics of
the individual works they represent.

Turning now to the most striking differences between the
two periods, we find, on the one hand, a clear increase in the
category of adventure and mystery stories, and on the other,
a decline in works concerned with sexual intrigue and *galanterie*.
The former category includes, for the period 1796–1800, quite
a high proportion of English Gothic novels in translation. This
effectively demonstrates that any discussion of readers' preferences must take account not only of native works but also of
translations. And while the re-edition figures confirm an aspect
of taste already familiar to historians of literature, the vogue of

the Gothic novel, the relation between these figures and those for the conventional sentimental love-story can help us to see that the Gothic novel was by no means overwhelming in its impact on the public's reading habits.

As for the decline in the re-editions of novels of *galanterie,* this is a matter on which a comparison with the figures for new novels may throw some light. Production of new works of this type, calculated as a percentage of the total output of new works, shows a progressive falling-off from over 15% in the 1750s to about 9% in the 1770s; after a slight lift in the 1780s, the figure for the last decade is some 8%. However, even if a decreasing number of novelists were choosing to write such works in the 1770s, the booksellers of that decade clearly assumed that this kind of work still stood high in public favour.

The discussion of these last two categories of novel shows, I believe, the chief ways in which the statistics of re-editions can be useful. With all their drawbacks and complications, such statistics can still help us to obtain a more accurate picture of readers' preferences than we would gain from the history and statistics of new works alone. The picture comes to us via the judgement of printers and booksellers; but since their very livelihood depended largely on such assessments, who could have a greater interest in faithfully following every shift and fluctuation of the reading public's taste?

THE MERCHANT ON THE FRENCH STAGE IN THE 18TH CENTURY, OR THE RISE AND FALL OF AN 18TH CENTURY MYTH

R. Niklaus

CHOLARS have become increasingly aware that the good merchant of the eighteenth century is a myth which has its *raison d'être* in a more complex society than we have hitherto thought. The fact is that merchants in France as in England were rich or poor, good or bad and without any special claim to a higher moral code than other members of the community. The myth of the good merchant is no better founded than the corresponding myth of the aristocratic libertine which Warren Roberts has striven to debunk in *Morality and Social Class in Eighteenth-century French Literature and Painting* (Toronto, 1974). Eighteenth-century education still stressed conventional morality and continued to leave its strong mark on women who suffered the greater shock when leaving school and entering a social life characterised by widespread immorality. Often only the outward seeming of Christian behaviour remained, but lip-service was paid to the old morality and virtues associated in the public eye with an upper-class golden age in which honour was a strong motivating force with the duel as its formal manifestation. In the consciences of many there remained a yearning for virtue which we find reflected in countless works and which contributed significantly to the success of *La Nouvelle Héloïse*. The values of the merchant class as presented on the stage reflect those which the aristocracy had forsworn, and the new social morality of the *philosophe,* which linked free-thinking, sentiment and an upright way of life, is not merely a rationalist's counterblast to the 'Christian' ethics, but a nostalgic return to the *mores* of an earlier period before the lowering of moral standards had manifestly set in.

As Dr. Norma Perry has pointed out in her article 'French and English merchants in the Eighteenth-Century: Voltaire revisited' *(Studies in Eighteenth-Century French Literature,* Exeter, 1975) merchants are an ill-defined group since they comprise prosperous financiers at one end and mere chandlers at the other, and their status varied greatly.[1] M. Jubb has reminded us in the October 1976 number of the Newsletter of the British Society for Eighteenth-Century Studies that the landed classes, too, differed widely and that there was considerable intermingling between the two groups at different social levels. In any case the number of merchants of every description was growing rapidly in France as well as in England, but mercantilism was doubtless of greater social significance in England where the total population was so much smaller, and was soon to rise to greater heights. Whether Voltaire in the *Lettres philosophiques* and subsequent writings founded his view of the English merchant on the opinions of his British and Huguenot friends, or whether he cunningly fostered the myth of the honourable and highly honoured English merchant for the purposes of home propaganda, he showed

---

1.   See M. Vovelle & D. Roche, 'Bourgeoisie, Rentiers and Property Owners. Elements for defining a social category at the end of the XVIIIth century,' *New Perspectives on the French Revolution: Readings in Historical sociology,* New York, 1965. See also N. Perry, 'The expatriate syndrome: Voltaire and his London acquaintances,' British Society for XVIIIth-century studies, *Newsletter 9* (June 1976) for Voltaire's misconception of the English merchant.

hind-sight when he stressed the great future of mercantilism, bringing this fact home to his countryman through constant reiteration. In France society was more stratified than in England and commerce and industry judged to be more degrading. The French merchant had no legal status, being lumped with the Third Estate. His aspirations, though, were similar to those of his English counterpart: he sought to make his fortune, or at least a better living than the peasant or the artisan, and to wrest some form of recognition for his services. The orthodox view hearking back to Guizot, that the French Revolution was essentially a conflict between the aristocracy and the bourgeoisie, has been recently upheld by marxists such as Albert Mathiez, Georges Lefebvre and V. Volguine *(Le Développement de la pensée sociale en France au XVIIIe siècle,* Moscou, 1975), but it has been successfully challenged by Alfred Cobban, P. Gay and other contemporary historians. The bourgeois endeavoured to ape the aristocrats whose values and aspirations they shared and yearned for the higher status they felt they deserved. For long the Third Estate sought to rehabilitate the nobility rather than to abolish it.[2] To understand XVIIIth-century society we need to bear in mind that the Ancien régime was caste-ridden, but not class-ridden, a distinction that XIXth and XXth century developments have blurred. The wealthy trading community's aspirations were clearly set out by Daniel Defoe in some four pages of *The Complete English Tradesman* (1726). He sees the rich bourgeois 'coming every day to the Herald's office, to search for the Coats of Arms of their ancestors, in order to paint them upon their coaches, and engrave them upon their plate, embroider them upon their furniture, or carve them upon the pediments of their new houses...' In practice these men governed the country. In France they enjoyed the

2.   See G. Taylor, 'Non-capitalist wealth and the origins of the French Revolution,' *American Historical Review,* 72 (January 1967), pp. 469–96.

protection of Louis XV who distrusted the nobility as much as
Louis XIV. Robe and sword often joined forces and in the
decade before the Revolution the King was obliged by them to
refrain from ennobling *roturiers* of merit, thereby antagonising
the bourgeoisie which found itself increasingly precluded from
important offices and, by an edict of 1781, from the army.[3]
But the King constantly needed to raise big loans from the
financiers and in 1757, and again in 1767, proposed the establishment of a new social class — the *noblesse commerçante*
which Coyer had put forward in 1756. This proposal, sensible
in itself, might have solved his dilemma, but ultimately it would
have reinforced the caste system without granting the bourgeois
the full recognition he desired. The bourgeois were anxious to
acquire land and offices which conferred titles of nobility. The
British practice of distributing occasional peerages and more
frequent baronetcies and knighthoods was a more effective way
of answering their aspirations.

For most of the century the merchants as a whole seem
to have been reasonably well off and content. Often more
prosperous than the provincial squires or the nobles at court
they commonly lived beyond their means and shared the tastes
of the aristocrats whose way of life they endorsed. Monsieur
Jourdain gives way to Turcaret. There is little evidence that they
espoused the ideas of the *philosophes* before their glorification
in print and on the stage. Voltaire certainly showed wile as well
as perspicacity in setting up the English merchant as a new ideal.
He created an effective myth: that of the merchant-philosopher
respected by all, making the wheels of society turn smoothly,
raising the standard of living of his fellowman and striving for
peace throughout the world. In his promotion of free trade
Voltaire had none of the reservations of Adam Smith who

---

3.   Cf. E.G. Barber, *The Bourgeoisie in XVIIIth-century France*, 1955.
      See also G. Richard, *Noblesse d'affaires au XVIIIe siècle*, 1974.

feared that the mercantile system would restrict the volume of trade by promoting monopoly and would favour the producer at the expense of the consumer *(The Wealth of Nations,* ed. E. Thorold Rogers, Oxford, 1880, v. ii, pp. 208—17). Liberal at heart, God-fearing (but no Roman Catholic), upright in all his transactions, he was a moral man full of compassion for the unfortunate ones of this world. He held a lofty view of marriage and the idea grew that to be happily married one needed to be a bourgeois. This idealistic picture of the bourgeoisie fitted in perfectly with the prevailing anglomania and also with the conception of a *drame bourgeois.* In his theory of *drame* and in his two plays, firmly founded on family virtues, Diderot deliberately sought to associate the rising mercantile class with the new social morality destined to replace the outworn Christian ethic. He sensed a moral and social revolution from which Rousseau also benefitted, and wished to replace worship in church by attendance at the theatre. 'Ils ont leurs sabbats, nous aurons aussi les nôtres,' *(Œuvres complètes de* Diderot, ed. Assézat-Tourneux, vii, p. 109), he wrote. His actors were ordinary men and women performing against a backcloth of morality reinforced by sentimentality. The ploy could not fail, and even an audience that was not significantly more bourgeois than at the beginning of the century was moved to applaud a way of life it did not pursue. As for those in authority, tired of fighting a nobility always eager for office, they were not disposed to view critically the rise of a new, more moral class of people who would be running the state. The merchants, however, tended to demand greater rewards as they saw themselves eulogised precisely when the government had less to give, and as they became better educated they grew increasingly resentful. But for a time at least the myth of the good merchant suited all except the lower nobility who resented the usurpation of morality by an inferior breed of men.

It is this myth which we see unfolded on the stage and

recorded by F. Gaiffe in *Le Drame en France au XVIIIe siècle* (Paris, 1910). He failed, however, to situate his account in its true social perspective. He oversimplified the evidence the signification of which he did not fully bring out, and his overall interpretation is too facile. For playwrights such as Nivelle de La Chaussée were no democrats and John Lough has shown that the *drame* is not strictly middle-class. The merchant on the stage reflects steps in his social and political standing. The good merchant remains a representative figure not so much as an epitome of his class, but as a great *cheval de bataille* in a war of propaganda.

In hearking back to Lillo and Moore's English prototypes the French writers of *drames* did more than provide themselves with respectable forerunners, they fostered their own philosophic purposes as no doubt Steele, Defoe, Gay and others who wrote in defence of merchants. Dr. N. Perry has rightly emphasized that the factors that made the success of the English plays were not at all those upon which the *philosophes* seized. Their concern was rather to bring out political implications favourable to the bourgeoisie and essentially in line with the tenets of the enlightenment.

A certain ambiguity over the true status of the bourgeois was at the time an advantage. In Steele's *Conscious Lovers,* as Dr. Perry has noted, the honourable and esteemed merchant, Mr. Sealand, exclaims : 'We merchants are a species of gentry...' Likewise, in *Le Philosophe sans le savoir,* M. Vanderk *père* turns out to be a nobleman. This inconsistency from the standpoint of the *philosophes'* general thesis is commonly ascribed to timidity or to the need to placate an essentially aristocratic audience[4] which could never exceed 2000 on any one night. Another reason may well have been Sedaine's desire to associate

---

4.   J. Lough, *Paris Theatre Audiences in the XVIIth and XVIIIth Centuries,* London, 1957.

what was best in the old aristocratic ideal with his own idealised picture of an upright merchant. A sense of honour and love of country of a golden age still remembered needed to be transposed into a contemporary setting. Furthermore, the new conjugal family, already well-established in England as Ian Watt has pointed out *(The Rise of the Novel,* London, 1957), was to take over from the cold, selfish patriarchal family derived from feudalism, and to promote a finer moral code. The duel, palpably anachronistic, had still kept a hold on the consciences and the imagination of many Frenchmen and did not seem incongruous to Sedaine or to his audiences. We find a duel again in Saurin's bourgeois tragedy entitled *Béverley* (1767).

The newly-found, happy society which Durkheim first traced to England, was endorsed by Rousseau in *La Nouvelle Héloise.* In promoting, after Richardson, the concept of an ideal, united family, Rousseau furthered the confusion between bourgeois and aristocratic values by making M. de Wolmar an aristocrat. Marmontel in the *Contes moraux* was prompted to act in the same manner. Of course the effort to associate merchant morality with the highest standards of a bygone aristocracy was to rebound to the advantage of the bourgeoisie and enhanced the chances of a successful confrontation between the myth of the perfect merchant and the myth of the aristocratic libertine. In the war that was being waged, Sedaine was playing a winning card. He was making a somewhat blatant attempt to dignify the middle-class way of life coupled with an effort to bring at least a section of the aristocracy into the charmed circle of a new intellectual and moral *élite.* We find the same endeavour in Beaumarchais's *Les Deux Amis, ou Le Négociant de Lyon* (1770).

Let us recall a few landmarks in the career of the merchant on the French stage. We see at first the evil effects of money on character and on society. The arrogant and greedy *financier* or rather *fermier général* makes his first appearance in Robbe's play *La Rapinière* (1682) and in Boursault's *Le Mercure Galant* (1683) a *commis des gabelles* supplements his earnings with a little theft of 200,000 fr. Griffard, the *financier* in Dancourt's *La Foire de Besons*, Farfadet in *La Foire Saint-Germain* (1796), Rapineau, the *sous-fermier* in Dancourt's *Le Retour des officiers* (1697), Griffet in Boursault's *Esope à la Cour* (1701) are all deplorable characters epitomised in 1709 by the *traitant* Turcaret who is shown at the zenith of his power. The succession of unpleasant *financiers* is then broken until much later in the century when Mercier presents Dortigny in *L'Habitant de la Guadeloupe*. The merchant as such, however, makes his first fleeting appearance with M. Coquelet in Regnard's *Les Ménechmes* and is given a major part in Nivelle de La Chaussée's *L'Homme de fortune* (1751). It is only after Paul Landois's *Silvie*, the first French *tragédie bourgeoise*, that *le négoce* comes to the fore as seen in *Le Philosophe sans le savoir* (1765), the masterpiece of the new genre. We know that the public had some difficulty in adjusting itself to the presentation of high finance on the stage, witness its poor response to the figures and financial transactions presented in *Les Deux Amis*[5]. Sedaine's own skill may be gauged from his success in placing commercial terms such as *usances, remises, escompte* and *rescription* in the mouths of his characters, without even

5.   Beaumarchais, Preface to *Le Mariage de Figaro:*
      Entre autres critiques de la pièce, j'entendis dans une loge, auprès de celle que j'occupais, un jeune 'important' de la cour qui disait gaiement à des dames, 'l'auteur, sans doute, est un garçon fripier qui ne voit rien de plus élevé que des commis des femmes et des marchands d'étoffes, et c'est au fond d'un magasin qu'il va chercher les nobles amis qu'il traduit à la scène française!' Hélas, monsieur, lui dis-je en m'avançant, il a fallu du moins les prendre où il n'est pas impossible de les supposer. Vous ririez bien plus de l'auteur s'il eût tiré des vrais amis de l'Œil-de-Bœuf ou des carrosses ? Il faut un peu de vraisemblance, même dans les actes vertueux.

raising a murmer from his audience.

In a plot typical of the period, that of Dampierre's *Le Bienfait rendu ou le Négociant*, the *négociant* Orgon will forget what the comte de Bruyancourt owes him, if only the comte will consent to give his daughter Angélique in marriage to Orgon's nephew Verville. *Le Fabricant de Londres* by Falbaire deals with matters of business as do *Le Juge* and *La Brouette du vinaigrier* by Mercier. Terms like *bénéfices, pertes, inventaires, billets à ordre, échéances* and *banqueroute* become common on the stage. All these *négociants* are taken from varying backgrounds, but they are all honest. If they are rich they have acquired their fortune legitimately. If they become ruined it is owing to unforeseen circumstances or to unscrupulous dealers whom *le drame* leaves in the wings so as not to tarnish the glorious image of *le commerce*. The dramatists, with the exception of Chamfort, saw business as Mercier saw virtue in his preface to *La Brouette du vinaigrier:* 'Aux yeux de Poète rien donc ne sera grand que la vertu, rien ne sera vil que le vice.' Their ideas are clearly those of the *philosophes* of their day. Had not Voltaire noted that a *négociant* 'est quelquefois un législateur, un bon officier, un ministre public'?[6] Clairville says to Dorval in Diderot's *Le Fils naturel* (1757) when faced with the prospect of a life of poverty with his beloved Rosalie: 'Je commercerai'. To which Dorval replies: 'Avec le nom que vous portez, auriez-vous le courage ? ' And Clairville rejoins: 'Il est d'autres états qui mènent rapidement à la richesse; mais le commerce est presque le seul où les grandes fortunes soient proportionnées au travail, à l'industrie, et aux dangers qui les rendent honnêtes.' Social criticism more far-reaching than that of Voltaire or Diderot has to await 1775 when Mercier in *La Brouette du vinaigrier* speaks of 'l'inégalité des conditions' and seeks to restructure the social order drastically. But towards the middle of the century, as in

6.   Voltaire, *Œuvres complètes*, ed. L. Moland, 1877, t. I, p. 547.

L'Homme de fortune (1751) by Nivelle de la Chaussée, the
social change is confined to presenting on the stage a bourgeois
problem, that of social preferment through marriage. Satire of
social hypocrisy takes precedence over propaganda on behalf
of commerce. The same can be said of *Le Véritable Père de
famille* which consecrates the triumph of the *négociant* Géronte,
whilst the *financier* saves the situation in Beaumarchais's *Les
Deux Amis.* Voltaire in *L'Ecossaise* (1760) offered a rather
unusual character in the person of Freeport. A good bourgeois,
he has Christian standards and helps the needy. Voltaire cannot
refrain from poking fun at him in spite of the goodness of his
heart, but the important point is that Voltaire endowed his
character with a virtue, generosity, that is at once attractive
and seemingly realistic. The fact that Voltaire chose an English-
man reinforces the point in the *Epître dédicatoire* to Falkener
which serves as a preface to *Zaïre:* that in England businessmen
were held in high esteem.

Lillo's The *London Merchant or the History of George
Barnwell,* first produced in London in 1731, was to make a
remarkable impact on French drama, and at least six plays may
claim to have been inspired by this work[7]. But the adaptations
by the French led to fundamental changes. In many of these
plays the bourgeois setting is turned into a noble one and in
Mercier's *Jenneval,* Thorowgood is converted into a barrister.
But the historical importance of Lillo's play and its translation

7.   Cf. Anseaume, *L'Ecole de la jeunesse ou le Barnvelt français,*
      1765; Falbaire, *Le Fabricant de Londres,* 1771; Blin de Sainmore,
      Orphanis, 1773; La Harpe, *Barneveldt,* pub. in *Œuvres,* 6 v.,1778;
      L.S. Mercier, *Jenneval ou le Barneveldt français,* pub. 1769, perf.
      1776, 1781. T. Lillo's play inspired Dorat to write an *héroïde* and
      Mme de Beaumont a novel. The play itself was first translated by
      Clément in 1748 without the last two scenes which were judged too
      daring, but these were included in his second edition in 1751. See
      also *Nouveau Théâtre anglais,* t. I, London, Nourse, 1767.

into French by Clément in 1748 lies in presenting a new ideology, a compound of Calvinism and mercantilism[8]. The playwrights, however, who were prepared to extol the *esprit mercantile* felt it necessary to play down English attitudes to religion and morals associated with Protestantism. They retained Lillo's eulogy of international trading which Sedaine and Beaumarchais also echoed. Sedaine goes even further than Lillo when he makes Vanderk exclaim: "Quel état, mon fils, que celui d'un homme qui d'un trait de plume se fait obéir d'un bout de l'univers à l'autre!" and after pointing to the advantages of being able to trade without cash on the strength of his financial standing and credit, he allows himself to be carried away by his dream: 'Ce n'est pas un peuple, ce n'est pas une nation qu'il sert; il les sert toutes et en est servi; c'est l'homme de l'univers.' And the *honnête négociant* 'ramène à la paix par la nécessité du commerce' *(Le Philosophe sans le savoir,* Act II, sc. 4). Sedaine did not wish to overthrow the social order. Professor Haydn Mason rightly asks whether the play is not an aristocratic *drame bourgeois* which blurs the commonly held distinction between the bourgeois and the aristocratic class *(French Studies,* October 1976). Sedaine is concerned with portraying the *homme de bien.* None of the other *négociants* or *hommes de bien* presented on the French stage before or after are either so convincing or so virtuous. This may be due to the playwright's ability to project himself unselfconsciously into a character which retained many of the peculiarities of the aristocrat and also epitomised the ideal of an age. Whilst Sedaine successfully incorporated the mercantile philosophy into the action of the play, we have to await Belloy's *Le Siège de Calais* (1765) for an unambiguous defence of the bourgeois

8.   See H. Hamard, *Revue de Littérature comparée,* 1965, vol. 39, p. 589.

position. With Haydn Mason we believe that E. Guibert-Sledziewski has grossly oversimplified the issues in *Le Philosophe sans le savoir (Dix-huitième Siècle* 7, 1975, pp. 259—74) when she tries to stress a confrontation between two generations of bourgeois represented by Vanderk *père* and Vanderk *fils* reacting differently against the aristocracy. She has failed to set the play in its contemporary intellectual, political and social context or in relationship to the presentation of the bourgeois on the French stage.

Les Deux Amis, a very tedious *drame,* first presented 13 January 1770, makes financial dealings the pivot of the play. This was an innovation, but the public was apparently unready to cope with 'négocier des effets,' 'suspendre des paiements,' 'mettre les scellés' and to hear about 'les apprêts de ses soies de ses plantations de mûriers,' and such words as 'bordereau', 'fonds', 'titres' and 'faillite' constantly repeated. The play had only ten performances in Paris, but was more successful in Bordeaux. Yet, as one wag put it: 'l'argent circule sans produire aucun intérêt.' Aurelly, the Lyons merchant, aspires to the nobility, but still continues in business. Less shrewd and more dogmatic than Vanderk, he is an *homme bienfaisant* who enjoys philosophising. Vanderk had placed the soldier above the merchant, but Aurelly declares:

> 'Et tout l'or que la guerre disperse, qui le fait rentrer à la paix? Qui osera disputer au Commerce l'honneur de rendre à l'Etat épuisé le nerf et les richesses qu'il n'a plus? Tous les citoyens sentent l'importance de cette tâche, le négociant seul la remplit. Au moment que le guerrier se repose, le négociant a le bonheur d'être à son tour l'homme de la patrie.' (Act II, sc. 10).

Beaumarchais affirmed that the play was written for *négociants* 'et, en général, pour honorer le Tiers Etat.' Aurelly stands out as the good, but not the perfect merchant.

By way of contrast Chamfort's *Le Marchand de Smyrne* (1770) shows us a Turkish slave-trader without moral scruples. As in *La Jeune Indienne* (1764), Chamfort argues against gold and riches in society. The play is imbued with patriotism and sentiment, and, although Chamfort does not worship the money-making slave-trader, he conjures up a rosy picture. Kaled, the Turk, is an exception on the French stage, but his reception by the public suggests a divergence of opinion on the concept of the *marchand* among the spectators if not among the propagandists of the enlightenment.

With *La Brouette de vinaigrier* (1776), the high-class *négociant* Delomer loses definitively his social preeminence, and the myth of the good merchant is in decline. He has to yield first place to Dominique, a mere *vinaigrier*. The *Préface* repays study. In the first paragraph Mercier says:

> le fait est plaisant et sert à prouver que l'orgueil des rangs, si haut, si intraitable dans ses discours, sait s'humaniser à propos, et qu'il ne s'agit au fond que des conditions pécuniaires (ed. R. Aggéri, Lib. Larousse, 1972, p. 32).

A social critic a century earlier would have blamed inequality on a person's birth, but now money is to blame. Mercier expounds his egalitarian, politically orientated views, arguing that:

> tout ce qui mêle les différents états de la société, et tend à rompre l'excessive inégalité des conditions, source de tous nos maux, est bon politiquement parlant. Tout ce qui rapproche les citoyens est le ciment sacré qui unit les nombreuses familles d'un vaste état, qui doit les voir d'un œil égal. La même loi qui défend aux frères de s'allier à leurs sœurs, devrait peut-être interdire aux riches de s'allier aux riches (ibid., p. 33).

In a sense both Delomer and Dominique are merchants, but the well-born merchant is challenged by a more moral, lower-class member of society who believes in hard-earned money and puts his faith only in solid gold, not in paper. International trade, fostered by the investment of capital, whether savings or unearned income, is not advocated. Dominique's conception of business is made to contrast favourably with that of Delomer who is a speculator, even though Dominique would never be able to continue to amass gold without diversifying into new and profitable lines of business. Delomer for his part goes bankrupt and low-class simplicity is seen to triumph over high-class manipulation when Dominique wheels his vinegar barrel on the stage to the spectators' surprise and visual delight. In the barrel is the gold which will save Delomer from ruin and enable the two's respective offspring to marry. Delomer has to agree that 'Il (Dominique) est plus heureux, plus tranquille que moi.' The representative of the Tiers Etat and spokesman of the proletariat does not, however, capitulate to social egalitarianism, but shows the brotherly respect of one businessman for another. 'Le commerce, mon cher Dominique,' says Delomer, 'est semblable à une mer tantôt calme et tout-à-coup orageuse. Les mêmes vents qui font voler votre vaisseau l'engloutissent. J'ai fait naufrage sous un ciel qui paraissait serein' (Act III, sc. 4, *Ibid.,* p. 104).

Mercier is not primarily concerned with the evil influence of money on society. He wishes above all to show that the moral dominance of the big-businessman is over. The merchant can no longer be viewed as an avant-garde hero, but must be seen as a conservative and outmoded figure. Having put the seal on his social propaganda Mercier became more concerned with forthright revolutionary political sentiments.

The myth had now run its full course. The *négociant* never again appears on the stage or indeed in literature in quite the same way. After the Revolution, business is an accepted factor in French life and a realistic conception of its role and its practitioners was to be recorded in the tribulations of a self-made Père Goriot and in the decline and fall of César Birotteau. A little after Balzac, Dumas *fils* was to present *La Question d'argent.* More poignant is the bitter portrayal of the heartlessness of business in Henri Becque's *Les Corbeaux* and in Octave Mirbeau's *Les Affaires sont les affaires.* By then the wheel had truly come full circle. The optimism with which business enterprise had been greeted had turned very sour, and with its increasingly questionable benefits it had brought about the appalling conditions which Zola was to describe so forcefully in many of his novels.

But the *philosophes* and the *dramaturges* in their age made the *négociant* an important member of society. The *négociant* was singled out as one who might work for the benefit of society as distinct from the *financier,* and, by pandering to his vanity, the *philosophes* enlisted his support. The merchant's power for good, his ability to be generous and enrich others, to help his king and country, and to promote international peace, required to be stressed for political reasons, and held out dramatic possibilities which needed to be exploited if success in the theatre and with the avant-garde was to be achieved. Unfortunately for the dramatists business itself is neither dramatic nor does it of itself generate emotion. Only individual businessmen, well characterised, can be the raw material of good theatre. Moreover, the dramatists had not studied the implications of trade and business seriously. They were content with the novelty of presenting a good merchant on the stage, the rewards attending hard, honest toil and virtue in its several forms. They had no difficulty in finding the material for attacks on the idle, unproductive nobility and, indirectly, on the church which could no longer claim a monopoly for its ethic. Their views are, therefore, valid as the reaction of *philosophes* to a contemporary but transient phenomenon. Their ideas cannot be made to apply outside the context which gave rise to them. They contributed to sapping the establishment, but the ultimate beneficiaries of the philosophical trend which was reflected on the stage were, in fact, the little men with their small *entreprises,* self-righteously doing their honest day's work, or so they proclaim not without some hypocrisy, whom many would consider as the biggest reactionary, anti-intellectual force in France to-day. So with the Revolution of 1789 the good merchant vanishes from the stage, the rogues portrayed by Lesage at the beginning of the century and by Rétif de la Bretonne at the end replace the virtuous Vanderks; and the hope of building a new lay society on something more than self-interest properly understood founders as had the Christian faith in the brotherhood of men.

GLANES ENCYCLOPÉDIQUES
J. Proust

Paulo minora canamus.

1

E sont des portraits dont les òriginaux ne subsistent plus".
Diderot a fait dans l'article *ENCYCLOPÉDIE* (1755), le meilleur résumé qu'on puisse donner de l'histoire des descriptions des arts de l'Académie des sciences: 'Qu'un homme [c'est Réaumur] consume une partie de sa vie à la description des arts; que, dégoûté de cet ouvrage fatigant, il se laisse entraîner à des occupations plus amusantes et moins utiles [comme l'histoire naturelle], et que son premier ouvrage demeure renfermé dans ses portefeuilles: il ne s'écoulera pas vingt ans qu'à la place des choses nouvelles et curieuses, piquantes par leur singularité, intéressantes par leurs usages, par le goût dominant, par une importance momentanée, il ne retrouvera que des notions incorrectes, des manœuvres surannées, des machines ou imparfaites, ou abandonnées. Dans les nombreux volumes qu'il aura composés, il n'y aura pas une page qu'il ne faille retoucher, et dans la multitude des planches qu'il aura fait graver, presque pas une figure qu'il ne faille redessiner. Ce sont des portraits dont les originaux ne subsistent plus.' [1]

1. Diderot, *Œuvres complètes,* éd. par J. Assézat et M. Tourneux, Paris, Garnier, 1875–1877, t. XIV, pp. 423–423.

Ce résumé est corroboré par le témoignage de Joly, garde
du Cabinet des estampes à la Bibliothèque du roi, que Françoise
Gardey a publié pour la première fois en 1964.[2]
Le contenu des 'portefeuilles' évoqués par Diderot et par
Joly est aujourd'hui réparti entre trois dépôts au moins: la
bibliothèque de l'Institut de France, le Cabinet des estampes de
la Bibliothèque nationale, l'Arsenal. J'ai étudié moi-même il y
a quelques années les dessins et les planches du premier de ces
fonds.[3] C'est lui qui a fourni également le meilleur de la documentation utilisée dans l'introduction à *L'Univers de l'Encyclopédie*.[4] On y a naturellement puisé pour la grande édition des
Œuvres complètes en cours de publication chez Hermann.
    Le deuxième fonds contient les planches du métier à bas
ayant appartenu à la collection de Marolles,[5] et surtout un lot
de planches préparées pour les *Descriptions* de l'Académie des
sciences, venant pour partie de la collection de Beringhen,
partie... *de Diderot lui-même.* Ce lot a été sommairement
décrit dans l'article de Françoise Gardey, déjà cité, et il mériterait
une étude approfondie, s'il est vrai, comme le suppose l'auteur,
que soixante-quatre planches 'portent une annotation manu-
scrite à l'encre, d'une certaine petite écriture bien proche de

2.   'Quelques planches des *Descriptions des arts et métiers* de
      l'Académie des sciences, au Cabinet des estampes', *Nouvelles de
      l'estampe*, 1964, 5—6, p. 167 et suivantes. Cette publication ronéo-
      typée n'a qu'une diffusion restreinte et l'étude de Françoise Gardey
      est passée inaperçue de beaucoup de spécialistes. Ses conclusions,
      et les pistes de recherche qu'elle ouvre méritent pourtant d'être
      largement connues.
3.   'La documentation technique de Diderot dans l'*Encyclopédie*',
      Revue d'histoire littéraire de la France, juillet-septembre 1957,
      pp. 335—352; *Diderot et l'Encyclopédie*, Paris, Colin, 1967,
      pp. 54—56, et 183—188.
4.   Paris, Les Libraires associés, 1964, avec une introduction de
      Roland Barthes, Robert Mauzi, Jean-Pierre Seguin, Françoise Gardey.
5.   Voir J. Proust, 'De l'*Encyclopédie* au *Neveu de Rameau:* l'objet
      et le texte,' *Recherches nouvelles sur quelques écrivains des lumières*,
      Genève, Droz, 1972, pp. 273—291.

celle de Diderot, sinon la sienne, et semblent former un lot d'origine commune.'

Le troisième fonds se trouve à la bibliothèque de l'Arsenal (Gr. Fol. 114, 1 et 2). Plusieurs des documents reproduits dans *L'Univers de l'Encyclopédie* en proviennent. Leur caractéristique la plus remarquable est de porter souvent des annotations et des révisions de Réaumur. Elles nous font entrer, mieux que la simple confrontation des dessins et des gravures de l'Institut, par exemple, dans le long et minutieux travail de mise au point des planches de l'Académie. De tout ce travail accumulé l'*Encyclopédie* a été la première bénéficiaire.

Grâce à l'extrême obligeance de Jean-Pierre Seguin, on trouvera ci-contre quatre planches gravées *inédites* ayant fait partie des portefeuilles de Réaumur, et conservées aujourd'hui à l'Arsenal.

La première est une épreuve du 'coutelier'. Elle est surchargée d'annotations au crayon (peu lisibles sur le cliché) et à l'encre. Elle porte en outre des indications marginales. Par exemple, en haut: 'mesurer exactement les angles des differentes scies, et les mettre icy en leurs mesures.' Certains dessins sont également corrigés, par exemple en T–T2. La seconde est le tirage définitif de la gravure précédente. Les ajouts et les corrections de l'épreuve y sont incorporés; la planche est signée: Regnier pour le dessin, Haussard pour la gravure. La date de 1717 correspond à la période d'activité maximale de Réaumur.

La troisième illustration est une épreuve du 'taillandier'. Ni l'indication 'dessiné par Bretes, et Chaufourier', ni la date '1716' (d'ailleurs rayée) ne sont reportées sur le tirage définitif. Celui-ci, en revanche, est signé du graveur Lucas, bien connu des lecteurs des *Descriptions* de l'Académie des sciences.

2.

Quelques aspects de la création littéraire chez Diderot.

Sous ce titre, j'avais essayé en 1964 de montrer qu'il ne fallait pas faire deux parts dans l'œuvre de Diderot, l'une, noble, qui contiendrait les romans et les œuvres philosophiques ou esthétiques, l'autre, mercenaire, qui serait essentiellement constituée par l'*Encyclopédie* et ce qui s'y rattache (comme la *Lettre sur le commerce de la librairie*).[6]

En fait, de 1748 à 1772 au moins, la circulation entre l'*Encyclopédie* et les autres œuvres de Diderot a été incessante. En voici deux nouvelles preuves.

L'article *ÉCLECTISME, publié en 1755, contient une longue citation latine de Brucker, au sujet de Plotin, à laquelle on devrait toujours songer lorsqu'on lit un texte de Diderot sur l'enthousiasme. Il s'agit d'ailleurs d'un portrait de Plotin par Porphyre, son disciple. Mais Diderot voulait en faire un portrait type de l'enthousiaste et a modifié le texte de Porphyre a cette fin. Voici côte à côte le texte de Brucker (Porphyre) et le texte de Diderot. On a mis en italique dans le second les mots ou expressions modifiés ou ajoutés.

BRUCKER	DIDEROT
Ex quo Plotini charactere, quem depinxit his verbis Porphysius, hominis ingenium miro ardore inflammatum et nescio qua ambitione ductum sese judicii habenis subtraxisse, et objectorum magnitudine captum et abreptum sibi saepe ipsi non fuisse praesentem,	Quorum *ingenium miro ardore inflammatum, et nescio qua ambitione ductum, sese judicii habenis* coerceri aegre fert et indignatur; qui *objectorum magnitudine capti et abrepti sibi saepe ipsi non* sunt praesentes; ex horum numero *qui non quid dicant*

6.   Dans *Six conférences...*, Chaire d'Histoire des créations littéraires en France [Jean Pommier], Collège de France, 1964, pp. 43–59.

recte concluditur, et Plotinus inter eos non immerito doctores refertur, qui non, quid dicant scribantque, perpendunt, sed cogitationum fertilissimarum fluctibus abrepti, amplectuntur, quicquid aestuanti imaginationi occurrit singulare et ab aliis diversum, licet judicio fulciatur nullo: quibus proprietatibus gaudere ingenia fanatica, norunt, quibus sacrae atque philosophicae historiae acta ignota haud sunt. [7]

sentiantve *perpendunt, sed cogitationum* vividissimarum *fertilissimarumque fluctibus* obvoluti, *amplectuntur, quidquid aestuanti imaginationi occurrit* altum, *singulare et ab aliis diversum,* fundamento *fulciatur* aliquo vel *nullo,* dummodo mentibus aliorum attonitis offeratur aliquid portentosum et enorme. [8]

On peut traduire le latin de Diderot ainsi: '[un de ces hommes] dont le génie enflammé d'une ardeur étonnante, et conduit par on ne sait quelle ambition, tolère mal d'être bridé par le jugement et s'en indigne; qui, absorbés et transportés par la grandeur des objets qui se présentent à eux, sont souvent absents d'eux-mêmes; de ceux qui ne pèsent avec scrupule ni leurs paroles ni leurs sentiments mais qui, enveloppés par les flots d'une pensée particulièrement vive et féconde, embrassent tout ce qu'une imagination bouillonnante leur suggère de profond, de singulier, d'inouï. Peu importe que leurs visions soient fondées, pourvu qu'elles offrent aux esprits étonnés l'image du prodige et de la démesure'.

Ce texte, à sa date, est incontestablement à mettre en parallèle avec le début du second entretien sur *Le Fils naturel,*

7.   Brucker, *Historia critica philosophiae,* Leipzig, 1742–1744, t.II, p. 224. Désigné ci-après en abrégé *Brucker.*

8.   Diderot, *Œuvres complètes,* éd. par R. Lewinter, Paris, Le Club français du livre, t.XIV, p.113. Cette édition sera désignée ci-après par l'abréviation *Lewinter.*

et avec le chapitre des 'mœurs' du discours *De la poésie dramatique* ('La poésie veut quelque chose d'énorme, de barbare [etc.]').

Dans un registre moins grave, on trouve d'autre part dans l'article ZEND-AVESTA, rédigé entre 1762 et 1765, le récit suivant, emprunté comme le reste à Anquetil du Perron (*Journal des savants*, juin et juillet 1762): 'Arrivé à Surate, M. Anquetil trouva les parsis divisés en deux sectes animées l'une contre l'autre du zèle le plus furieux. La superstition produit partout les mêmes effets. L'une de ces sectes s'appelait celle des *anciens croyants*, l'autre celle des *réformateurs*. De quoi s'agissait-il entre ces sectaires qui pensèrent tremper toute la contrée de leur sang? De savoir si le *penon* [en parsi; *penum*], ou la pièce de lin de neuf pouces en carré, que les parsis portent sur le nez en certains temps, devait ou ne devait pas être mise sur le nez des agonisants.' Et Diderot ajoute: '*Quid rides? mutato nomine de te fabula narratur*' [Pourquoi rire? sous un nom différent ce conte parle de vous].

Le 'conte' se retrouve en effet avec quelques retouches burlesques dans le chapitre XVI des *Bijoux indiscrets*, intitulé 'Vision de Mangogul', et publié pour la première fois dans l'édition Naigeon des *Œuvres* de Diderot, en 1798. Il commence ainsi: 'Ce fut au milieu du caquet des bijoux qu'il s'éleva un autre trouble dans l'empire; ce trouble fut causé par l'usage du *penum*, ou du petit morceau de drap qu'on appliquait aux moribonds. L'ancien rite ordonnait de le placer sur la bouche. Des réformateurs prétendaient qu'il fallait le mettre au derrière [etc.]'. La satire, à sa date (1762 au plus tôt), était tout à fait transparente: elle visait les *billets de confession,* une des armes les plus redoutées de la répression antijanséniste au XVIIIe siècle.

3.
'Notre Magot prit pour ce coup
Le nom d'un port pour un nom d'homme'.[9]

De Naigeon à Roger Lewinter, les éditeurs successifs des
articles fournis par Diderot à l'*Encyclopédie* ne semblent pas
avoir pris garde à quelques bizarreries qui en rendent parfois
le texte cocasse. En fait, ils en ont bien décelé quelques-unes,
mais de crainte de mettre le doigt dans un engrenage fatal à
leur repos, ils ont préféré gommer subrepticement... et passer.
Ils se disaient sans doute—et ils n'avaient pas toujours tort — que
les dix derniers volumes du dictionnaire avaient été imprimés
à la hâte, que les épreuves n'avaient pas été revues, et que le
typographe en avait pris tout à son aise. C'est ainsi que Roger
Lewinter améliore *sans le dire* l'édition Assézat en imprimant
'Constantin, Abbon' dans l'article JESUS–CHRIST[10], 'Cicéron'
(entre crochets carrés, marque d'un scrupule méritoire, mais
trop peu explicite) dans l'article MÉGARIQUE[11],'Pforzheim' dans
l'article PYTHAGORISME[12], 'Kublai Kanni' dans l'article
SARRASINS[13], 'Zénon de Sidon' dans l'article STOICISME[14],
'Fincin' et 'Pic' dans l'article SYNCRÉTISTES[15]. On lit dans
l'*Encyclopédie*, et Tourneux comme Assézat avait laissé imprimer
respectivement: 'Constantin Abbon' *(Brucker,* III, 641–643,
parle bien de deux personnages, *'Constantinus floriacensis'* et
'Abbo, floriacensis abbas', c'est-à-dire Constantin et Abbon, du
monastère de Fleury); 'Ceuto'; 'Pforzen'; 'Kublat, Kanm' (en
deux mots, alors qu'il s'agit bien, dans *Brucker,* III, 118, de
Koubilaï khan - il orthographie *'Kublai Kanni'*—, le petit-fils de

9.   La Fontaine, *Le Singe et le Dauphin.*
10. *Lewinter,* XIV, 357.
11. *Lewinter,* XIV, 529.
12. *Lewinter,* XIV, 702.
13. *Lewinter,* XIV, 742.
14. *Lewinter,* XIV, 848.
15. *Lewinter,* XIV, 861.

Gengis khan, fondateur de la dynastie chinoise des Yuan); 'Zénode, Scion' (en deux mots encore); 'Fran. Pic' (comme s'il s'agissait du nom propre Pic et de l'abréviation d'un prénom comme François).

M. Lewinter s'arrête d'ailleurs curieusement en chemin, lorsqu'il corrige l'article *CASUISTE, rétablissant comme il convient le nom d'Iribarne—dont l'*Encyclopédie* a fait Tribarne-, mais laissant Acozier et Dealkoser où il faudrait Achokier et Dealkozer.[16] Et pourquoi corriger Pforzen en Pforzheim si on laisse passer sans commentaire la phrase imprimée dans l'*Encyclopédie:* 'Reuchlin naquit à Pforzen en Suisse, en 1455'? Pforzheim se trouve en effet en Allemagne, dans le pays de Bade. On voit bien comment Diderot s'est mépris; il avait lu trop vite, dans *Brucker,* IV, 358: '*Pforzhemii, oppido Sueviae, in Badensi ditione sito...*'

Mais pourquoi imprimer encore 'Alliac', dans l'article SCOLASTIQUE, un nom qui se lit 'Assiac' dans l'*Encyclopédie*? M. Lewinter se sera sans doute reporté à l'*Historia critica philosophiae*, où l'on trouve en effet '*Petrus de Alliaco*', et non point '*de Assiaco*'. Mais *Petrus de Alliaco* n'est pas plus Pierre de Alliac que Pierre de Assiac. Il s'agit en réalité du cardinal Pierre d'Ailly, dit de Marteau des hérétiques et l'Aigle des docteurs de France, qui vécut à la fin du XIVe et au début du XVe siècle. Comme on voit, la latinisation des noms français par Brucker, et leur remise en français par Diderot—qui neuf fois sur dix ignorait de qui il pouvait s'agir—imposent à l'éditeur de ses articles un travail de décryptage assez délicat.

Assézat avait laissé passer dans l'article ARABES une bévue de taille: 'Je ne nie pas que depuis Islamime l'érudition et la philosophie n'aient été extrêmement en honneur chez ces peuples'. Il en avait même aggravé l'effet en mettant en note à Islamime: 'Mahomet'.[18] Naturellement, Islamime n'a jamais

16. *Lewinter*, XV, 143.
17. *Lewinter*, XIV, 803.
18. *AT*, XIII, 314.

existé. Diderot lisait dans *Brucker*, I, 213: '*Et Arabibus quidem post Islamismum* [etc.]'. Roger Lewinter a eu le bon goût de s'aviser qu'on parlait tout bonnement de l'Islam, et il a maquillé le texte de manière à produire un sens acceptable: 'Je ne nie pas que depuis l'islamisme [etc.]'[19]

Mais pour une bévue repérée, combien de bizarreries encore, que la grande édition en cours ne corrigera certainement pas toutes. S'est-on demandé par exemple ce que c'était que ces 'schystes' dont parle l'article *CHAVARIGTES[20], le 'sicuto' dont parle l'article *JAPONOIS ('ceux qui se dirigent par le sicuto ou la voie philosophique')[21] ; qui étaient exactement 'Anlegisus' et 'Egobart', dans l'article JESUS–CHRIST[22], ou Lambert Danée, dans l'article MOSAIQUE[23]; dans quelle partie du monde, en quel temps ont vécu les 'Islalites' chez qui passa Zoroastre après s'être instruit dans les sciences orientales? [24]

Où trouvera-t-on, dans une encyclopédie de l'Islam, les noms d'"Asaria' et de 'Mutazali', cités avec l'autorité de Maïmonide dans l'article SARRASINS? [25] Y trouvera-t-on la secte des 'aspahanites', ou celle des 'al-sharestans'? [26] Qui est encore ce 'Michel Montanus', accusé d'athéisme, et dont Thomasius aurait eu l'imprudence d'entreprendre l'apologie?[27]

19. *Lewinter*, XIV, 10. Il faut bien dire 'maquillé', car il ne s'agit pas seulement d'une *s* malencontreusement sautée à l'impression et heureusement rétablie. Roger Lewinter a *aussi* remplacé la majuscule par une minuscule et ajouté l'article, sans même le mettre entre crochets.
20. *Lewinter*, XIV, 48.
21' *Lewinter*, XIV, 325.
22. *Lewinter*, XIV, 357.
23. *Lewinter*, XIV, 535.
24. Art. *PERSES, Lewinter*, XIV, 590.
25. *Lewinter*, XIV, 731.
26. *Lewinter*, XIV, 737 et 750.
27. Art. *THOMASIUS, Lewinter*, XIV, 895. Dans tous les exemples cités depuis la note 20, le texte de l'édition Lewinter est conforme à Assézat, à Naigeon, et à l'*Encyclopédie*. Ce sont donc des bizarreries qui ont la vie dure.

Dans tous les cas, il faut recourir à l'*Historia critica philosophiae* pour comprendre de qui ou de quoi il est question. Diderot lisait vite, on le sait, son imprimeur a travaillé vite, nous le savons aussi, mais cela n'explique pas tout et il faudra se demander un jour sérieusement si *l'acte de lire,* au XVIIIe siècle, mettait en jeu les mêmes mécanismes cérébraux et les mêmes données culturelles que pour nous. Il faudra faire un jour une histoire de la lecture.

Quoi qu'il en soit, voici ce que nous devons lire dans les articles que je viens d'énumérer, si du moins nous nous attachons à leur contenu manifeste. Les 'schystes' sont tout simplement les Chiites, par opposition aux Sunnites, les uns et les autres formant les deux courants majeurs de l'Islam. 'Sicuto' est un mot forgé, peut-être par contamination avec le *sicut* latin, sur le mot japonais *siuto* que Brucker avait lui-même trouvé dans l'*Histoire du Japon* de Kämpfer. Kämpfer disait: '*Siuto* dans le sens littéral signifie la voie ou la méthode des Philosophes. *Siudosja* [japonais *jyūdōja*] ou au pluriel *Siudosju* sont les philosophes qui suivent cette méthode.' Brucker a lu respectivement, ou laissé imprimer *siuto, sindosiuista,* dont Diderot a fait à son tour *sicuto et sendosivistes.* [28]

Anlegisus, Egobart, Danée n'ont jamais existé. Sous le premier nom il faut lire *Ansegisus (Brucker,* III, 626); c'est l'abbé de Fontenelle, auteur du premier recueil des capitulaires des rois. Sous le second, *Agobardus,* archevêque de Lyon mort en 840 (*ibid.*). Sous le troisième, Lambert Daneau, auteur d'une éthique chrétienne publiée à Genève en 1582 (*Brucker,* IV, 626: en latin '*Lambertus Danaeus*'.

Les 'Islalites' de l'article *Perses* ne sont que des Israélites (*Brucker,* I, 146: '*inter Israëlitas*').

'Asaria' n'a jamais existé. Le mot *asaria,* que Brucker a effectivement trouvé dans Maïmonide, est un pluriel arabe qui

---

28.   Je dois ces éclaircissements sur l'article *JAPONOIS à M. Ichikawe Shin-ichi, professeur à l'Université Waseda de Tokyo.

désigne les disciples d'Aschari (Eschiari, Al-Asshari dans l'*Encyclopédie*). Diderot les appelle indifféremment *Ascariouns* (voir l'article qui porte ce titre) ou *assharites* (dans le contexte même où figure le nom imaginaire d'Asaria). Il n'a jamais existé non plus de 'Mutazali'. Ce nominatif pluriel, chez Brucker, désigne ceux que Diderot appelle ordinairement les 'mutazalites' ou les 'motazalites' (Brucker écrit aussi *'Mutazalitae'*). L'invention des 'asphahanites' est plus étrange. Diderot les a imaginés à partir d'une note de Brucker énumérant les différents courants du droit islamique (III, 97—98, note *a*). Brucker cite deux personnages, David d'Ispahan (*Aspahaniensis*) et Abu Hanifa, célèbres pour leur dispute au sujet de l'usage de la raison. De là deux sectes, évidemment. Celle des Hanéfites (Diderot écrit Hanifites) était connue comme une sous-division du courant sunnite. Le nom de la second a été construit sur le même modèle, mais Diderot ne s'est aperçu qu' *'aspahaniensis'* n'était pas un nom propre. Quant aux 'al-sharestans', ils sont nés d'une grossière méprise sur le latin de Brucker. Al-Sharestan est un personnage historique. Son autorité est souvent invoquée dans le *Specimen historiae Arabum,* traduit par Pocock de l'arabe d'Aboul Faradj, ou Bar Hebraeus. Brucker écrit tout naturellement: '*Al Sharestani fide* [...] *refert auctor* [etc.]' [sur la foi d'Al-Sharestan, l'auteur rapporte que...] Diderot a pris ce génitif singulier pour un nominatif pluriel. *Quandoque bonus dormitat Homerus...*

Il est plus surprenant qu'il n'ait pas reconnu Montaigne dans le 'Michel Montanus' de l'article THOMASIUS. Il est vrai que le savant auteur de l'article paru en 1971 dans les *Studies on Voltaire*[29] ne l'a pas reconnu non plus![30]

---

29. Hartmut Häusser, 'The Thomasius article in the *Encyclopédie*,' *S.V.E.C.,* 1971, vol. LXXXI, pp. 177—205.
30. Le nom apparaît p. 191 dans la réfutation d'une thèse sur Thomasius défendue en 1931 et selon laquelle Diderot se serait inspiré du *Zedler's Universal-Lexikon* pour son article: '*Close*

Une note plaisante, pour clore provisoirement ce chapitre infini. Aucun des lecteurs de l'article *HOBBISME ne s'est troubler par le début d'un paragraphe qui se lit ainsi dans l'édition Lewinter: '[Hobbes] guérit de cette maladie, et l'année suivante il publia ses traités *De la Nature humaine* et *Du Corps politique*. Sethus Wardus, célèbre professeur en astronomie à Séville, et dans le suite évêque de Salisbury, publia contre lui une espèce de satire [etc.]'.[31] Ce personnage est Seth Ward, II vécut de 1617 à 1689 et fut successivement évêque d'Exeter et de Salisbury. Nulle trace d'un passage à Séville dans la carrière de cet honorable ecclésiastique. On sait en revanche qu'il fut *Savilian Professor of Astronomy* à Oxford. La qualité de *Savilian Professor* le dispensait de donner des cours *ex cathedra* à l'Université. Diderot lisait exactement dans *Brucker, IV, 2,* 156: '*vir celeberrimus Sethus Wardus,* tunc astronomiae professor Savilianus [c'est moi qui souligne], *postea episcopus Sarisbiensis*'. Il a pris le titre de la chaire pour le nom d'une ville espagnole. Il était d'autant moins excusable que Brucker parlait encore, deux pages plus loin, des *Savilian Professors,* à propos de Hobbes lui-même et des cours qu'il publia à leur intention en 1655.

30. *analysis and comparison of the Zedler text with Diderot's showed, however, that names and proper nouns like* Michaële Montanus [c'est moi qui souligne] *and Friedrich Hoffmann, which appear in Brucker and Diderot, are missing in Zedler'.*
31. P. 280. Même texte chez tous ses prédécesseurs et dans l'édition originale de l'*Encyclopédie*.

Fig. I. Arsenal: Cliché Giraudon 169

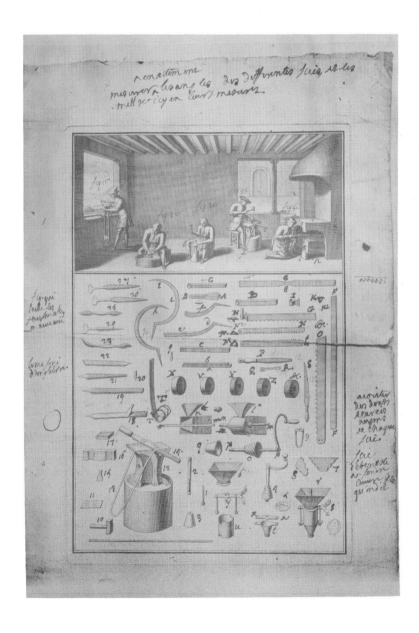

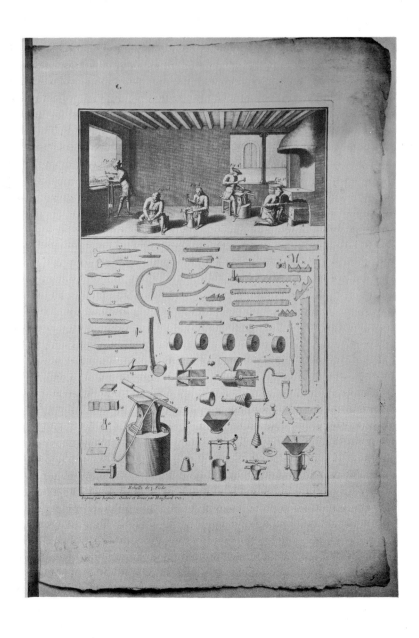

Fig. III. Arsenal: Cliché Giraudon   171

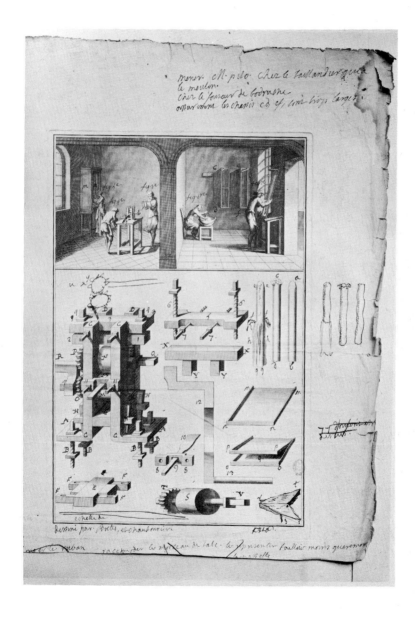

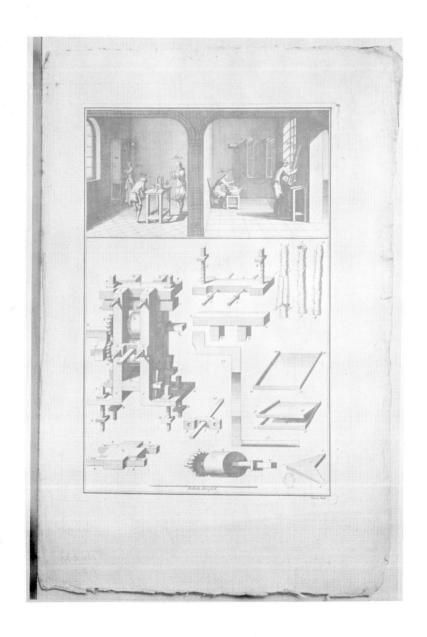

LACLOS AND STENDHAL

G.E. Rodmell

ULL knowledge of a writer's circle of literary acquaintances is seldom easy to come by, and in the case of Laclos the lack of such knowledge is so great that it becomes one of the most exasperating facets of the 'Laclos enigma', to use the term coined many years ago by Emile Henriot[1]. We know that Laclos had some connection with Mme Riccoboni (the letters which they exchanged after the appearance of *Les Liaisons dangereuses* in 1782 are sufficient proof of this), and there is some evidence that this association may have been of long standing, in that in her first letter to Laclos Mme Riccoboni implies that she is a family friend: 'Je ne suis pas surprise qu'un fils de M. de Chauderlos écrive bien. L'esprit est héréditaire dans sa famille'[2]. There is, however, no trace in Laclos's correspondence of anything like a close literary friendship[3]. Indeed, allusions to other writers are not especially numerous in Laclos's letters, although it is possible to detect in them signs that he was particularly prone

1. E.Henriot, 'L'Enigme Laclos', in *Temps*, 11 November, 1930. See also the same author's *Les Livres du second rayon: irréguliers et libertins*, Paris, 1925, pp. 313–338.
2. In Choderlos de Laclos, *Œuvres complètes*, ed. M.Allem, Paris, Bibliothèque de la Pléiade, 1951, p. 710.
3. See Laclos, *Lettres inédites*, ed. L. de Chauvigny, Paris, 1904.

to admiration of Jean-Jacques Rousseau, for all that Armand Hoog, not by any means unreasonably, argues that 'à proprement parler, en plein bouleversement préromantique, cet officier représente la pointe extrême et comme le dernier feu - éblouissant, glacé - de l'art et de l'analyse classiques'[4].

It is disappointing not to be able to demonstrate beyond doubt that a personal relationship existed between Laclos and significant writers of prose fiction whom he may well have had the opportunity of meeting: the Marquis de Sade or Benjamin Constant, for example. There is some evidence, tantalisingly thin though it is, that Laclos may indeed have known the 'divin Marquis'. On 27 March, 1794 Sade was transferred from prison at Saint-Lazare to Picpus, where Laclos had been incarcerated since 5 November of the previous year on account of his close association with the Duc d'Orléans. Sade was released on 15 October, Laclos on 3 December: in other words, the two of them shared the same prison for almost seven months. Despite attempts which have been made to erect on this foundation a complex edifice, the principal decorative features of which would be that the two writers quarrelled, that Sade deliberately excluded mention of Laclos's name from his *Idée sur les romans,* and indeed that Sade set out to *'refaire* le roman des *Liaisons dangereuses'* and to demonstrate that he could outdo Laclos in a field which Sade considered his own[5], there is no real evidence to substantiate any such theory. Which, of course, is not necessarily to deny the existence of parallels between certain aspects of the work of the two men.

Similarly, although Benjamin Constant, who was born in 1767, may well have met Laclos (who was his senior by a quarter

4. *Les Liaisons dangereuses,* ed. A.Hoog, 2 vols., Paris, Editions du Bateau ivre, 1946, I, xii.
5. See G.Lély, 'Sade a-t-il été jaloux de Laclos? ', in *Nouvelle Revue française,* June 1953, p. 1128.

of a century or more) at some such place as the home of Madeleine-Augusta Pourrat, the wife of a prosperous Lyonnais banker, who was certainly well known to both of them, there is irritatingly little in the way of hard evidence that the author of *Les Liaisons dangereuses* exerted any direct influence on the creative writing of the author of *Adolphe,* although one may well be tempted to see similarities between certain aspects of these two works.

Both Sade and Constant may well have met Laclos (Constant observed in a letter to Mme de Charrière dated 9 March, 1790 that in a conversation with a thoroughly stupid pedagogue by the name of Boutemy, who denied that *Les Liaisons* had been written by Laclos and who, indeed, called into question the very existence of Laclos himself, he had replied, 'Mais Monsieur, j'ai dîné, moi, avec Mr de Laclos..., j'ai vu à Paris Mr de Laclos et toute la société qui l'avait vu faire son roman'[6]. Equally, it is possible that another writer, arguably more significant in many ways than either Sade or Constant, namely Stendhal, may have known Laclos. Whether he did or not may well, in the end, not be all that important, but there can be little doubt that *Les Liaisons dangereuses* was not without its importance so far as the writings of Stendhal are concerned.

The name of Laclos may have come to the ears of the young Henri Beyle very early on indeed. That Laclos was known to Stendhal's family, probably in consequence of his military service in Grenoble, seems well enough attested. A. and Y. Delmas point out, for example, that it was Stendhal's grandfather, Dr. Gagnon, who ensured Laclos's election as a corresponding member of the Lycée des Sciences et des Arts of Grenoble[7].

6. Quoted in full in G. Rudler, *La Jeunesse de Benjamin Constant (1767–1794),* Paris, 1909, pp. 205–6.
7. A. & Y. Delmas, *A la Recherche des 'Liaisons dangereuses',* Paris, 1964, p. 106.

Laclos's letter of thanks, dated 16 fructidor, an X (3 September, 1802) is to be found in the town library there[8]. Dubois-Fontanelle, the young Beyle's master at the École Centrale in the same town, held *Les Liaisons dangereuses* in high esteem[9]. Stendhal himself claims to have met the ageing General Laclos in Italy, although it has to be admitted that his references in this connection are somewhat confusing. In *Souvenirs d'égotisme,* he claims to have met Laclos in a box at La Scala, Milan. Henri Martineau shows that this meeting could only have taken place during the second fortnight of September, 1800, or the second week of April, 1801[10]. Matters are further complicated by a note in *De l'Amour* in which Stendhal seems to situate the meeting not in Milan but in Naples: 'Il faut avoir entendu parler l'aimable général Laclos, Naples, 1802' (II, 75). This apparent contradiction may well, in itself, raise doubts in the minds of the wary concerning the authenticity of Stendhal's claim to have met Laclos at all, especially since, as both Martineau and Mistler point out[11], the meeting cannot have taken place in Naples, since Stendhal did not set foot in that city until 1811, whereas Laclos died in 1803. Moreover, when Stendhal wrote his *Journal* in 1811, he began chapter XIV with an analysis of his life in Milan after the Battle of Marengo (14 June, 1800), and there he says,

8. Bibliothèque de Grenoble, R. 7591. Published in *Petite Revue des bibliophiles dauphinois*, vol. 5, no. 2, 1951, p. 58.
9. See J.G. Dubois-Fontanelle, *Cours de belles-lettres*, 4 vols., Paris, 1813, IV, 232.
10. Stendhal, *Souvenirs d'égotisme*, Paris, Divan, 1927, p. 131 and p. 398, n. All subsequent references to the works of Stendhal, unless otherwise stated, will be to the Divan edition (ed. H. Martineau), and will be incorporated into the body of the text.
11. See Henri Martineau, *Petit Dictionnaire stendhalien*, Paris, Divan, 1948, p. 283, and *Les Liaisons dangereuses*, ed. J. Mistler, Monaco, 1948, p. xviii.

> Je n'avais jamais vu le monde, pas le plus petit bout mais en
> revanche j'avais senti tous les romans possibles, et entre autres
> l'*Héloïse*; je crois que dans ce temps j'avais lu *les Liaisons
> dangereuses* et j'y cherchais des émotions (IV, 244).

That is all he has to say of Laclos and his novel in connection
with Milan. There is no mention here of a meeting in a box at
La Scala, as there is in *Souvenirs d'égotisme:* the general's
name is not even mentioned. Beyle was certainly capable of
romanticising himself to the greater glory of Stendhal, and one
is perhaps somewhat inclined to say with Mistler,

> Nous espérons qu'on ne nous accusera pas de scepticisme
> systématique si nous disons que la rencontre d'Henri Beyle et de
> Laclos a dû avoir lieu dans l'imagination de Stendhal, entre
> 1811 et 1832.[12]

Be that as it may, there can be no doubt that Stendhal
allowed his imagination to play freely on Laclos and his novel.
He claims to have seen, when visiting the Marquis Berio in
Naples, a manuscript by Laclos which consisted of a chronicle
of the scandals of the day (a possible preparatory notebook for
Les Liaisons (*De l'Amour*, II, 159): unfortunately there is no
other reference to this mysterious manuscript. He claims that,
as a child, he was fed on 'noix confites' by the original of
Laclos's Mme de Merteuil, a certain Christine-Marie-Félicité de
Montmaur (*Vie de Henry Brulard*, I, 86–7 & II, 217–8): the
question of the existence of real-life originals for Laclos's
characters is a dubious one, and there are no grounds at all for
accepting this story of Stendhal's at face value. He identifies a
certain Mme de Blacons as the original for Cécile de Volanges
(*Henry Brulard*, I, 86–7): this story is equally unsubstantiated.
The whole process of seeking originals for the characters of
Les Liaisons is a search for a needle in a haystack, and indeed
the needle may well not even exist.

However, the extent to which Stendhal was intrigued by

12. J. Mistler, p. xviii.

Laclos is amply attested to by the traces of *Les Liaisons dangereuses* to be found in his work. His essay, *Du Caractère des femmes françaises,* which was not published until 1909 [13], was written in 1803 when Stendhal was only twenty, or in other words when he had just returned to Grenoble from Italy, where he claims to have met Laclos himself. It is a very superficial, extremely bookish exercise, a sort of would-be manual of seduction. The observation that 'il y a un cérémonial dans l'amour; nos seuls maîtres en ce genre sont les romans que nous lisons' (an intriguing observation from one who had sought 'des émotions' in Laclos's novel), is explicitly linked with *Les Liaisons dangereuses:*

> Pour la confection des plans de campagne, on peut consulter les grands auteurs. Par exemple, sur le problème: jouer l'amour auprès d'une jeune fille de 18 ans, le Danceny des *Liaisons;* — auprès d'une dévote de 28, le Valmont du même...[14]

Stendhal's other direct reference to *Les Liaisons* in this immature work runs as follows: 'Valmont le dit: c'est le cœur qui nous donne les plus grands plaisirs' [15]. A. and Y Delmas are quite correct when they state that in fact Valmont never says this [16]. They may well, on the other hand, be less correct in suggesting that this remark may be a reminiscence of Valmont's somewhat disenchanted observations after the act of charity which he deliberately performs in the knowledge that this will enhance his reputation with Mme de Tourvel, who has put a spy on his tail. If so, it is a very muddled reminiscence indeed. What Valmont remarks on this occasion, in a letter to Mme de Merteuil, runs as follows:

13. Stendhal, *Du Caractère des femmes françaises,* published by P. Arbelet in 'Le Cathéchisme d'un roué', in *Revue politique et littéraire,* 19 June, 1909, pp. 769—773.
14. Stendhal, *Du Caractère des femmes françaises,* p. 772.
15. Stendhal, *Du Caractère des femmes françaises,* p. 771.
16. A. & Y. Delmas, p. 109.

J'avouerai ma faiblesse; mes yeux se sont mouillés de larmes, et
j'ai senti en moi un mouvement involontaire, mais délicieux.
J'ai été étonné du plaisir qu'on éprouve en faisant le bien; et je
serais tenté de croire que ce que nous appelons les gens vertueux,
n'ont pas tant de mérite qu'on se plaît à nous le dire (*Les
Liaisons dangereuses*, Letter XXI).

In other words, there is little difference between the 'virtuous'
such as Mme de Tourvel and the 'vicious' such as Valmont: it is
merely that they gain their pleasure by different means — and
there is perhaps an implication that the performing of 'good
works' is just as much a method of exerting one's dominion
over others as are the activities of the *roué,* just as much an
expression of vanity. Valmont's remark can be seen as a
swingeing indictment of those who take the line that that which
gives pleasure is by definition morally good. But is it acceptable
as the likely source of Stendhal's misquotation? It is noteworthy,
for example, that there is no direct reference to ' le cœur' in
this remark of Valmont's. There are other passages in Laclos's
novel which may perhaps be considered more probable sources.

One might adduce, for example, an extract in which
Valmont is describing to Mme de Merteuil his early impressions
of Mme de Tourvel:

> Vous le dirai-je? je croyais mon cœur flétri, et ne me trouvant
> plus que des sens, je me plaignais d'une vieillesse prématurée.
> Madame de Tourvel m'a rendu les charmantes illusions de la
> jeunesse. Auprès d'elle, je n'ai pas besoin de jouir pour être
> heureux (Letter VI).

Another possible source of Stendhal's remark is a later passage,
again from a letter written by Valmont to Mme de Merteuil,
in which the Vicomte expatiates on the nature of love:

> En effet, si les premiers amours paraissent, en général, plus
> honnêtes, et comme on dit plus purs; s'ils sont au moins plus
> lents dans leur marche, ce n'est pas, comme on le pense,
> délicatesse ou timidité, c'est que le cœur, étonné par un sentiment
> inconnu, s'arrête pour ainsi dire à chaque pas, pour jouir du
> charme qu'il éprouve, et que ce charme est si puissant sur un
> cœur neuf, qu'il l'occupe au point de lui faire oublier tout
> autre plaisir... (Letter LVII).

But by far the most likely source of the words inaccurately
ascribed by Stendhal to Valmont comes much later in the novel,
in the last paragraph of Valmont's final letter to Danceny:

> Ce que j'ajoute encore, c'est que je regrette Madame de
> Tourvel; c'est que je suis au désespoir d'être séparé d'elle; c'est
> que je paierais de la moitié de ma vie, le bonheur de lui consacrer
> l'autre. Ah! croyez-moi, on n'est heureux que par l'amour
> (Letter CLV).

It should not be assumed that Valmont is here sincerely baring
his own heart. In this letter, he assures Danceny that since his
return to Paris he has been working unremittingly to bring
Danceny and Cécile de Volanges together. Now, he says, thanks
more to the love which Cécile feels for Danceny than to his own
skill, he is able to report that 'tous les obstacles sont surmontés,
et votre bonheur ne dépend plus que de vous'. Danceny thus
has the choice between 'une jeune fille timide, qui n'a pour elle
que sa beauté, son innocence, et son amour', and the 'agréments
d'une femme parfaitement usagée [i.e. Mme de Merteuil]'. In
other words, this letter is a ploy to ensure that Danceny will
abandon Mme de Merteuil in favour of Cécile, thus bringing
humiliation upon the Marquise. It is in fact one of the last
manœuvres in the central battle in this novel between Mme de
Merteuil and Valmont. Its tone is consonant with that of
earlier dealings which Valmont has had with Danceny (see
Letters LVII and LX) and its final paragraph is an attempt to
appeal to the heart of Danceny who, despite his 'nouveaux
principes' as a *coureur de jupes* is still, deep down, to use Mme de
Merteuil's expression about him, too much of a Céladon
(Letter LI) ever to become a successful *roué* in the class of
either the Marquise or the Vicomte. Valmont himself, echoing
Mme de Merteuil, had earlier described Danceny as 'ce beau
héros de Roman' (Letter LVII), and at this late stage Danceny
still thinks that Mme de Tourvel is proving 'inexorable' to
Valmont (Letter CLVII), just as he is prepared to accept that

Cécile is still 'innocente'. Danceny is still, in many respects, an innocent abroad. Valmont, however, hedges his bets by appealing not only to the Céladon in Danceny but also to the new 'Danceny d'aujourd'hui, arraché par les femmes, courant les aventures, et devenu, suivant l'usage, un peu scélérat': at the very least, he says of Cécile, 'c'en est une de plus'. Thus Letter CLV is a trap set for Danceny with a view to ensuring the defeat of Mme de Merteuil by Valmont, and it should certainly not be thought, on the basis of such examples as these from the text of *Les Liaisons* (and still less on the basis of Stendhal's inaccurate quotation from that work) that Valmont is, in the last analysis, an 'homme sensible'.

One simply cannot accept D.A. Coward's thesis that Laclos's Vicomte is 'the Rake Reformed By Love and dies in an odour of sanctity'[17]. Although it may be true that Mme de Tourvel makes a greater impact on Valmont than he likes to admit, the fact remains that his heart is indeed 'flétri' and not 'neuf', that when he speaks of the illusions of youth he does indeed see them as illusions, and that, as he himself puts it, 'Je ne sais pourquoi, il n'y a plus que les choses bizarres qui me plaisent' (Letter CX). Mme de Merteuil, who, as part of her campaign to assert her superiority over Valmont, repeatedly twits him with being in love, gives a fair indication of his capacity in this regard when she writes to him, after he has succeeded in seducing Mme de Tourvel,

> ... ce que j'ai dit, ce que j'ai pensé, ce que je pense encore, c'est que vous n'en avez pas moins de l'amour pour votre Présidente; non pas, à la vérité, de l'amour bien pur ni bien tendre, mais de celui que vous pouvez avoir; de celui, par exemple, qui fait trouver à une femme les agréments ou les qualités qu'elle n'a pas; qui la place dans une classe à part, et met toutes les autres en second ordre; qui vous tient encore attaché à elle, même alors

17.   See D.A. Coward, 'Laclos and the Dénouement of the *Liaisons dangereuses*', in *Eighteenth-century Studies*, vol. 5, no. 3, Spring, 1972, p. 437.

que vous l'outragez; tel enfin que je conçois qu'un Sultan peut le ressentir pour sa Sultane favorite, ce qui ne l'empêche pas de lui préférer souvent une simple Odalisque [a reference to the *fille d'opéra*, Émilie] (Letter CXLI).

On the subject of Valmont's sensibility, one can certainly go no further than this, and in going even thus far one needs to exercise caution, for Mme de Merteuil is far from being a ˙disinterested commentator on her accomplice's character. There are signs of a possible influence of Laclos throughout the writings of Stendhal. The famous division of love into four categories in the opening chapter of *De l'Amour* is, methodologically as well as in content, very much of the eighteenth century, and one is almost tempted to ask oneself whether Stendhal's search for 'émotions' in Laclos's novel may not have contributed something to it. Whether love as it is depicted in *Les Liaisons dangereuses* falls principally into the second category, that of *amour-goût*,

> ... celui qui régnait à Paris vers 1760, et que l'on trouve dans les mémoires et romans de cette époque, dans Crébillon, Lausun, Duclos, Marmontel, Chamfort, Mme d'Épinay, etc., etc.,

and of which Stendhal says, 'Il est vrai, si l'on ôte la vanité à ce pauvre amour, il en reste bien peu de chose', or whether it falls into the fourth category, *amour de vanité*, concerning which Stendhal remarks,

> L'immense majorité des hommes, surtout en France, désire et a une femme à la mode, comme on a un joli cheval, comme chose nécessaire au luxe d'un jeune homme,

is perhaps difficult to say (*De l'Amour*, I, 27—9). But then, as we have seen, Stendhal himself has to use the word 'vanité', which is crucial in terms of all the principal characters of Laclos's novel, when he is discussing *amour-goût* and, as he says a little later in the same chapter of *De l'Amour*, 'Au reste, au lieu de distinguer quatre amours différents, on peut fort bien admettre huit ou dix nuances' (I, 31). Broadly speaking, then, these are the two categories of love with which *Les Liaisons* deals. These labels are particularly applicable, perhaps, to Valmont's relationship with Mme de Merteuil and to Mme de Merteuil's with Prévan, although to some degree they can be applied to Valmont's seduction of Cécile and Mme de Tourvel. Of the other two categories, one at any rate is present in the pages of Laclos's novel. We can see, in Mme de Tourvel's utter devotion to Valmont, once she has given herself to him, an example of *amour-passion,* described by Stendhal as 'celui de la religieuse portugaise, celui d'Héloïse pour Abelard'. Nothing as simple as an example of the remaining category, *amour-physique,* characterised by Stendhal in the following terms, 'A la chasse, trouver une belle et fraîche paysanne qui fuit dans les bois... On commence par là à seize ans', is to be found in *Les Liaisons.* No innocent gambolling in the woods here. Everything in this world is tainted.

It has to be remembered, of course, that Stendhal was thoroughly steeped in the literature and thought of the eighteenth century, from Crébillon *fils* to the *idéologues,* and so one has to be cautious about attributing too much to the influence on him of any one writer. Yet there can be no doubt that Laclos fascinated him, and surely it is not unreasonable to suggest that *Les Liaisons* played a by no means insignificant part in his evolution.

In the second chapter of *De l'Amour* (I, 32 *et seq.*), he describes the stages in the birth of love, and it is here that he introduces his theory of *cristallisation:*

> ... La première cristallisation commence.
>
> On se plaît à orner de mille perfections une femme de l'amour de laquelle on est sûr; on se détaille tout son bonheur avec une complaisance infinie. Cela se réduit à s'exagérer une propriété superbe, qui vient de nous tomber du ciel...
>
> Ce que j'appelle cristallisation, c'est l'opération de l'esprit, qui tire de tout ce qui se présente la découverte que l'objet aimé a de nouvelles perfections...

En un mot, il suffit de penser à une perfection pour la voir
dans ce qu'on aime...

Un homme passionné voit toutes les perfections dans ce qu'il
aime...

It does not seem unduly fanciful to suggest that Mme de Merteuil
puts forward something remarkably like this theory of
cristallisation in at least two of her letters. In the first passage,
which appears in a letter to Mme de Volanges, the Marquise is
dealing with women in general terms. She writes,

J'ai rencontré, comme vous pouvez croire, plusieurs   femmes
atteintes de ce mal dangereux [love] ; j'ai reçu les confidences de
quelques-unes. A les entendre, il n'en est point dont l'Amant ne
soit un être parfait; mais ces perfections chimériques n'existent
que dans leur imagination. Leur tête exaltée ne rêve qu'agréments
et vertus; elles en parent à plaisir celui qu'elles préfèrent: c'est
la draperie d'un Dieu, portée souvent par un modèle abject:
mais quel qu'il soit, à peine l'en ont-elles revêtu, que, dupes de
leur propre ouvrage, elles se prosternent pour l'adorer (Letter CIV).

Mme de Merteuil may be writing here in general terms; it is
nevertheless true that what she describes is precisely what
happens to Mme de Tourvel who, after having resisted Valmont
for reasons which are basically an amalgam of religious
conventionality and vanity, finally succumbs to him and literally
treats him as her God ('Je l'aime avec idolâtrie, et bien moins
encore qu'il ne le mérite' (Letter CXXXII)). Mme de Merteuil,
of course, has her own reasons for depreciating Mme de Tourvel,
but it is interesting that Stendhal himself assesses the Présidente
in terms which would have delighted Mme de Merteuil. In
De l'Amour he observes,

C'est uniquement pour ne pas être brûlée en l'autre monde, dans
une grande chaudière d'huile bouillante, que madame de Tourvel
résiste à Valmont. Je ne conçois pas comment l'idée d'être le
rival d'une chaudière d'huile bouillante n'éloigne pas Valmont
par le mépris (II, 137).

The second passage in question, which occurs in a letter
to Valmont, is also relevant to the liaison between the

Présidente and the Vicomte. It takes the form, however, not of
strictures on Mme de Tourvel's state of mind, but of yet another
accusation by Mme de Merteuil that Valmont himself is in love,
and a consequent demand for the sacrifice of the Présidente:

> J'exigerais donc, voyez la cruauté! que cette rare, cette étonnante
> Madame de Tourvel ne fût plus pour vous qu'une femme ordinaire,
> une femme telle qu'elle est seulement: car il ne faut pas s'y
> tromper; ce charme qu'on croit trouver dans les autres, c'est en
> nous qu'il existe; et c'est l'amour seul qui embellit tant l'objet
> aimé (Letter CXXXIV).

The reason Mme de Merteuil, and for that matter Valmont, are
anxious not to allow their sentiments to become involved is
their insistence on an intellectual control of their lives (an
ambition shared to some degree by a number of Stendhal's
characters, including Julien Sorel and Lamiel), a determination
to see things as they are, by the cold light of reason. They would
agree with Stendhal that 'du moment qu'il aime, l'homme le
plus sage ne voit plus aucun objet tel qu'il est' (De l'Amour,
I, 65) [18].

There are signs of the presence of Laclos in Stendhal's own
prose fiction. Armance, which appeared in 1827 and which is,
like Les Liaisons, the first novel of a man in his forties, contains
one direct reference to Laclos. This appears as a consequence
of the Commandeur de Soubirane's plot to prevent the marriage
of Octave and Armance by means of a forged letter purporting
to be from Armance to her friend Méry de Tersan:

18.   See also De l'Amour, I, 64: 'Voilà la raison morale pour laquelle
       l'amour est la plus forte des passions. Dans les autres, les désirs
       doivent s'accommoder aux froides réalités; ici ce sont les réalités
       qui s'empressent de se modeler sur les désirs'. A third passage from
       Les Liaisons which might be cited in connection with the Stendhalian
       notion of cristallisation is the one quoted above from Mme de
       Merteuil's Letter CXLI (see above p. 182).

... M. de Soubirane avait emplóyé deux jours à faire un modèle de lettre pétillant d'esprit et surchargé d'idées fines, réminiscence de celles qu'il écrivait en 1789.

Notre siècle est plus sérieux que cela, lui dit le chevalier [de Bonnivet], soyez plutôt pédant, grave, ennuyeux... Votre lettre est charmante; le chevalier de Laclos ne l'eût pas désavouée, mais elle ne trompera personne aujourd'hui. —Toujours aujourd'hui, aujourd'hui! reprit le commandeur, votre Laclos n'était qu'un fat. Je ne sais pourquoi vous autres jeunes gens vous en faites un modèle. Ses personnages écrivent comme des perruquiers, etc., etc.

Le chevalier fut enchanté de la haine du commandeur pour M. de Laclos; il défendit ferme l'auteur des *Liaisons dangereuses*, fut battu complètement, et enfin obtint un modèle de lettre point assez emphatique et allemand, mais enfin a peu près raisonnable (*Armance*, pp. 298—9).

This reference to Laclos supports one's belief that his influence on Stendhal was not insignificant. The implications of this conversation are entirely to the advantage of Laclos, defended as he is by the intelligent Chevalier de Bonnivet (who has about him something of Valmont) and attacked by the Commandeur de Soubirane, described elsewhere as 'cette âme vulgaire' (*Armance*, p. 42).

A number of critics have, over the years, seen parallels between *Les Liaisons dangereuses* and *Le Rouge et le noir,* and it is not intended here to attempt a detailed examination of Stendhal's novel in the light of that of Laclos. It is clear that there are facets of Julien's character which suggest an apprentice Valmont. If Valmont can compare himself with Turenne or Alexander the Great, no doubt Julien Sorel can, in his fantasy view of himself, draw a parallel with Bonaparte. He does draw up a plan of seduction which he tries, clumsily, to put into operation in terms of Mme de Rênal (*Le Rouge et le noir,* I, 142—3). By far the clearest example, however, of a 'manual of seduction' in *Le Rouge et le noir* is that given to Julien by his friend Korasoff, of whom we are told that 'l'art de séduire est son métier' (II, 300), and who is an eighteenth-century *roué* who has strayed into the nineteenth century. If Julien himself never quite makes the grade as a *roué*, it is equally true that he never entirely loses the mechanistic habits of thought associated with that profession in so much eighteenth-century erotic literature, a certain icy detachment, an idea that people can be reduced to formulae and, by extension, that methods of manipulating people can be clinically worked out. There may be a passionate side to Julien, but this other aspect of him is very important, and is present in him from the early days of his career. But if calculation plays a part in Julien's relationship with Mme de Rênal, it plays a still greater part in his pursuit of Mlle de La Mole, and his campaign by blindly-copied letters against Mme de Fervaques (which is in fact part of this pursuit in accordance with the principles laid down by Korasoff) is a vivid example of a person being used as a puppet: 'Il adressait la parole à la maréchale, mais son but unique était d'agir sur l'âme de Mathilde' (II, 315). Parallels can be drawn, too, between Mme de Rênal and Mme de Tourvel, and even between Mathilde de La Mole and Mme de Merteuil.

In *La Chartreuse de Parme,* when Ranuce-Ernest IV remarks of Gina Sanseverina, 'Il faut avoir cette femme..., c'est ce que je me dois, puis il faut la faire mourir par le mépris' (*La Chartreuse,* II, 16), his thoughts, and the attitude which they imply, closely parallel Valmont's attitude towards Mme de Tourvel, if one makes allowances for the different positions of the characters in the two novels. The Prince's methods are cruder, but the determination to place the woman at his mercy is the same (compare his remark, quoted above, with Valmont's cry concerning Mme de Tourvel in Letter IV, 'Voilà ce que j'attaque, voilà l'ennemi digne de moi'), and the ultimate casting-off of La Sanseverina in his plan is the fulfilment of the *roué's* code as exemplified by Valmont's use of the 'Ce n'est pas ma faute' letter (see Letters CXLI–CXLII). We find something of the same attitude in Fabrice del Dongo himself. He may suffer from

vanity only 'par accès' (*La Chartreuse*, I, 270), but he does
suffer from it, like Laclos's characters, and there is in him a
coldly cerebral attitude akin to that of Valmont, together with
a desire for domination, in his *galanteries* in Naples and in the
La Fausta affair in Bologna, although it must be admitted, that
despite Fabrice's own fears there is in him (as there is in Julien
Sorel) a passion, a capacity or at any rate a desire for love, which
is not found in Valmont, and which finds expression in his
relationship with Clélia Conti. Even here, though, there are
parallels to be drawn between the tactics of Fabrice and those
of Valmont. Valmont sends Mme de Tourvel the *lettre timbrée
de Dijon*, so that she will think it comes from her husband
(*Les Liaisons*, Letter XXXVI[19]). Fabrice, 'poussé à bout par
l'excès de sa mélancolie et par ces regards de Clélia qui
constamment se détournaient de lui', adopts a not dissimilar
stratagem:

> Un jour, à la tombée de la nuit, Fabrice, habillé comme un
> bourgeois de campagne, se présenta à la porte du palais, où
> l'attendait l'un des domestiques gagnés par lui; il s'annonça
> comme arrivant de Turin, et ayant pour Clélia des lettres de
> son père (*La Chartreuse*, II, 394).

Fabrice may be more 'romantic' as a hero: his tactics are those
of Laclos's *roué*. [20].

Clélia's interpretation of her vow never again to see
Fabrice (II, 395–6) may suggest that the foundations of her
religious faith are no more substantial than those on which
Mme de Tourvel's faith rests, but what is more interesting about
Clélia in terms of Laclos is that her attitude towards Fabrice,

19.   See also *Les Liaisons dangereuses*, Letter XXXIV.
20.   It is true that this incident comes after the seduction of Clélia, that
      Valmont has none of Fabrice's melancholy, except by affectation,
      and that Fabrice presents the letter himself. Nevertheless, it is not
      impossible that the basic device springs from a recollection of
      Laclos's novel. One can put it no more strongly than that.

before she becomes his mistress, is remarkably similar to the Présidente's view of Valmont. Clélia remarks,

Je n'eus point le courage de quitter la forteresse et je suis une fille perdue, je me suis attachée à un homme léger: je sais quelle a été sa conduite à Naples: et quelle raison aurais-je de croire qu'il aura changé de caractère? Enfermé dans une prison sévère, il fait la cour à la seule femme qu'il pût voir, elle a été une distraction pour son ennui. Comme il ne pouvait lui parler qu'avec de certaines difficultés, cet amusement a pris la fausse apparence d'une passion. Ce prisonnier s'étant fait un nom dans le monde par son courage, il s'imagine prouver que son amour est mieux qu'un simple goût passager, en s'exposant à d'assez grands périls pour continuer à voir la personne qu'il croit aimer. Mais dès qu'il sera dans une grande ville, entouré de nouveau des séductions de la société, il sera de nouveau ce qu'il a toujours été, un homme du monde adonné aux dissipations, à la galanterie, et sa pauvre compagne de prison finira ses jours dans un couvent, oubliée de cet être léger, et avec le mortel regret de lui avoir fait un aveu (*La Chartreuse*, II, 201–2).

There are, of course, inevitable differences (not the least of which is the fact that Clélia charitably assumes that Fabrice's feelings for her, however temporary, are genuine), but this passage, and perhaps more especially the last sentence of it, closely parallels Mme de Tourvel's feelings and, indeed, to some degree (in the reference to the convent), her subsequent history, Mme de Tourvel is just as aware of Valmont's past record as Clélia is of that of Fabrice, and the similarities between the passage quoted above and certain of the Présidente's observations are striking. The following passage is a good example:

De retour à Paris, vous y trouverez assez d'occasions d'oublier un sentiment qui peut-être n'a dû sa naissance qu'à l'habitude où vous êtes de vous occuper de semblables objets, et sa force qu'au désœuvrement de la campagne... Y pouvez-vous faire un pas sans y rencontrer un exemple de votre facilité à changer...? Vous demander de ne plus vous occuper de moi, ce n'est donc que vous prier de faire aujourd'hui ce que déjà vous aviez fait, et ce qu'à coup sûr vous feriez encore dans peu de temps, quand même je vous demanderais le contraire (*Les Liaisons*, Letter L).

Valmont is in the country, Fabrice is in prison. That apart, there is a remarkable similarity between the two situations. Mme de Tourvel would certainly have sympathised with Clélia's uneasiness.

It is in the heroine of the unfinished *Lamiel*, however, that we find the clearest example of a Laclosian character in the work of Stendhal. Lamiel is a truly remarkable female character, striving after lucidity, and comparable (despite her lowly social origins) with both the Marquise de Merteuil and and Cécile de Volanges. It may be objected that the Marquise and the young Cécile are two very different characters, but it should be remembered that at one point, if only briefly, Mme de Merteuil contemplates making Cécile her assistant and apprentice. Moreover, it is clear that Laclos was in Stendhal's mind when he wrote this work: in his plan for *Lamiel*, Stendhal makes a direct reference to the author of *Les Liaisons* [21]. In certain notes made in 1840–1, Stendhal states the essence of Lamiel as being 'le dégoût profond pour la pusillanimitié...; suivant elle une âme de quelque valeur devait agir et non parler' (*Lamiel*, pp. 293–5). This could be applied equally to Valmont and Mme de Merteuil, although, like Stendhal's other characters, Lamiel has a passionate side to her nature, upon which Stendhal insists (pp. 294–5), and which differentiates her from Laclos's creations.

Vanity and *ennui* once again play prominent parts in this work. Vanity, as Stendhal himself points out, is 'la seule passion de Sansfin' (p. 300), and *ennui* is a term which regularly appears – it is, for example, Sansfin's diagnosis of Lamiel's disease (p. 92). The relationship between Dr Sansfin, 'ce don Juan bossu' (p. 5), and Lamiel is an exceptionally fascinating one

---

21.   'Sansfin arrange la reconnaissance de Lamiel par un vieux libertin de l'école de Laclos sans principes et sans un sou, M. le Marquis d'Orpierre...' *(Lamiel,* p. 290). The novel also contains a character named Prévan (p. 268).

for any student of Laclos. Sansfin, in effect, embarks upon the task of providing Lamiel with a catechism of debauchery. The first step in this enterprise is Sansfin's endeavour to take complete control of Lamiel's mind, an operation very similar to that undertaken by Mme de Merteuil in respect of Cécile de Volanges:

> Bientôt Lamiel fut convaincu que ce pauvre médecin d'une figure aussi burlesque était le seul ami qu'elle eût au monde. En peu de temps, par des plaisanteries 'bien calculées, Sansfin réussit à détruire tout l'affection que le bon cœur de Lamiel avait pour sa tante et son oncle Hautemare (p. 90).

His tactics, on occasion, are very different from those of Laclos's character. He resorts, for instance, to the use of terror. But the aim is the same, the exercise of total dominion over his apprentice:

> Toute son âme était remplie du bonheur d'avoir réduit la jeune fille à l'état de *complice*. Il l'eut engagée aux plus grands crimes qu'elle n'eût pas été davantage sa complice... (p. 94).

Such was the fate of Cécile in the hands of Mme de Merteuil, and even more so, subsequently, in the hands of Valmont.

Sansfin's principles are indeed remarkably similar to those of Laclos's characters. The emphasis on pleasure is there (one is reminded of Valmont's reflexions after he has performed his self-conscious act of charity), as is the recognition, of which even Mme de Merteuil is aware, of a woman's need to keep up social appearances [22]. Sansfin remarks to Lamiel,

> Il y a donc doublement à gagner à écouter la voix de la nature, et à suivre tous ses caprices: d'abord l'on se donne du plaisir, ce qui est le seul objet pour lequel la race humaine est placée ici-bas; en second lieu l'âme fortifiée par le plaisir, qui est son élément véritable, a le courage de n'omettre aucune des petites comédies nécessaires à une jeune fille pour gagner la bonne opinion des vieilles femmes en crédit dans le village ou dans le quartier qu'elles habitent (pp. 110–111).

In this rarefield world of both Laclos and Stendhal, pleasure

22. See *Les Liaisons dangereuses*, Letter LXXXI.

comes not through the emotions but by the imagination working on the senses.

Other striking similarities between Sansfin's principles and those put forward in *Les Liaisons* are to be found. Sansfin counsels Lamiel that 'il ne faut jamais écrire' (p. III). Mme de Merteuil makes a point of saying that when Belleroche comes to her *petite maison* he is given 'un billet de moi, mais non de mon écriture, suivant ma prudente règle' (*Les Liaisons*, Letter X; see also Letter LXXXI). The letters from the Marquise which help to make up Laclos's novel must, of course, be seen as the exception to this rule, but we have no need to consider their existence as an example of lack of verisimilitude. There is a very good explanation for their existence given in the novel itself, and this explanation leads us to the next similarity between *Les Liaisons dangereuses* and Sansfin's principles. Sansfin tells Lamiel that

> ....le danger de la doctrine du plaisir c'est que celui des hommes les porte à se vanter sans cesse des bontés que l'on peut avoir pour eux. Le remède est facile et amusant, il faut toujours mettre en désespoir l'homme qui a servi à vos plaisirs (*Lamiel*, p. 111).

Mme de Merteuil adopts one method to 'mettre en désespoir' Prévan; she uses another in respect of Valmont, and it is this which enables her to express herself freely to him in her letters. As she tells him,

> Descendue dans mon cœur, j'y ai étudié celui des autres. J'y ai vu qu'il n'est personne qui n'y conserve un secret qu'il lui importe qui ne soit point dévoilé...... Nouvelle Dalila, j'ai toujours comme elle, employé ma puissance à surprendre ce secret important... A la vérité, je vous ai... livré tous mes secrets: mais vous savez quels intérêts nous unissent, et si de nous deux, c'est moi qu'on doit taxer d'imprudense (*Les Liaisons*, Letter LXXXI).

Thus it is that, despite appearances, Mme de Merteuil can assert, in this same letter, that 'celle de ne jamais écrire' is one of the principal precautions she takes. Similarly, Sansfin warns Lamiel that

... il ne faut jamais témoigner de confiance à une femme, si l'on
n'a en mains le moyen de la punir de la moindre trahison. Jamais
une femme ne peut ressentir d'amitié pour une autre femme du
même âge qu'elle (*Lamiel*, p. 111).

Mme de Merteuil, long before Sansfin, had laid down this
principle in anticipation of Valmont's argument that she was
after all in the hands of her maid-servant. In the same Letter
LXXXI she says of this girl, 'J'ai son secret', and goes on to
explain that she has in her possession an official order which
could be used at any moment to have the girl shut away.

Lamiel, despite the fact that her social origin is very
different from that of Mme de Merteuil, nevertheless manifests
attitudes remarkably similar in certain respects to those of
Laclos's Marquise. Like her, Lamiel is essentially a cerebral
character, a fact which is clearly brought out by her creator:
'Le lecteur pense peut-être que Lamiel va prendre de l'amour
pour l'aimable abbé Clément, mais le ciel lui avait donné une
âme ferme, moqueuse et peu susceptible d'un sentiment tendre'
(*Lamiel*, p. 114). The novels which she reads warn her against
love, but without making it clear what love is. This, not
surprisingly, arouses in her a curiosity about the subject. Her
approach, however, remains essentially intellectual:

> Elle n'avait aucune disposition à faire l'amour; ce qu'elle aimait
> par-dessus tout, c'était une conversation intéressante. Une
> histoire de guerre, où les héros bravaient de grands dangers et
> accomplissaient des choses difficiles, la faisait rêver pendant
> trois jours, tandis qu'elle ne donnait qu'une attention très
> passagère à un conte d'amour... Lamiel n'était attentive qu'aux
> obstacles que les héros rencontraient dans leur amours (pp. 126–7).

The community of spirit between Lamiel and Laclos's Marquise
and Vicomte here is closer than at first sight may seem to be
the case. The interest in obstacles, the importance of surmounting
obstacles, is crucial in the psychology of Laclos's characters.
It is not so much the actual enjoyment of the victim which
matters to Mme de Merteuil or to Valmont, as the *pureté de
méthode* which each demonstrates in overcoming the obstacles,

the skill and effectiveness of the campaign. It is not insignificant that they frequently write in military jargon and on occasion liken themselves to the great military leaders of the past, declaring that 'conquérir est notre destin' (Letter IV), any more than it is insignificant that Lamiel should reveal such a lively interest in stories of war.

The sterility of human relationships which is apparent in Valmont and Mme de Merteuil (and indeed in *Les Liaisons* as a whole) is akin to the discovery made by Lamiel as a result of the experiments which, like Mme de Merteuil, she deliberately makes in the sexual domain. The word 'experiment' is important. Lamiel and Mme de Merteuil have a similarly detached approach to the subject of love. Lamiel's uncle, Hautemare, warns her of the dangers of walking in the woods with a young man:

> 'Eh bien! j'irai me promener au bois avec un jeune homme,' se dit Lamiel...
>
> 'Je veux savoir absolument,' se dit-elle, 'ce que c'est que l'amour. Mon oncle dit que c'est un grand crime, mais qu'importent les idées d'un imbécile tel que mon oncle? C'est comme le grand crime que trouvait ma tante Hautemare à mettre du bouillon gras dans la soupe du vendredi... Il faut convenir que tout ce que disent mes pauvres parents Hautemare est cruellement bête. Quelle différence avec les paroles du docteur (*Lamiel*, pp. 128–9).

Lamiel suffers from somewhat stupid, superstitious guardians much as Cécile de Volanges suffers from a stupid, hypocritical mother. In consequence, each comes to place her trust in *roués,* Lamiel in Dr Sansfin, Cécile in Mme de Merteuil and, subsequently, Valmont. Lamiel, however, is considerably more intelligent than Cécile, and an altogether stronger personality. The fact that 'elle n'avait aucune disposition à faire l'amour', coupled with her observation, 'Je veux savoir absolument ce que c'est que l'amour', seems directly to echo Mme de Merteuil's remark about her own youth in the brilliant autobiographical Letter LXXXI: 'Ma tête seule fermentait, je ne désirais pas

de jouir, je voulais savoir; le désir de m'instruire m'en suggéra
les moyens'. The parallel becomes even clearer when we compare
the actual steps taken by Lamiel to educate herself in these
matters with Mme de Merteuil's statements in Letter LXXXI.
Lamiel's first experiment is with a drunk whom she
allows to kiss her. Her 'Quoi! n'est-ce que ça' *(Lamiel,* p. 178)
is identical with Julien's exclamation after becoming Mme de
Rênal's lover *(Le Rouge et le noir,* I, 153). 'Experiment' is
certainly the word to use of this episode, and also of the
subsequent and more important episode in which Lamiel goes
off to the woods with Jean Berville, and if we make suitable
allowances for the directness and relative simplicity of a country
girl, even one of Lamiel's astounding calibre, the parallel with
Mme de Merteuil's manipulation of lesser mortals becomes
apparent enough. Lamiel deliberately controls Berville's actions
throughout the scene:

> Mène-moi me *promener au bois...* Embrasse-moi, serre-moi dans
> tes bras... Allons-nous-en; toi, va-t'en jusqu'à Charnay, à une lieue
> de là, et ne dis à personne que je t'ai mené au bois *(Lamiel,*
> p. 179)[23].

Later, she meets him again. He makes the advances this time,
and scratches her with his beard. Lamiel is not prepared to
become the dominated partner: she repulses him, but says that
she will meet him again, tells him where and when to meet
her, and offers him money. The pattern is repeated:

> —Embrasse-moi, lui dit elle.
> Il l'embrassa, Lamiel remarqua que, suivant l'ordre qu'elle lui
> en avait donné, il venait de se faire faire la barbe; elle le lui
> dit.
> —Oh! c'est trop juste, reprit-il vivement, mademoiselle est la
> maîtresse; elle paye bien et elle est si jolie!
> —Sans doute, je veux être ta maîtresse.
> —Ah! c'est différent, dit Jean d'un air affairé; et alors sans
> transport, sans amour, le jeune Normand fit de Lamiel sa maîtresse
> (p. 181).

23.   Stendhal's italics. On the same page we have learned that 'le curé
       défendait surtout aux jeunes filles *d'aller se promener au bois'.*

All this shows, on a cruder, more rustic plane, a remarkable similarity to the technique of Mme de Merteuil, not only in her early education, but also in her subsequent treatment of members of the male sex, from Belleroche to Prévan and to Valmont himself. They are the *things,* the instruments on which she plays. Both Lamiel and Mme de Merteuil take certain precautions against discovery, although admittedly the steps taken by Lamiel are inexpressibly clumsy by comparison with those of the Marquise. Each ensures that she is in control, and above all each is essentially cerebral in approach.

Between her first and second interview with Berville, when she has so far done no more than kiss him, Lamiel goes to see her confessor:

> Elle raconta au saint prêtre sa promenade dans le bois; elle n'avait garde de rien lui cacher, dévorée qu'elle était par la curiosité.
>
> L'honnête curé fit une scène épouvantable mais n'ajouta rien ou presque rien à ses connaissances (pp. 179–80).

In Letter LXXXI of *Les Liaisons dangereuses,* Mme de Merteuil tells how she too went, in her mood of scientific inquiry, to see her confessor. She shows rather more imagination in her approach:

> Je sentis que le seul homme avec qui je pouvais parler sur cet objet, était mon Confesseur. Aussitôt je pris mon parti; je surmontai ma petite honte; et me vantant d'une faute que je n'avais pas commise, je m'accusai d'avoir fait *tout ce que font les femmes.* Ce fut mon expression; mais en parlant ainsi je ne savais en vérité quelle idée j'exprimais. Mon esprit ne fut ni tout à fait trompé, ni entièrement rempli; la crainte de me trahir m'empêchait de m'éclairer: mais le bon Père me fit le mal si grand, que j'en conclus que le plaisir devait être extrême; et au désir de le connaître succéda celui de le goûter.

Mme de Merteuil continues, 'Je ne sais où ce désir m'aurait conduite'. However, at this precise moment her marriage was arranged: 'sur-le-champ la certitude de savoir éteignit ma curiosité, et j'arrivai vierge entre les bras de M. de Merteuil'.

We have already seen where this same desire led Lamiel — back to the woods with Jean Berville, to become his mistress. The two women are equally objective in their conduct of the experiment, although there is a slight difference in the reactions. Lamiel, as she had done after her first kiss, expresses disappointment:

> —Il n'y a rien d'autre? dit Lamiel.
> —Non pas, répondit Jean.
> —As-tu eu beaucoup de maîtresses?
> —J'en ai eu trois.
> —Et il n'y a rien d'autre?
> —Non pas que je sache...
> —Quoi! l'amour n'est que ça? ...... Lamiel s'assit et le regarda s'en aller (elle essuya le sang et songea à peine à la douléur).
>
> Puis elle éclata de rire en se répétant:
> —Comment, ce fameux amour, ce n'est que ça! *(Lamiel*, pp. 181—2).

In this respect above all Lamiel is, as Henri Martineau describes her, 'une sorte de Julien femelle'[24]. There are here, too, certain similarities with Mme de Merteuil's reaction to the same experience. Laclos's Marquise writes,

> Cette première nuit, dont on se fait pour l'ordinaire une idée si cruelle ou si douce, ne me présentait qu'une occasion d'expérience: douleur et plaisir, j'observai tout exactement, et ne voyais dans ces diverses sensations que des faits à recueillir et à méditer.

If she admits that, after the first objective experiment, 'ce genre d'étude parvint à me plaire', the enjoyment is still cerebral, and she decides to

> ... donner un champ plus vaste à mes expériences. Ce fut là [i.e. on her husband's country estate], surtout, que je m'assurai que l'amour que l'on nous vante comme la cause de nos plaisirs, n'en est au plus que le prétexte (Letter LXXXI).

And indeed, for that matter, despite her initial sense of

---

24. H. Martineau, in *Armance. Lamiel*, Paris, F. Hazan, 1949, p. 213.

disappointment, Lamiel too is not slow to indulge in further experiments, particularly with the young Duc Féodor. She remains as much in control of her relationship with this young aristocrat as she had remained in control of the peasant Jean Berville: 'Lui était fou d'amour. Elle passait sa vie à inventer des tourments' (*Lamiel,* p. 189). These torments, which demonstrate her desire for domination, can be extremely capricious in character. For example, to humiliate the Duc she insists that he wear black, and when he asks why she makes him do this, she explains, 'Un de mes cousins vient de mourir; il était marchand de fromage'. He agrees to put on the melancholy costume, and Lamiel embraces him: 'Le pauvre enfant pleura de joie. Mais Lamiel n'éprouva d'autre bonheur que celui de commander' (p. 190). Her attitude towards the young Duc is indeed essentially the same as her attitude towards Jean Berville: 'Quant au duc, elle le regardait par curiosité et pour son instruction' (p. 194).

One striking difference between Lamiel and Mme de Merteuil lies in Stendhal's observation about his heroine to the effect that 'l'épigramme était chose absolument inconnue dans sa bouche' (p. 269). It is perfectly true that stylistically there is no comparison between the two women. Psychologically, however, if we make the necessary allowances for differences of plot and social context, and for the theme of the provincial hero/heroine which is foreign to Laclos's novel, then the similarities are there for all to see.

There can be no doubt that Stendhal was imbued with the writings of the eighteenth century and, whatever the truth may be about his having met Laclos, there can be no doubt that he was familiar with the latter's work, or at any rate with his one novel. The points which differentiate these two writers one from the other may well be at least as significant as those which throw light on a certain community of attitude, but nevertheless the similarities cannot and should not be overlooked, and they have to do with a fascination of emotional sterility or the fear of it. The principal differences between the two writers may perhaps be put as follows. Although Stendhal places considerable emphasis on individualism and on the ability of the mind and imagination to control the heart (where Laclos's characters speak of destiny ('conquérir est notre destin...'), Julien Sorel speaks of duty, 'un devoir héroïque'(*Le Rouge et le noir*, I, 97)), it remains true that in Stendhal's heroes and heroines there is a warmth, a capacity or at any rate a desire for tenderness such as exists also in Constant's Adolphe, a reluctance entirely to abandon the heart to cerebral activity, which is not to be found in Laclos's Marquise and Vicomte. Moreover, there is a great deal of Stendhal himself in Julien Sorel, in Fabrice and, for that matter, in Lamiel. The same cannot, despite a recurring tendency amongst critics over the years to identify Laclos and Valmont, be said of the author of *Les Liaisons dangereuses* and his characters. A Romantic Revolution had intervened in the years separating Laclos's single masterpiece from the great works of Stendhal.

A MINISTER'S FALL AND ITS IMPLICATIONS:
THE CASE OF CHAUVELIN (1737–1746)

J.M.J. Rogister

ERMAIN Louis Chauvelin, keeper of the seals and minister of foreign affairs was dismissed on 20 February 1737. This event formed the subject of an article published nine years ago, but it may be re-examined here because fresh evidence helps to reveal some of its lesser known aspects and far reaching implications within the political system of the *ancien régime*[1].

The main argument of the article published in 1968 was that Chauvelin had been dismissed not so much on account of his alleged intrigues with the court of Spain, but because his adherents in the *Parlement* of Paris were trying to create trouble there and to discredit the new first president, Louis Le Peletier. They were attempting to bring about an assembly of the chambers of the *Parlement* to force a debate on the content of the latest remonstrances and on the disgraceful scenes which, so it was claimed, had recently attended the burial of a Jansenist canon

*   I wish to thank the Research Fund Committee of the University of Durham for a grant which enabled me to carry out the research that forms the basis of this paper.

1.   J.M.J. Rogister, 'New light on the fall of Chauvelin', *English Historical Review*, lxxxiii (1968), 314–330. I wish to thank the Editor and Longman Group Ltd for permission to use some material which appeared in this article.

at Douai. The resultant crisis had culminated in the dismissal of Chauvelin, according to the evidence of one of the *avocats généraux*. Daguesseau de Plainmont (the youngest son of the chancellor), whose autograph memoirs contain a detailed account of these developments.[2] Some corroboration of his account was provided by the printed correspondence of the chancellor with his son.[3] By means of new evidence, it is possible to explore three different aspects of Chauvelin's fall. First, there is the question of the minister's standing on the eve of the event and of his personal involvement in the actions of the *Parlement*. Secondly, there is the matter of Cardinal de Fleury's role and of that of the princes of the blood in an affair that seems to be closely connected with the question of the choice of an eventual successor to the cardinal as the king's first minister. Finally, one can examine the problems which faced Chauvelin after his fall.

* * * *

It emerges from several contemporary accounts that Chauvelin's dismissal had been expected for several weeks before it occurred. The minister himself seems to have received a warning possibly nine or ten days before the event. In the

2.   *Ibid.* pp. 319 and 324—27.
3.   pp. 323—4. My claim (p. 323, n. 8) that the chancellor's letters printed in 1823 by Rives were written to Daguesseau de Plainmont is now confirmed by an examination of a volume of manuscript copies of these letters which was unknown to me in 1968. Moreover, it now appears that Rives did not publish all the letters from the chancellor to the *avocat général,* and some of the unpublished ones supply further details concerning the final stages of the *parlementaire* crisis of 1737; see Bibliothèque historique de la ville de Paris, MSS no. (cote provisoire) 5538, pp. 466—9.

archives of the Ministry of Foreign Affairs there is an unsigned
note dated only 'le 10^{ii} ' which reads as follows:

> Les raisons sont toujours les mesmes.
>
> Les entretiens a la sourdine ne roulent depuis avanthier que sur
> votre disgrace qu'on regarde comme infaillible.
>
> Mad^{me} la C [omtesse] de Toulouse, dit-on a resté longtemps
> avec le Roy à ce suiget [sic].
>
> Tous vos amis sont en mouvement pour tâcher de parer le
> coup.
>
> Mme de Carignan a fait de vains efforts pour faire prévenir
> M^r le Cardinal sur votre compte.
>
> Vous avés travaillé deux heures avec lui pour commencer a lui
> remettre les affaires dont vous êtes chargé.
>
> Les uns prétendent que vous serés déplacé inssesament
> [sic].
>
> Les autres veulent que ce ne soit qu'après la publication de la
> paix.
>
> On veut s'être aperçu qu'en vous retirant avec M^r le Card.....
> il ne vous écoute que d'un air froid et sans vous regarder.[4]

This note emanated clearly from one of Chauvelin's spies. The
suggestion that the minister might be dismissed 'inssesament'
must have put him on the alert, and the account of the activities
of the Comtesse de Toulouse and of the Princesse de Carignan
is plausible.[5] At the same time, the information is possibly

---

4. Archives du ministère des affaires étrangères, Paris [hereafter AAE],
    Mémoires et documents: fonds France, 1310, f. 417.

5. The role of the comtesse de Toulouse is treated in the course of this
    paper. The princesse de Carignan (1690–1766) was a daughter of
    Victor Amadeus II of Savoy by his mistress, the comtesse de Verrue.
    In 1714 she married the Prince de Carignan, of a cadet branch of the
    House of Savoy. The Carginans left Savoy in some haste in 1718 and
    settled in Paris, where the princesse obtained a pension of 160,000
    livres to compensate her for the loss of her possessions. By all
    accounts she and her husband were an unscrupulous pair who
    engaged in speculation and intrigue. The Savoie-Carignans had
    family connexions with the House of Condé dating from the
    previous century, and the princesse de Carignan worked in their
    interest. In 1740 her son married a princess of Hesse-Rheinfels who
    was a sister of the duchesse de Bourbon. Mme de Carignan had some
    influence with cardinal de Fleury.

misleading in its reference to Chauvelin's official relations with Fleury at this time. These seem to have been marked by a spirit of mutual confidence as late as 6 February, if one judges from a note sent by Chauvelin to Fleury that day. Chauvelin wrote that he was enclosing some papers for His Eminence, 'dont M. de Bussy luy rendra compte si elle le permet', and he added: 'Je ne perdray pas icy mon tems, J'ay bien a travailler'. Fleury's reply was made in the margin after he had seen Bussy at Issy and it does not suggest that relations were strained between him and Chauvelin:

> Je trouve encore bien des difficultés sur la prise de posséssion de la Lorraine et le Sr de Bussy vous les expliquera. La conduite du canton de Berne est des plus insolentes [illegible word] Je vous enverrai la réponse qu'il leur fait avec une copie pour vous. [6]

Moreover, if Fleury was waiting for the conclusion of the negotiations which were to give Lorraine to the deposed king of Poland before having Chauvelin dismissed, as some historians have suggested, then this reply also does not suggest that he was hastening those negotiations. If one hardly gets the impression from the exchange that the two were now in deadly enmity or that Chauvelin was handing in his portfolio, as the anonymous informant stated, one has to recognise that by all accounts Chauvelin's position was no longer very strong by this time. Yet the decision to dismiss him was probably determined by the chain of events that started at the *Parlement* on 13 February.

Some reports addressed by Hérault, the *lieutenant de police,* to Chauvelin on the initial stages of the crisis in the *Parlement* have also come to light.[7] It may be interesting to analyse them in view of a statement made in a memoir of 1763 by Pasquier, then a senior member of the *grand'chambre.* After claiming that at the time of his fall Chauvelin was planning a

6.   AAE, Mémoires et documents: France 1309, f. 94.
7.   *ibid.* ff. 119—20.

reform of the *Parlement,* Pasquier referred to Hérault as one who, in his words, 'n'avoit pas peu contribué à la disgrace de ce ministre'.[8] These allegations cannot be substantiated. On 14 February, Hérault reported to Chauvelin that the chambers of *enquêtes* and *requêtes* had decided to ask the first president to call an assembly of the chambers to discuss the Douai affair. Hérault's report confirms Daguesseau de Plainmont's claim that Le Peletier had already decided to grant their request in order to steal a march on them. Hérault also suggested to Chauvelin that any judicial proceedings in the Douai affair could probably be stopped by getting the *procureur général* of the *Conseil* of Arras to make a formal complaint on the grounds that the affair fell within the attributions of his court.[9] Chauvelin cannot be blamed for the fact that this suggestion was not followed. Hérault had also put it to Fleury, and the latter had told him to discuss the question with the chancellor. Daguesseau thought the suggestion was good but that no use could be made of it because of sudden developments at the *Parlement,* where the assembly of the chambers had ended in a deadlock as a result of Le Peletier's refusal to allow a debate on the Douai affair once he had announced that only the *grand'chambre* was entitled to deal with the case.[10] Hérault's reports confirm that, as one would have expected, Chauvelin had been kept informed of Le Peletier's intention to grant the request for an assembly of the chambers. Neither the minister nor the *lieutenant de police* knew in advance that the first president did not intend to allow any debate to take place. As it was Le Peletier's conduct that determined the course of events at the *Parlement* on 15

8.   Bibliothèque nationale, Paris, Cabinet des manuscrits, n.a. fr. 7,981: 'Mémoire sur les changemens qui ont été projettés pour réformer la discipline du Parlement', f. 353^V. A note on the first folio of this manuscript reads: 'Mr Pasquier Le Père conseiller au Parlement, 9bre 1763'.

9.   AAE, Mémoires et documents: France 1309, f. 119.

10.   *Ibid.* ff. 123–4: Hérault to Chauvelin, 15 Feb. 1737 (5.30 p.m.).

February, it is unlikely, to judge from the evidence, that Chauvelin gained any information from Hérault that he could usefully have betrayed to Le Peletier's opponents there. It is possible that he did betray the scheme to get the *Conseil* of Arras to intervene, though the outcome shows that it was unnecessary for him to have done so. Daguesseau de Plainmont was certainly of the opinion that Chauvelin tried to embarrass Le Peletier's position two days later. On 16 February the first president had changed his tactics in the face of the continued opposition of the *enquêtes* and *requêtes* and had asked the Government to intervene with an *arrêt du conseil* removing the Douai affair out of hands of the *Parlement*. At Versailles on the 17th, the ministers (including Chauvelin) decided instead to send a *lettre de cachet* to the *gens du roi* enabling them to ask the assembly of the chambers for all the documents in the case. The ministers then changed their minds and fell back on Le Peletier's original idea for an *arrêt du conseil* after Daguesseau de Plainmont had convinced the chancellor that to ask the assembly of the chambers for the documents in the Douai affair was tantamount to a recognition of its right to deal with the case. Chauvelin had been very surprised to learn of this change of plan, and Dageusseau de Plainmont was convinced that the idea of a *lettre de cachet* had been nothing but 'un nouveau tour du garde des sceaux'.[11] Hérault had written to Chauvelin on 15 February: 'Vous avés grande raison de dire qu'il y a à s'attrister et à s'affliger sur tout ce qui se passe'.[12] However, it is possible that such phrases had served to conceal intrigues and indiscretions on the minister's part which Hérault may have uncovered and exposed. What is striking about Chauvelin's subsequent conduct is that he gave the impression

11.   Rogister, p. 322.
12.   AAE, Mémoires et documents: France 1309, f. 121: Hérault to Chauvelin, 15 Feb. 1737 (7.30 p.m.).

of being guilty of some offence. The day after his fall his friend, the dowager Princesse de Conty went to see him at Grosbois, and she reported back to Fleury:

> J'ay trouvés *un homme*[13] qui m'a surpris par *son silence.* J'avoue qu'à sa place je dirais quelquechose; je ne murmurerois pas contre mon maître, mais j'en appellerois à lui même sur *les bruits du publique.* Je fis même en particulier ce que je pus pour le faire parler non pour le servir, mais pour le justifier; j'en ay eu pour toute réponce qu'il me prioit de trouver bon *qu'il ne me répondit* pas. J'ay dinê et et [sic] *repartit* après.[14]

* * * *

The new evidence is particularly interesting where it bears upon Fleury's role and on that of the princes of the blood. The date of 17 February when the ministers met to discuss the *arrêt du conseil* seems also to have been that on which it was decided to dismiss Chauvelin. The cardinal went to his place of retreat at Issy on 18 February, having told Chauvelin to attend to some business that day, which was a Monday; Chauvelin having seen the ambassadors the following day intended to be back at Versailles on the Wednesday. It now seems that the scenario for his removal had been prepared before the cardinal left for Issy on a visit that was probably intended to allay the foreign minister's suspicions. The first piece of evidence is a letter that Fleury wrote on his arrival at Issy. The name of the person to whom it was addressed is not known, but from the contents of the letter it is possible to suggest that he may have been involved in the arrangements for Chauvelin's subsequent

13. Words in this and other letters in France 1309 are underlined in ink; and this was possibly done by Fleury himself. I have reproduced them in italics.
14. France 1309, f. 134: dated 22 Feb. 1737 in a different hand.

transfer to his country seat at Grosbois under escort:

+ a Issy ce 18e février 1737

> Sa Majesté vous ayant choisi, monsieur, pour exequater [sic]
> une commission qui regarde son service, elle m'a ordonné de vous
> écrire de sa part de vous rendre demain au soir chès m^r le
> Comte de Maurepas pour recevoir ses instructions et agir en
> conséquence comme il vous le dira. Vous connoissés, monsieur,
> mes sentiment pour vous.

(s) le Card de Fleury[15]

The recipient would thus have seen Maurepas on the night of
19 February. Before Chauvelin could leave for Versailles the
next morning, Maurepas called on him at 6 a.m. with the
letter of dismissal, and shortly afterwards the fallen minister
was escorted by a troup of musketeers to Grosbois.[16]

While he was at Issy, Fleury also wrote to the First Prince
of the Blood, the duc d'Orléans, to give him advance notice of
Chauvelin's fall:

> Je serois fasché, monsieur, que votre altesse sérénissime apprit
> par le public le parti que le Roy a pris d'envoier demander
> demain au matin par m^r le Comte de Maurepas les sceaux et la
> démission de sa charge de sécrétaire d'état [sic]. Je me réserve à
> avoir l'honneur d'en expliquer plus en détail à V.A. les motifs
> et les raisons. Si j'avois été à Versailles, je l'aurois fait moi-même
> et je prens seulement la liberté de la supplier de tenir la chose
> secrète jusqu'a ce que j'aye des nouvelles de la mission de m^r de
> Maurepas. Il ne me reste qu'a assurer V.A. de mon respect très
> humble et de mon parfait dévouement.

(s) le Card de Fleury

A Issy ce 19 février

Le Roy ne s'est pas encore déterminé sur le choix d'un sécrétaire

15. *Album von Handschriften berühmter Persönlichkeiten vom
     Mittelalter bis zur Neuzeit*, ed. K. Geigy-Hagenbach, Basel, 1925,
     p. 82.
16. Narbonne, *Journal des règnes de Louis XIV et Louis XV de l'année
     1701 à l'année 1744*, ed. J.A. Le Roi, Paris, 1866, p. 404.

d'état.[17]

The duke replied the next day:

> Je crois, monsieur, que V.E. n'est pas en peine de ce que je pense sur le changement qui vient d'arriver *dans le ministère* et je suis persuadé qu'elle trouvera les *sentiments assez uniformes sur cet évenement.* Je la remercie de l'attention qu'elle a eu de m'en prévenir. Je suis parti de Versailles ne scachant rien et comptant de n'y revenir qu'après les jours gras, mais pour peu que V.E. veuille changer quelque chose à ma marche elle scait que je suis toujours disposé à faire tout ce qu'elle me conseillera et à luy donner dans touttes les occasions les preuves de ma véneration et de mon amitié.
>
> (s) Louis d'Orléans[18]

The duc d'Orléans' reply is now in the archives of the Ministry of Foreign Affairs alongside letters sent the same day to Fleury by other leading members of the royal family. The discovery in a private collection of Fleury's original letter to the duc d'Orléans strongly indicates that these other letters were also replies to similar missives from the cardinal. Those replies were far less reassuring than the one Fleury received from the duc d'Orléans. The dowager princesse de Condé, still known as 'Madame la Duchesse', mother of the former prime minister, the duc de Bourbon (Prince de Condé), wrote back indignantly:

> Il est certain, monsieur, que la disgrace de m^r Chauvelin me fait de la peine. Vous aviés voulu que je fusse de ses amies et j'en fus. Je vous avoue qu'il y a encore une chose qui m'en fait beaucoup, qui est que *nous ayant promis à mon fils et à moi que vous ne feriés rien que de concert avec nous,* nous ayons apris la

---

17.   Archives du château des Ormes, Les Ormes-sur-Vienne (Vienne) now deposited at the Bibliothèque Universitaire, Poitiers (1977): file of cardinal de Fleury's letters to the comte d'Argenson. Fleury first dated his letter as the 18th and then altered it to the 19th. The comte d'Argenson was at this time chancellor to the duc d'Orléans, and this fact may explain the presence of Fleury's letter to the duc among his papers. I wish to record my gratitude to the marquis d'Argenson for allowing me to consult his family papers.

18.   AAE, Mémoires et documents: France 1309, f. 127.

chose faitte; mais comme malgré ce que je vois et ce que je scay des moyens qui ont amené ce qui vient d'arriver, je conserve toujours une grande confiance en *vous* et en vos paroles [illegible word] je me garde bien de vous condamner sans vous entendre, et je continue de vous prier *de vouloir bien ne rien arrêter sans nous entandre.* Aussy, il y va de la *tranquillité du reste de mes jours, de l'honneur et de la seureté* [sic] *des princes du Sang et du bien l'état;* je connois vostre attachement pour ce dernier article, et l'amitié que j'ay pour vous me persuade que vous en avés assés pour moy pour avoir attantion à ceux qui me me regarde.

(s) Louise Françoise de Bourbon

Mr de Lassay a répondu sur le champ à ce que vous m'avés mandé pour luy, mais mon fils n'avoit pas encore receu votre lettre à neuf heures du soir.¹⁹

Madame la Duchesse's daughter, the dowager princesse de Conty, was even more forthright:

Je suis affligée, monsieur, de la disgrace de *m^r Chauvelin.* Vous savés qu'il étoit de *mes amis.* Je voudrois bien l'aler [sic] voir. Je vous prie de me mander si je le puis sans de plaire [sic] au roy.²⁰

(s) Louis Elisabeth de Bourbon

Madame la Duchesse herself returned to the attack two days later, when she learned that Amelot de Chaillou had been appointed as Chauvelin's successor as foreign minister. The reference to Le Peletier des Forts, uncle 'à la mode de Bretagne' of the first president and a former controller general, in her letter is interesting; she wrote to Fleury:

Il faut avoir une confiance aussy aveugle que celle que j'ay en vous, pour croyre que *m^r Amelot du Chaillou, ayant été placé par m^r des Forts* et étant son parent ne soit pas seulement de *la cabale;* mais enfin il n'est qu'un *sécrettaire d'état.* Pour le

19. *Ibid.* ff. 130—1. The marquis de Lassay was perhaps the lover and certainly the adviser of Madame la Duchesse. The duc de Bourbon's reply is missing, though it is clear that he wrote (Rogister, p. 326).
20. f. 129: dated 20 Feb 1737 in a different hand.

premier ministre, j'espère bien n'en point voir d'autre que vous, mais je désire ardament [sic] de voir le *gouvernement de l'état assuré* pour *quand on aura le malheur de vous perdre*, et je ne le désire que pour le bien de l'état et pour que *celuy de mes enfants* soit assuré. Ils pourroient se trouver dans une *terrible situation* sy les choses tournoient comme tout le monde le dit et comme les apparances donne lieu de le croyre. Vous m'avés promis de *veiller à nos intérest* [sic]. Ils ne peuvent estre en de meilleurs mains, mais je vous en parleray souvent, car tout ce que je vois me fait trembler.[21]

All these letters confirm Daguesseau de Plainmont's suggestion in his memoirs that Cardinal de Fleury had for some time been contemplating a solid plan of government which would take effect after his death. The *avocat général* thought Fleury did not intend to be succeeded by a prime minister but preferred that the king should put his trust in a prince of the blood, 'qui lui serviroit de conseil et qui auroit plutôt une Inspection genéralle qu'un véritable ministère'. It now seems likely that it was the death of a senior member of the council, the duc d'Antin, in November 1736 which forced the cardinal to think of a replacement and also to raise the question of his own succession.[22]

There were few candidates to choose from, if the intention was to restrict the choice to members of the royal family. The duc d'Orléans was already in the council, but he was still a young man and was doubtless beginning to reveal his limitations; however, he was in a position to create difficulties if he did not like Fleury's scheme. The duc de Bourbon (prince de Condé) had been prime minister, but Fleury had brought about his fall in 1726 and the king did not want him back; his son was only a year old; his brothers and his nephew, the prince de Conty, were young men. There was, however, an obvious choice, the comte de Toulouse, son of Louis XIV and Madame de Montespan. A capable sailor and a seasoned administrator (having been

21.   ff. 132–3.
22.   Rogister, pp. 324 and 330 (note 2). The duc d'Antin was the half-brother of the comte de Toulouse.

governor of Brittany since 1695), Toulouse was on very good terms with Louis XV. To the orphan king, Toulouse and his wife (a Noailles who had been previously married to the duc d'Antin's son) became 'oncle' and 'tante'; to the huntsman king, Toulouse was an experienced *grand veneur;* to the solitary king, unhappy in his marriage, the comtesse de Toulouse was a confidante; and to the king in need of a lively circle of friends, the comtesse de Toulouse contributed the gaiety of her house at Rambouillet and the presence of her young d'Antin and Noailles relatives. It was in this circle that Madame de Mailly emerged as the king's mistress around the time of Chauvelin's fall.

Whatever advantages the comte de Toulouse possessed, the obstacles to placing him in the council were great. He was a 'légitimé' and like his late brother, the duc du Maine, he had been excluded during the Regency from the royal succession for which Louis XIV had once made them eligible. The chief opposition to his elevation to a position of power in 1737 came from the princes of the blood who felt that their interests might once again be threatened. The duc d'Orléans maintained a relatively neutral position, but the House of Condé, deprived of a place in the council by the dismissal of the duc de Bourbon, was openly hostile to any scheme that favoured the comte de Toulouse. The irony of the situation was that the prime mover of the Condé faction, namely Madame la Duchesse, was herself a child of Louis XIV by Madame de Montespan and a sister of the comte de Toulouse. However, she saw it as her duty to protect the interests of her sons and of her grandson, the prince de Conty. Thus, battle was joined between the factions, with Chauvelin being considered as their ally in the government by the Condés, and the Toulouse faction doubtless relying for its support on the comtesse de Toulouse's influence with the king and on the assistance of her brother, the maréchal de Noailles (who was openly hostile to Chauvelin). The Le Peletier

family seem to have been working in the Toulouse interest. [23]
It is in this context that Chauvelin's dismissal and the attendant
correspondence between Fleury and the princes and princesses
of the blood has to be understood.

In his memoirs Daguesseau de Plainmont claimed that the
comte de Toulouse was informed of the intended arrangement
by the king himself the night before Chauvelin's dismissal. [24]
What is still not clear, however, is why the comte de Toulouse
was not after all brought into the council. Whether by design
or because the House of Condé had raised such a strong protest,
the king and Fleury made no further moves. However, it is
possible that they were waiting for the situation to calm down,
and that they intended to bring the comte de Toulouse into
the council later in the year, perhaps when the court moved to
Fontainebleau in the autumn. [25] If so, they counted without
the vigilance of the indefatigable Madame la Duchesse and the
worsening health of the comte de Toulouse. She wrote to
Fleury on 3 July concerning new efforts on the part of
'la cabale' to bring the comte de Toulouse into the council and
eventually to make him prime minister; she exposed the
scheme as an attempt to use Toulouse's poor state of health as
an excuse to make his promotion seem less significant. The
Noailles were behind the move, she claimed, and the duc
d'Orléans would doubtless support it because of the influence
which the comtesse de Toulouse's nieces had over him. [26] But

23. In this connexion it is interesting to note the friendly tone in which
    the comte de Toulouse wrote to Le Peletier des Forts when he
    ceased to be controller general of the finances in 1730: 'Je ne pouvois
    apprendre Monsieur une nouvelle qui me fachât davantage que celle
    de vostre retraitte'; Charavay sale catalogue (bulletin) n. 752 (April
    1974), p. 56.
24. Rogister, p. 324.
25. A suggestion made in the well-informed *Anecdotes curieuses de la
    Cour de France sous le règne de Louis XV*, ed. P. Fould, Paris, 1905,
    pp. 114—7. The author of this work is François-Vincent Toussaint.
26. Presumably they were the daughters of the maréchal de Noailles:
    the marquise de Caumont, the duchesse de Villars, the princesse
    d'Armagnac, and the comtesse de la Marck.

the cardinal loved the state and the king too much, Madame la Duchesse continued,

> pour que je puisse craindre que vostre bonté vous entraisne
> à favoriser un projet aussy dangereux et dont le premier pas
> seroit aussy humiliant pour moy et pour toute ma maison que
> de voir un légittimé dans le conseil pendant que mes enfans et
> petits enfans en seroient exclus.[27]

A few months later her fears were laid to rest, the comte de Toulouse had to undergo a painful operation from which he did not recover. He died on 1 December.

Why had Fleury, and presumably the king, limited the choice of a potential prime minister to the royal family and why had they attached so much importance to its reactions to Chauvelin's removal? It must not be forgotten that it was not until the late 1750s that the succession ot the throne was firmly assured in Louis XV's line. The king had no brothers, and it was becoming apparent by 1737 that the dauphin would remain his only son. If the king and this child of eight had died at that time, the problem of the succession could easily have been raised with all the European complications familiar to students of the Treaty of Utrecht.[28] Hence, the princes of the blood were still powerful figures who wished to protect their interests and eventual claims on the succession, especially against the illegitimate descendants of Louis XIV whose right to that succession had once been recognised. Fleury had to treat them and their numerous clientèle with care and seeming impartiality.

After 1737 the situation changed. First, the death of the

---

27. AAE, Mémoires et documents: France 1310, ff. 165—6.
28. Any accidents that happened to the king were an instant source of
     alarm; see, for instance, the concern displayed by Fleury when
     reporting one of them to the archbishop of Paris on 1 April 1737;
     it was a harmless incident but one which, he wrote, 'n'a pas laissé
     de nous allarmer infiniment dans le premier moment que nous
     l'avons scu' (Bibliothèque Mazarine, Paris MSS 2358, p. 667).

comte de Toulouse meant that the cardinal had to soldier on until his death in 1743 and that the king came to take a greater responsibility for the conduct of affairs. The only significant changes that were made in the ministry came in 1742, when cardinal de Tencin and the comte d'Argenson were brought into the council: the first in order to offset the chancellor's influence in the religious question, and the second because he was a competent administrator who belonged to the 'safe' Orléans faction. These changes did not affect the *status quo*. After Fleury's death, the maréchal de Noailles was brought into the council and he exercised considerable influence there, though not to the exclusion of all other. The king was by then his own prime minister. Secondly, the princely factions lost their leaders and figureheads. The comte de Toulouse was dead. The duc de Bourbon died in 1740, followed by Madame la Duchesse three years later; the new prince de Condé was a minor and his two uncles did not carry much weight. The duc d'Orléans became a recluse and was finally dropped from the council in 1741. Only Madame la Duchesse's other grandson, the young prince de Conty, showed signs of ambition and ability, a rare combination in the royal family at that time. Louis XV employed him but never placed him in the council. Only the dauphin was made a member of it after the duc d'Orléans ceased to be invited to its meetings; Louis XV had thus excluded the princes of the blood from the seat of government.

* * * *

Far from the princely intrigues, the fall of Chauvelin had some little-known implications for the victim himself. In June 1737 he was moved to Bourges, and on 31 January 1743, possibly as a result of an incautious letter to the king on the death of Fleury, he was exiled first to Issoire and then, in April, to Riom.[29] His wife accompanied him to the depths of the Auvergne. After a year in Riom, Chauvelin wrote a plaintive letter to Maurepas on 3 April 1744: 'quelque déplorable que soit ma situation, quelque sincère que soit mon repentir, s'ils ne peuvent toucher Sa Majesté, ne puis-je pas espérer qu'elle se laissera fléchir? ' He pleaded his wife's ill-health and his inability to do anything for the establishment of his son and three daughters. He hoped the king would show mercy on these whom he described as 'les victimes innocentes de mes fautes'.[30] But the king was unmoved and did not see fit to change the situation. Chauvelin took his disappointment bravely, merely asking Maurepas to remind the king at an appropriate time of their plight.[31] In December 1744 Louis XV allowed him to move to Orléans, an outpost of civilization.[32] Chauvelin's friend, the marquis d'Argenson, had become foreign minister a month earlier. In May 1745 Madame Chauvelin, now recovered, wrote to him. Her husband, she told him, was now seriously ill; the doctors at Orléans were no good and those in Paris were not readily available. She enclosed a letter from one of them and asked the minister to intercede with the king to allow Chauvelin to return to Grosbois where he could receive proper medical attention.[33] D'Argenson had to refer the matter officially to Maurepas, which he did, pointing out that the

29. Barbier, *Chronique de la Régence*, iii, 420–1; Argenson, *Journal et Mémoires*, ed. Rathery, iv. 59.
30. Archives nationales, Paris 257 AP 21 (Papiers Maurepas), dossier 5, liasse 2, no. 1. For a copy of Maurepas's undated reply see 1bis.
31. *Ibid.* no. 2: letter to Maurepas, 20 April 1744.
32. *Ibid.* no. 3: Chauvelin to Maurepas, 13 Dec. 1744; and *Lettres de M. de Marville, lieutenant général de police, au ministre Maurepas (1742–1747)*, ed. A. de Boislisle, Paris, 1896–1905, i. 108, note 2.
33. AN, 257 AP 21, dossier 5: Madame Chauvelin to the marquis d'Argenson, 23 May 1745. She wrote to Maurepas on 3 June enclosing a note from Chauvelin's doctor in Paris: dossier 5, liasse 3, no. 2.

king had been moved by her letter.[34] It would appear that the king now made it a condition of Chauvelin's return to Grosbois that he should give up the *présidence à mortier* which he had kept in the *Parlement.*[35]

Chauvelin claimed that he had only kept this office in the hope that his son might succeed him. The son had turned out to be a bad character, and, in any case, Chauvelin needed to sell the office in order to provide dowries for his three daughters. He was probably quite willing to comply with the king's wishes. However, his problem was that if it became known that he could only return to Grosbois on condition that he sold his office, he would have difficulty in selling it at a good price. He and his wife wanted an improvement in his circumstances to accompany his negotiations for the sale.[36] As Chauvelin was now committed to selling the office, the king saw the justice of their request and allowed him to return to Paris in February 1746.[37] Five months later, Chauvelin sold his *présidence* to Gilbert, the *premier avocat général,* for 550,000 *livres,* exactly 100,000 *livres* less than he had paid for it in 1718.[38] It is unlikely that impersonal economic trends had affected the sale of what was still a valuable office. The disgrace of Chauvelin was something that even his return to Paris could not entirely obliterate where potential, and doubtless hard-headed, purchasers were concerned. The fallen minister had one consolation: the Parisian doctors performed wonders, for Chauvelin lived on until 1762.

34.   *Ibid.*: letter of 30 May, 1745.
35.   See Madame Chauvelin's letter to Maurepas (with an enclosure in Chauvelin's hand) of 12 December [1745]; dossier 5, liasse 3, nos. 1 and 1ª.
36.   *Ibid.*
37.   *Ibid.* liasse 2, nos. 4 and 5: Chauvelin to Maurepas, 13 and 12 Feb. 1746.
38.   See J. Francois Bluche, *Les Magistrats du parlement de Paris au xviiie siècle (1715–1771),* Paris, 1960, p. 168.

* * * *

From fresh evidence it has been possible to explore some of the aspects of Chauvelin's fall which were only hinted at in an earlier article. The crisis in the *Parlement* remains the most important single clue to his dismissal, though his guilt still cannot be established precisely. The new evidence links the event more closely to the question of Fleury's succession and serves to clarify the role of the cardinal and of the respective princely factions. Finally, Chauvelin's plight after his dismissal tells its own revealing account of the practical implications for a minister and, in his case, also a *parlementaire,* of a fall from royal favour.

LA *SCÈNE DE STUPÉFACTION* DU *BARBIER DE SÉVILLE*

J. Scherer

'EST Beaumarchais lui-même qui l'appelle ainsi, dans la *Lettre modérée sur la chute et la critique du Barbier de Séville*. Il y souligne la réussite de 'la scène de stupéfaction de Bazile, au troisième acte, qui a paru si neuve au théâtre et a tant réjoui les spectateurs.' La satisfaction particulière de l'auteur devant cette onzième scène de l'acte III est loin d'être isolée. De nombreux critiques contemporains ont exprimé une admiration toute spéciale pour ce moment de la comédie. Grimm écrit dans sa *Correspondance littéraire* dès mars 1775: 'La scène d'imbroglio où Basile semble arriver pour déconcerter tous les projets du comte Almaviva et où on l'intrigue si bien qu'il ne sait plus qui l'on veut tromper est une des plus excellentes scènes qu'il y ait au théâtre, et l'idée en est tout à fait neuve'. En décembre de la même année, la *Correspondance littéraire*, à l'occasion d'un jugement plus général, revient sur cette même scène: 'Nous ne craindrons point de dire que cette pièce peut être mise à côté des meilleures farces de Molière, que si le fond en est moins philosophique, l'intrigue en est adroite et que les plus grands maîtres de l'art n'auraient point désavoué la scène de Basile.' Le rédacteur des *Annonces, affiches et avis divers* écrit le 9 août 1775: 'L'un des meilleurs *Imbroglio* que je connaisse au théâtre est cette apparition de Basile, qui n'étant prévenu de rien est à tout moment près de découvrir le stratagème du Comte; c'est sa surprise et le sang-froid si plaisant avec lequel il prend l'argent du Comte pour garder le *tacet;* enfin la manière dont, sans entrer dans le mystère du déguisement, il paraît y participer par son seul silence. Et cette naiveté du même: *Qui diable est-ce qu'on trompe ici? Tout le monde est dans le secret.* Si ce n'est là de véritable comique, nous confessons que nous n'y entendons rien'. Une anecdote rapportée par *Le Courrier* d'Avignon du 1er décembre 1775 montre combien cette scène avait profondément frappé un public d'habitués: 'L'acteur qui jouait le rôle de Basile le rendit si bien qu'il fut universellement applaudi; le lendemain il parut dans un autre rôle et y fut trouvé si mauvais qu'une voix du Parterre lui cria: *Basile, allez vous coucher, vous n'êtes pas dans votre assiette ordinaire.* A l'instant, toutes les voix firent *chorus,* et Basile alla se coucher'. Plusieurs années plus tard, Voltaire craindra encore une mésaventure semblable et n'osera pas appeler Basile un personnage de sa tragédie d'*Irène;* il remplacera son nom par celui de Léonce. Il n'est pas jusqu'à Collé, qui pourtant n'aime pas Beaumarchais, qui ne se joigne à ce concert de louanges. 'La scène de Basile, dans le troisième acte du *Barbier de Séville,* écrit-il, est de la première force, et digne du génie de Molière' [1].

La convergence de ces jugements, si elle n'est pas arbitraire, doit s'expliquer par l'efficacité particulière des ressorts dramaturgiques de cette scène. M. Niklaus a attiré l'attention sur l'originalité de la scène, qui, écrit-il, 'is... worth examining for the revelation it offers of Beaumarchais' structural skill'[2]. Nous voudrions compléter ses remarques par une analyse plus détaillée.

1. Tous ces textes sont cités, mais non rapprochés les uns des autres, en différents endroits du livre d'Enzo Giudici, *Beaumarchais nel suo e nel nostro tempo: Le Barbier de Séville,* Rome, 1964. Voir aux pages 407, 419, 433, 494 note 108 et 510.
2. Robert Niklaus, *Beaumarchais, Le Barbier de Séville,* Londres, 1968, p. 43.

Bazile arrive, en cette scène 11 de l'acte III, à un moment de particulière émotion pour les personnages qui sont en scène. Figaro vient de casser volontairement le nécessaire à raser de Bartholo et de lui dérober la clef de la jalousie. Le Comte ne parvient pas à donner à Rosine l'explication pourtant indispensable et urgente au sujet de sa lettre, qui est maintenant entre les mains de Bartholo. Chacun de ces quatre personnages fait face à un problème difficile, qu'il ne domine pas. Bazile apporte avec lui un problème nouveau, qui se surajoute à ceux qui se posaient déjà. Par nature, et parce que Beaumarchais l'a construit ainsi, Bazile est un traître. La fonction de traître, représentée dans chacune des six pièces de Beaumarchais et entretenant souvent des rapports, discrets mais perceptibles et dénonciateurs, avec l'Eglise[3] est caractérisée, en ce qui concerne Bazile, par la possibilité qu'il a de s'engager dans les deux groupes d'intérêts opposés dont le conflit constitue la comédie. D'une part il est chargé de préparer, en résolvant les difficultés juridiques, le mariage de Bartholo avec Rosine; mais son zèle, en cette matière où la rapidité importe au premier chef, dépend, comme le montre la scène 8 de l'acte II, de la générosité de Bartholo. D'autre part, en tant que maître de musique, Bazile peut être remplacé, selon une tradition comique fréquente qu'a soin de rappeler la scène 2 de l'acte III, par un amant déguisé. Surtout, il est essentiellement corruptible, et agira pour celui qui le paiera le mieux. Le Comte, etant beaucoup plus généreux que Bartholo, doit donc l'emporter à la fin. De fait, il donnera deux bourses à Bazile lors de deux moments décisifs: au cours de la scène de stupéfaction pour le faire partir, et lors du dénouement, pour obtenir la signature sans laquelle son mariage n'était pas valable.

Mais quand Bazile fait son entrée imprévue au troisième acte, le Comte ne lui a encore rien donné. Ce qui est plus grave

3.   Je me permets de renvoyer sur ce point à ma *Dramaturgie de Beaumarchais*, 2 ème édition, Paris, 1970, pp. 217–19.

encore, il n'a établi avec lui aucun contact. A la scène 6 du premier acte, le Comte ignorait qui était Bazile. A la scène 8 du deuxième, rien, dans ce que dit Bazile, ne permet de penser qu'il a eu une relation quelconque avec le Comte. Au contraire, sa tirade sur la calomnie, comme le remarquent immédiatement Bartholo et à la scène suivante Figaro, est singulièrement inadaptée: l'arme de la calomnie se briserait sur une personnalité aussi en vue que celle du Comte, et Bazile est le seul à ne pas le comprendre. Encore au début du quatrième acte, Bazile affirme clairement qu'il ne connaît pas le Comte. C'est un peu à l'aveuglette que celui-ci élabore ses projets, et en particulier ses déguisements. Le premier, celui d'un soldat un peu ivre, n'est en rapport ni avec Bazile ni avec aucun autre personnage. Le deuxième, celui d'un prétendu élève de Bazile qui s'appellerait Alonzo, est mieux intégré, mais cette intégration n'entraîne pas la connaissance de celui qui devrait couvrir le stratagème et pose de ce fait de délicats problèmes. Rien, dans la scène 2 de l'acte III, n'indique que le Comte soit d'accord avec Bazile pour le remplacer dans la leçon de musique à donner à Rosine. Rien non plus n'indique que Bazile sache qu'il doive se prétendre malade. Le contraire serait impossible, puisque Bazile et le Comte ne se sont jamais vus. Le Comte ne se tire pas mal de cette situation difficile, parce qu'il est servi par son intuition. C'est lui qui invente, pour les problèmes juridiques du mariage de Bartholo, l'homme de loi dont la désignation reviendra comme un refrain dans la scène de stupéfaction. Il tombe juste en promettant pour le lendemain la solution des problèmes légaux; c'est aussi ce qu'avait promis Bazile à la scène 8 de l'acte II. En rusant comme il le fait, il retrouve aux yeux de Bartholo les chemins de la calomnie, ce qui l'authentifie, bien à tort, comme envoyé de Bazile.

Cette absence de relation entre le Comte et Bazile est fertile en rebondissements. Elle est pourtant bien peu vraisemblable. Dans une société réaliste, le Comte aurait acheté à l'avance un Bazile qui ne demande qu'à se laisser acheter au lieu d'attendre un renversement *in extremis* qui aurait pu ne pas se produire. Figaro était l'intermédiaire tout désigné pour cette transaction. Mais en agissant ainsi, Beaumarchais se serait privé de la tension comique de la scène de stupéfaction.

Figaro est moins démuni que le Comte devant l'arrivée inopinée de Bazile. Il l'est pourtant dans une certaine mesure, car il est l'auxiliaire du Comte et il ne sait pas tout ce qu'il devrait savoir pour pouvoir toujours répondre avec sécurité. Son embarras était déjà visible à la scène 5 de l'acte III, lorsqu'il devait répondre à Bartholo sur les bonbons qui auraient été envoyés à 'la petite Figaro'. Il fallait que Rosine lui 'souffle' la bonne réponse, et Figaro était ici sur le chemin de la stupéfaction. Si ce schéma de 'souffler' est si fréquent dans le théâtre de Beaumarchais[4], c'est qu'il résulte de l'absence de liaison entre des personnages qui devraient être alliés. Rosine n'a pas parlé davantage à Figaro des bonbons embarrassants que le Comte ne s'est concerté à l'avance avec Bazile, comme il aurait pu le faire. Le procédé s'épanouira de manière plus grave encore, ou plus féconde, dans le *Mariage de Figaro,* lorsque la Comtesse ne voudra pas informer Figaro de ses projets.

Rosine, voyant entrer Bazile, est *'effrayée'.* Elle sait en effet depuis la scène 10 de l'acte II que Bazile, agent de Bartholo, se fait fort de rendre possible dès le lendemain le mariage qu'elle redoute. Bartholo est le seul à n'avoir aucune raison de se troubler à l'arrivée de Bazile. Il peut l'accueillir avec le sourire. Mais il serait nuisible à l'effet comique que l'attitude de Bartholo diffère de celle des autres. Il faut que tous unissent leurs efforts pour repousser Bazile vers la coulisse. Or Bartholo a une raison, qu'il ne comprend pas au début de la scène mais que le Comte lui suggère opportunément, de s'associer à cette action: à la scène 2 de l'acte III, il s'est fait, après quelque

4.   Voir ma *Dramaturgie de Beaumarchais,* pp. 178–9.

hésitation, le complice du faux Alonzo, et il n'a pas intérêt à ce que Bazile, par des questions maladroites, révèle en présence de Rosine des machinations qui lui déplairaient.

Ainsi, tous les personnages ont de bonnes ou d'excellentes raisons de redouter l'intervention de Bazile et de chercher à le renvoyer au plus vite. Ce sont des nécessités, et même plusieurs ordres différents de nécessités, qui les assemblent, car ils sont loin d'être d'accord entre eux. Il y avait déjà trop de monde pour le confort de chacun, quand Bazile entrait. Chacun recherchait le tête-à-tête et personne ne l'obtenait. Pour les autres, Bartholo était déjà de trop, quand Bazile se révèle de trop pour eux tous.

Si les conditions de l'expulsion de Bazile se trouvent dans les motivations diverses des personnages, elles résident également dans les faits qui précèdent immédiatement son arrivée. Ces faits, qui emplissent la presque totalité de l'acte culminant dans la scène de stupéfaction, sont au nombre de trois: la leçon de musique de Rosine, qui occupe la scène 4, le rasage de Bartholo, remis à plus tard mais préparé dès la scène 5, et le vol de la clef de la jalousie par Figaro à la scène 10. Non sans quelque application, Beaumarchais a pu situer ces faits assez hétéroclites dans le même lieu, qui est celui de la scène. Ils recèlent tous des moyens dissimulés d'établir enfin un contact entre Rosine et le Comte. Bazile, qui ne peut connaître ces moyens ni ce but, risque évidemment de faire tout échouer par son arrivée imprévue. Sa seule entrée doit inspirer aux autres personnages et aux spectateurs une sorte de terreur comique. La puissance de cet effet et les soins dont il est entouré expliquent assez qu'il reste exceptionnel. Bazile est dans le *Barbier de Séville* un personnage rare; il n'intervient que dans cinq scènes de la comédie. Et la scène de stupéfaction est la seule de la pièce, en dehors de celle du dénouement, où soient réunis les cinq personnages qui y figurent.

L'importance et les raisons de la scène étant ainsi précisées, on peut en distinguer les moments successifs, que le texte rend très clairs. Ils sont au nombre de quatre, et montrent la progression de la parole au silence et du silence à l'absence: on veut d'abord que Bazile ne dise rien, puis qu'il disparaisse; et, paradoxalement, on y réussit.

Le premier mouvement est une rupture des communications. Bartholo, qui, ne s'est pas encore avisé des réactions possibles de Rosine devant des révélations déplaisantes, parle imprudemment à Bazile de ce qu'il croit être vrai: la maladie de celui-ci, le rôle d'Alonzo, sont pour lui réels. Il est donc pour la volonté de silence des autres un obstacle. Bazile, sentant peut-être combien le terrain est dangereux, ne répond ni oui ni non. Ses paroles sont parfaitement vides: 'le seigneur Alonzo... Me ferez-vous bien le plaisir... Mais encore... La leçon de musique...' Il ne fait que répéter ce qu'on lui dit ou commence des formules qu'il n'achève pas. Il évite soigneusement toute signification. Les mots qu'il prononce sont aussi proches que possible du silence. Il en dit toutefois encore trop pour les craintes des autres. Chacun s'emploie méthodiquement, à son tour, à rompre la communication dangereuse entre Bartholo et Bazile. Figaro, le premier, l'interrompt au nom de la barbe qu'il veut faire. Le Comte intervient ensuite. Il 'souffle' à Bazile ce qu'il doit dire, ou du moins accepter: la leçon de musique. De même, dans une situation tout à fait comparable, Suzanne dira plus tard à Figaro: 'Détourne, détourne!' [5] . Rosine se joint au chœur avec plus de conviction que d'invention en disant simplement à Bazile de se taire. La fête ne serait pas complète si Bartholo lui-même n'intervenait pas dans ce jeu des communications trompeuses. En une démonstration brillante qui ne pouvait pas avoir échappé à Beaumarchais, Molière avait prouvé dans l'*Ecole des Maris* que le moyen le plus comique de faire agir un geôlier est qu'il

5. *Le Mariage de Figaro*, acte II, scène 21.

participe activement à l'évasion de sa prisonnière. Sollicité par le Comte, Bartholo intervient donc à son tour, et dicte à Bazile ce qu'il doit dire: Alonzo est bien son élève.

Le deuxième mouvement est la feinte transmission d'une vérité. Soucieux de justifier son entrée, Bazile apporte une information qu'il croit nouvelle: l'arrivée d'Almaviva. On peut jouer avec ce problème, puisqu'en réalité il ne se pose pas. Chacun des personnages sait quelque chose sur Almaviva, mais croit que les autres l'ignorent. C'est pourquoi tous parlent bas, ce qui dénonce la tromperie aux yeux de Bazile. La situation est devenue circulaire et il est effectivement impossible, pour Bazile comme pour chacun des autres, de savoir qui l'on trompe vraiment.

De cette aporie généralisée Bartholo va sortir par la passion. Ce qui l'intéresse est son mariage, et il demande à Bazile, en un troisième mouvement, des nouvelles de l'homme de loi dont il espère les services. Malheureusement cet homme de loi n'existe pas. Il a été inventé par le Comte à la scène 2 de l'acte III. Ne pouvant parler de lui, on le chante, et la discussion impossible est remplacée par un refrain. Six répliques successives, très courtes, se terminent par les mots 'homme de loi'. Rime ou écho, le procédé est aimé de Beaumarchais, qui l'emploie fréquemment[6].

Tout ce que l'on pouvait 'dire' (sans rien dire, puisqu'il s'agit de mots sans contenu) est dit, et il est déjà étonnant que cet exercice sur du rien ait pu durer si longtemps. Il faut maintenant renvoyer Bazile. C'est à quoi va servir la maladie imaginaire qu'on lui attribue. Elle emplit le dernier mouvement, qui se subdivise en deux éléments. Dans le premier, les adversaires de Bazile accumulent les détails affirmant la réalité de cette maladie. Bartholo, le Comte, Figaro, soulignent l'imprudence du malade et, puisqu'il s'agit de chanter plus que de raisonner, le refrain se fait incantation: *Allez vous coucher*. Bartholo, qui

6. Voir ma *Dramaturgie de Beaumarchais*, pp. 167–71.

est médecin, ajoute l'idée que Bazile a la fièvre. Rosine suggère
que cette fièvre peut être contagieuse. Le deuxième élément
commence lorsque Bazile, qui se sait pourtant en bonne santé,
se laisse persuader par l'accord des autres. Il faut que la victime
consente à son élimination. Peut-être absurde logiquement,
cette attitude est humainement possible et dramaturgiquement
nécessaire. Elle est induite par les aspects musicaux, et presque
oniriques, des dernières répliques. 'Tous les acteurs' parlent
'ensemble', on redit 'Bonsoir' et le docile Bazile répond
'Bonsoir'.

   Le comique de la scène résulte d'abord de l'élimination
physique du personnage surnuméraire par des moyens excep-
tionnels. Bazile, homme libre, semble mu par la volonté vide de
personnages qu'il ne comprend pas. Est-ce pour lui que Diderot
a dit que l'oeil ne se voit pas? Est-ce à son intention que Sartre
a affirmé que l'homme n'existe que par le regard d'autrui?
Mais ces principes philosophiques ne sont ici que d'une application comique comme la situation elle-même. Une seconde source
de comique naît du contraste: l'enjeu est important pour les
personnages, mais la matière dont ils discutent est inexistante;
l'exécution doit être lente pour être savourée, mais les périls
sont pressants et leur déroulement rapide. Le jeu est trop
dangereux, l'équilibre trop instable pour qu'on puisse s'y attarder.
La tension entre les personnages est si forte qu'elle les condamne
à sortir au plus vite d'une situation hautement inconfortable. La
scène de stupéfaction a la même valeur dynamique engendrant
l'expulsion du personnage dangereux que, dans l'espace, le
schéma du 'troisième lieu', tel qu'il est illustré, par exemple, dans
le *Mariage de Figaro,* par la scène du fauteuil au premier acte ou
celle du cabinet au deuxième.

   La principale victime de la scène de stupéfaction est
Bartholo. Bazile s'en tire avec un aller et retour inutile. Mais
Bartholo, qui s'est laissé persuader de se joindre à la manoeuvre
de ses adversaires, va voir ceux-ci, délivrés de toute crainte pour
l'immédiat, se retourner immédiatement contre lui. L'acte

s'achèvera par son effondrement. La scène de stupéfaction est donc pour l'ensemble du rôle de Bartholo un tournant décisif. Avant, le personnage, intelligent, attentif, actif, semble un obstacle insurmontable; il le faut, pour l'animation de la comédie. Après, le même Bartholo, désorienté, angoissé, faillible, aura causé sa propre perte; il le faut, pour l'heureux dénouement.

Les contemporains ont donc eu raison de souligner l'importance et la réussite exceptionnelles de cette scène. Pour lui rendre complète justice, il aurait d'ailleurs fallu ne pas en limiter l'étude à l'analyse sèchement fonctionnelle que nous avons tenté d'en proposer. Il aurait fallu en rendre sensible une valeur quasi poétique, y trouver ce que M. Giudici relève dans l'ensemble de la comédie, un scintillement du style qui est à la fois cause et effet, dans le temps de la création, d'un climat, d'une atmosphère, d'un sens tout imaginaire (l'italien dit ici, avec une merveilleuse expressivité, 'fiabesco'), idéal et musical, dans lequel les contours opaques de la réalité perdent leur valeur...[7]

Dans l'histoire du théâtre enfin, le procédé si brillamment mis au point par cette scène aura une abondante postérité. L'élimination comique de l'importun, de l'homme en trop, deviendra un type de scène favori dans les comédies de Labiche, puis dans celles de Feydeau. Une récente comédie de boulevard, *Boeing Boeing,* est même contruite tout entière sur ce schéma maintenant éprouvé.

La fin du troisième acte du *Barbier de Séville* est tout illuminée par le rayonnement de la scène de stupéfaction, dont les effets se prolongent longuement. La scène 12, après avoir commenté ironiquement l'attitude de Bazile, en revient aux faits que la confrontation purement verbale qui précède avait momentanément fait oublier: la leçon de musique, la clef de la jalousie, le rasage de Bartholo. Mais elle traite ces thèmes avec

---

7. Je traduis ici un passage de Giudici, p. 598.

une hardiesse auparavant inconnue. Les amoureux ne se cachent plus et semblent même défier le tuteur. Le Comte, pour la deuxième fois, tente, trop lentement, de transmettre à Rosine l'information essentielle sur sa lettre. Malgré l'aide de Figaro, Bartholo les surprend, et à sa colère répond leur colère. Après tant de mensonges, la vérité éclate comme une délivrance. La scène 13 est pour l'essentiel faite d'échos: faute de bons arguments, les personnages insistent sur des répétitions qui étaient une des formes les plus visibles de la scène de stupéfaction. Ils répètent les gestes aussi bien que les mots, et le geste le plus indiqué, puisqu'ils n'ont proprement rien à dire, est, comme dans la scène de stupéfaction, de quitter la scène. Rosine est déjà sortie à la fin de la scène 12, Figaro et le Comte sortent à la fin de la scène 13. Bartholo reste seul. Son désarroi est marqué par l'intériorisation des paroles de ses adversaires: on l'a dit fou, il devient fou. Il évoque le 'diable', ce qui est probablement ici, non point une simple banalité mais un souvenir des fragments primitifs de ce qui deviendra le *Barbier de Séville;* un faux diable y jouait un rôle beaucoup plus cru que ce 'diable d'homme' qu'est ici le comte Almaviva.[8] Les figures de la dépersonnalisation évoquent aussi quelques grands égarements des comédies de Molière. En perdant l'esprit et en quelque sorte la conscience de lui-même, Bartholo éprouve l'angoisse existentielle du Sosie d'*Amphitryon* dépossédé de son Moi. En perdant le sentiment du lieu où il est et des hommes qui pourraient y vivre, il retrouve le délire d'interprétation d'Harpagon volé qui, dans l'*Avare,* cherche son voleur jusqu'en lui-même. *Tartuffe,* qui inspirera la *Mère coupable,* s'imposait pour finir. Comme Orgon se référait sans cesse à Tartuffe, Bartholo cherche Bazile, seul espoir dans cet écroulement. Mais Bazile n'est rien, la scène de stupéfaction l'a prouvé. Bartholo est désormais condamné.

8.   Sur ces fragments primitifs, voir E.J. Arnould, *La Genèse du Barbier de Séville,* Dublin et Paris, 1965, et les articles de M. René Pomeau et de M. Jean-Pierre de Beaumarchais dans la *Revue d'Histoire littéraire de la France* de novembre-décembre 1974.

SLEUTHING IN THE *ENCYCLOPÉDIE*
R.N. Schwab

ERE is a chapter in a continuing encyclopedic detective tale in which Professor Lough has played a crucial role. During the past few years his investigations into the documents associated with the *Encyclopédie* and mine into certain puzzles in the physical texts of the volumes themselves have fallen together, as if by pre-established harmony, to make possible solutions to various historical textual mysteries of the work. The focus of this account is upon the curious, partially counterfeited edition of the *Encyclopédie* which I have called the 'Riverside' edition, whose main characteristics will be rehearsed later in this essay. In entirely unexpected ways it has yielded up a trove of facts about the *original* work. Now new information has come to light about specimens of the 'Riverside' edition which refines and expands our knowledge about its history and opens the way for further discoveries about the encyclopedic project while it was still under the editorship of Diderot.

One of the aims of this essay is to suggest a general strategy for approaching the study of the history and texts of the *Encyclopédie* by recounting the ways in which certain encyclopedic riddles have presented themselves unexpectedly and have been unravelled in the course of studying a large number of sets. As will be seen, seemingly minute points of

difference from set to set have been the key to larger discoveries. An opinion expressed in our *Inventory of the
Encyclopédie* still seems an essential truth: the largest store of
untapped information about the *Encyclopédie* is in the
Encyclopédie itself; and one might refine that general proposition by asserting that an especially useful category of new
facts will yet be uncovered through a program of systematic
scrutiny of *individual sets,* which in turn can only be adequately
achieved through a world census of the *Encyclopédie*. Once we
have located a large share of the copies in existence we can
systematically apply some of the techniques used here of
analyzing internal textual evidence, with what I predict will be
fruitful results for our fuller understanding of the heroic work.
What has already been found through the examination of a few
specimens of the 'Riverside' edition may serve as an example of
the kinds of new information that can be unearthed about the
Encyclopédie as it was originally printed and as it was exploited
and distributed throughout the later eighteenth century; but
the possible discoveries are not limited to that edition.

Before going into elaborations on the case of the 'Riverside' counterfeit, it is necessary to sketch out the larger dimen-
sions of the problem of the texts of the *Encyclopédie*. Most of
us who were studying the work in the past two decades were
not at first aware there were mysteries about the physical
texts to be solved, and none of us knew the magnitude of them.
We discovered them by accident and by small, disconcerting
hints. For instance, in trying to isolate all of Diderot's starred
articles in the *Encyclopédie,* Professors Lough, Proust, and I
began to find that for the same article Diderot's asterisk would
be present in one set and missing in another. The suspicion
began to grow in my mind that we might be dealing with
variant and corrupted copies, and it became more and more
clear that not even the most elementary textual study had been
made of this great work, in spite of the axiom that we must

establish precisely the nature of our texts before we can proceed with the interpretation of them.

After suspecting with a sceptical eye, magnifying glass in hand, several dozen sets of the *Encyclopédie,* I was astonished to find that no two copies that came under my notice are precisely the same. It has held true throughout my experience with ever more copies that if one looks carefully enough one will always find at least some small, easily recognizable variation from set to set, and in several cases, there are crucial differences. Although aware that the standardization of mass-produced books to which we are accustomed did not come until after the eighteenth century, I was nevertheless surprised at first by the degree of difference from one copy to another. It became evident that — even taking into account practices in the printing craft of the eighteenth century — the *Encyclopédie* was peculiarly vulnerable to variations, owing to its immense bulk, the hectic conditions of its publications, the censorship by official censors and the scoundrelly publisher, Le Breton, the printing of different editions of the early volumes by the original publishers, the circumstance that subscribers customarily bought only the printed leaves and arranged for the binding of the volumes themselves, and the apparent desire of some collectors to possess unusual sets with extra pages. This speaks only of the original folio edition. The tangle is much complicated by the industrious projects of profitable contrafaction that started even as the volumes of the original plates were being produced, which entailed serious corruptions of the text. Thereafter, the ravages of time and the greed and cannibalism of booksellers led to peculiar matings of disparate sets, forging of pages, and mixtures of signatures from legitimate and spurious forms of the work. This process has continued into the present century, and the result is that one must be very careful to determine the state of the particular set upon which one is basing historical or critical scholarship.

But all is not chaos. Through the comparative study of dozens of individual sets and the proper deductions and correlations with documents, it ultimately became evident that overarching the swamp of variations from set to set there is the solid structure of five distinct editions of the *Encyclopédie* bearing the Paris-'Neufchastel' imprint, each with special, and sometimes critical, variations from the others. It was possible to isolate examples of three editions by the original publishers (two of them involving only the first volumes) and two contemporary counterfeits which we call the 'Riverside' and 'Geneva' editions respectively. The descriptions of these five editions are given in volume I of our *Inventory of the Encyclopédie*. With this instrument at our disposal it is now possible to undertake a rational world census of copies of the *Encyclopédie* and a systematic examination of each copy found. The following brief account of what was found in the Riverside set will, I think, demonstrate why this latter operation should be carried through, and it will set the terms by which the continued detective operations recorded in this essay may be understood.

The Case of the Riverside Set

The *Inventory of the Encyclopédie* (I, pp. 92 ff. in *Studies on Voltaire,* 80) describes the chance discovery that something was amiss with the asterisks in the early volumes of the copy at the University of California at Riverside. One pays particular attention to asterisks in the *Encyclopédie,* of course, because they are Diderot's sign of attribution at the beginning of many of his articles. Focusing a magnifying glass upon the suspicious characters I observed that there were blocks of pages in the first volume where the asterisks had only *five* points instead of the six-pointed ones found in all the tomes of the original work. From this seemingly absurdly small point (nay, lack of it) I was led to the recognition that the first seven volumes of the Riverside set were counterfeits from beginning to end and from there to the discovery of many other interesting facts about the history of the *Encyclopédie.*

Early on it was possible to establish that this variant was representative of a relatively widespread *type,* and ultimately, I tracked down four more specimens of it in the Peabody Library of Baltimore, the Library of the Taylor Institution at Oxford, the Allegheny College Library, and the Bibliothèque Publique et Universitaire in Geneva. While this essay was being completed, a copy has been recognized at the Newberry Library in Chicago, and I have a strong indication of the existence of still another set. It became evident immediately that this edition deserved careful study. It is more than a mere curiosity in the history of book piracy, for by a quirk of history copies of this partially counterfeited type yield the most important new information about the censorship and original texts of the *Encyclopédie* to be found outside the extra volume described in Gordon and Torrey's *Censoring of Diderot's Encyclopédie and the Re-established Text* (New York, 1947).

Here is a summary of the physical clues in the Riverside set, which we recorded as M. Poirot might have jotted them down.

1. Volumes I-III. Made up of two forms of counterfeited leaves all unlike those of any other edition.

   a. The main body of leaves has *six*-pointed asterisks.

   b. There are blocs of leaves and individual ones with *five*-pointed asterisks and printed in somewhat different type faces (e.g. in volume I, signatures A-G, pp. i-lij; L-P, pp. 81-120; 5H and 5M-5Z, pp. 793-800, 825-914).

Whence? Why? How?

2. Volumes IV-VII. Of still another counterfeit form with even cruder typography. *Whence? Why? How?*

3. Volumes VIII-XVII. Of the original edition, but with the
    Avertissement of volume VIII missing. Includes a sur-
    prising uncancelled version of vol. XI, pp. 736-737. *Why?*

4. Other peculiarities:

    a. All title pages from volume I through volume VII
        bear a variant form of the engraving of Minerva (see
        plate facing p. 822 of our *Inventory*, vol. IV), which
        appears only in volumes III, IV, and VI of these
        seven tomes in the original edition.

    b. Several pages reproduce the unrevised versions of
        cancelled pages in the original.

    c. The title page of volume III is dated 1753, whereas
        Papillon's engraving on the *Avertissement* immedia-
        tely following is dated 1767!

We shall draw the curtain on the tortuous paths of induction
and deduction, of listing clues and comparing texts, that followed
the recognition of these oddities, and contrary to all proper
canons of detective writing we shall rush forward to the
solution of the questions of their existence and source. From
the first, the inexhaustible Parisian entrepreneur, Panckoucke,
was the prime suspect as the source of the sets; the indubitable
motive, as it always was in his case, large profit. Enough was
known about the serpentine machinations of Panckoucke from
the researches of George Watts into editions of the *Encyclopédie*
to put him under immediate investigation. I had gone some
distance in working out a hypothesis about him when the
publication of the documents in Professor Lough's *Essays*
helped make virtually all parts of the puzzle suddenly snap
neatly into place and to convince me that Panckoucke was
indeed the culprit.

Here is the solution to the mystery of the 'Riverside'
edition that came out of this happy union of documents with
evidences in the physical texts. (Relate these points to those

in the list above.)

1. Volumes I-III are in the large part made up of none other than the long lost leaves of volumes that Panckoucke, sniffing profits in a counterfeited edition of the desirable and scarce item, had had printed up in Paris in 1770. Almost as the print dried on them they were impounded by the royal government and immured until 1776 in the Bastille in the company of many a famous and sordid prisoner. References to these three volumes weave in and out of the documents in Professor Lough's account of the stormy history of the Panckoucke-Cramer ('Geneva') edition, the spurious printing Panckoucke finally managed to have carried through in Geneva.

   a. The main body of these volumes was made up of leaves, all with *six*-pointed asterisks, that had survived the rigours of six years of imprisonment.

   b. The blocs of material with *five*-pointed asterisks were leaves that had to be counterfeited to fill in gaps in those rescued volumes possibly caused by dampness or vermin, or were not printed up in the first place. These leaves were printed in another establishment with a different type face.

2. Volumes IV-VII were produced in still another establishment to serve as a bridge between the three repaired Bastille volumes and the remaining volumes of the set.

3. Volumes VIII-XV were surplus stock of the original volumes obtained from the original publishers.

   The entire operation of putting together these patchwork quilt sets was perfectly predicted in 1772 by the shrewd Cramer: 'Monsieur Panckoucke observera, que les premiers Editeurs de Paris ont de reste, au moins, 600 tomes 8 à 17 de discours dont ils faisoient bon marché; de maniere que, si M. Panckoucke obtient un jour la

libération des tomes 1.2.3. il se procurera plus de 600 Ex.
complets, en imprimant les tomes 4 à 7.' (Lough, *Essays*,
p: 96.) This document gives us also the probable outer
limit of 600 for the number of sets of the 'Riverside' type
that might have been put into circulation.

4. The other peculiarities of the 'Riverside' type described in
    the list above can be easily accounted for by the fact that
    it was made up from a variety of sources.

Aside from the obvious value for collectors of knowing
what is and is not a counterfeit text, the recognition of the
'Riverside' form offers some special dividends. *The sets were
put together by someone who had access to the original
publishers' stock of leaves, even cancels and perhaps proof
pages.* Whoever assembled them clearly was concerned to attract
the interest of collectors. Because extra pages of leaves of the
texts before these were revised or censored in the cancels are
bound into several sets of the 'Riverside' type (Taylorian,
Allegheny, Riverside) we are able to reconstruct the original
versions of all the known cancels in the *Encyclopédie*. A
unique feature of the copy at the Riverside campus itself
provides a prime illustration of the valuable new information
about the *Encyclopédie* that can be retrieved from this edition.
The cancel of the pages in volume XI of that set which contained
the *abbé* Mallet's article PACIFIQUE was not carried through,
and we are now permitted to see what the surprisingly intolerant
original text of that critical article was before it was completely
revised by someone else. Using that information as one starting
point, Professor Walter Rex has brilliantly set forth a basic re-
evaluation of the work of Mallet in the original project and has
raised the possibility that other significant editorial changes
may have been made in the later volumes in articles having to
do with religion. ('"Arche de Noé" and Other Religious
Articles by Abbé Mallet in the *Encyclopédie*', *Eighteenth-
Century Studies*, 9 (1976), pp. 333 *et seq.*).

The copy of the 'Riverside' form of the *Encyclopédie* at the Library of the Taylor Institution has an unusually large number of cancelled leaves bound in an overt manner to the final, corrected versions of these leaves. Three of them in volume II have not yet been seen in any other copy, and no one would ever have known they were cancelled were it not for their presence in this set, for the final, cancelled versions were not marked with asterisks in the bottom margins as such cancels usually were. The lesson is manifest — there may be a multitude of unmarked cancelled texts, perhaps crucial ones, which have yet to be unearthed in sets of this form of the *Encyclopédie*.

Ancestry of the 'Riverside' Type: The Case of the Allegheny College Copy

Now we turn to an exceptionally important set of the *Encyclopédie* at Allegheny College which is a variant of the 'Riverside' type and which sundry deductions and reasonings lead us to believe is an immediate ancestor of the type. The trail of evidences becomes so involuted in this copy, the mysteries so thick, that one runs the chance of losing the reader (and oneself) altogether in an effort to untangle the skein. But we shall bravely try. This remarkable set, although related to the Riverside counterfeited form, has unique variations and peculiar mixtures of signatures and leaves from different editions. It is a veritable harlequin of remnants from the printing history of the *Encyclopédie*. We have been able to trace documents relating to the provenance of this copy back to 1818. Its known history is heroic enough, as can be seen in an article by H.W. Church in the Allegheny College *Alumni Bulletin,* pp. 207 *et seq.,* June, 1933. The set participated in an early wave of the American westward movement, borne by wagon train across the Allegheny mountains in 1822 from Cambridge, Massachusetts — sometimes on old Indian trails, it is reported — to the frontier settlement of Meadville, Pennsylvania. There it became part of the library for one of the very first colleges to be planted on the frontier beyond the Allegheny range. The learned Judge James Winthrop, once librarian of Harvard from 1722 to 1787, willed the copy as part of his large collection to Allegheny College in 1818. It is hinted that because he was not appointed to a chair in Mathematics and Natural Philosophy, Judge Winthrop passed over Harvard and gave the bulk of his library to the newly-established Allegheny College. Its founder and president was his old friend, the Reverend Timothy Alden, who had also been thwarted in an earlier contest for a professorship. Thus did Harvard lose out in acquiring one of the rarest sets of the *Encyclopédie*. The bequest to Allegheny College, along with the acquisition of two other fine collections, evoked the gentle envy of Thomas Jefferson, who was busy with the establishment of his own University of Virginia and wrote a handsome letter of congratulation to the Reverend Alden. Until 1954 Harvard, all unsuspecting, possessed only a copy of the Geneva counterfeit, the volumes of which were ultimately incarcerated deep in the dungeon of Widener Library among the clanking and clattering pipes.

We can pinpoint fairly accurately when Winthrop acquired the set through the following entry in volume IV of the William Bentley *Diary,* p. 181, 23 July 1813: 'Mr. Gleason the lecturer on Geography & occasional Univ. Preacher with me this day, as was also my old friend Judge Winthrop from Cambridge. Judge Winthrop has added to his rich Library, the French Encyclopedia, & he had collected a most valuable Library in general Literature.' What the provenance of the set was before that is unknown, but there is always the hope that it might sometime be clarified by documents. Other works having the same marbeling as the *Encyclopédie* in the Winthrop Library at Allegheny College bore the name of M. Gigot-D'Orcy, 'Receveur G^{ale} de Finances,' which might provide a clue on a long shot.

He was *inspecteur des mines* and *receveur général des finances,* a collector of insects, and an editor of works on insects, who lived from 1755 to 1793. (Beauvais, *Dictionnaire historique,* Paris, 1826, II).

Even in the absence of outside documents we can reconstruct something of the early history of the copy by applying the method of developing circumstantial evidences from the physical text itself. The finished set is expensively bound in eighteenth-century tooled calf, and it is among the few I have seen with gilt edges. When one inspects the contents with a suspicious eye one finds it is an extraordinary *mélange.* Whoever put the set together must have possessed a regular arsenal of leaves from nearly every folio form of the *Encyclopédie* bearing the Paris-' Neufchastel' imprint, from which he grafted together a highly saleable and desirable item. The prime suspect is once again Panckoucke, for he is known from the documents printed in Lough's *Essays,* to have had potential access to the whole store of material from the *magasin* of the original publishers, including remainders of some of the earlier volumes and up to six hundred left-over sets of volumes VIII through XVII of the original. We believe we have demonstrated that he produced the first three volumes of the 'Riverside' counterfeit and probably the next four, and he was the guiding spirit behind the printing of the Geneva one. Leaves and signatures from *all* these forms are to be found in the Allegheny set, and specimens of up to four different ones are mixed together in the same volume.

What makes this copy an outstanding treasure is the collection of cancelled leaves at the ends of volumes I, II, III, IV, VI, and VII. Next to the set owned by Douglas Gordon, which was probably Le Breton's or Diderot's own copy and includes an extra volume of documents and page proofs, the Allegheny College set is the most important known copy. That it must have come from somewhere close to the heart of the original enterprise is demonstrated by the existence in the extra leaf at the end of volume IV of two printed pages of the controversial suppressed article CONSTITUTION *UNIGENITUS* by the *abbé* Mallet. The only other specimen of this article that has come to light is in the extra volume of Mr. Gordon's set, where it is preserved in entirety.

Panckoucke, or whoever the shadowy producer of this set was, designed it to appeal to the tastes of collectors, who were then and always have been covetous of variant and unique pages of a famous work The extra leaves of the Allegheny College copy permit us to reconstruct the original states of all except three of the revised pages known to have been cancels by the presence of an asterisk on the lower margin in the original text of the *Encyclopédie*. And the set has the partial text of one of those three (CONSTITUTION). This is the richest trove of cancels from the original *Encyclopédie* yet to be uncovered. Some of the variant texts are highly interesting, as for instance the one with deleted remarks from Quesnay's article FERMIERS.

It was not only the *known* cancels that were represented in the Allegheny copy. Whoever assembled this set and added the extra leaves was able to draw on left-over excised pages that have never previously been suspected of being cancels. One of them, bound at the end of the seventh volume, gives us a hint of the author's identity for the article GÉNÉROSITÉ. The existence of this and other unmarked cancels to be found in the Taylor Institution specimen of the 'Riverside' edition opens the possibility that there may be a significant number of other such pages to be dug out of copies of this counterfeit.

Quite aside from the presence of the extra, cancelled pages, the physical history of the Allegheny College text is most interesting. For several reasons I surmise that this copy was one of the first made-up sets Panckoucke can be suspected of assembling after the release of his three impounded volumes in

1776. He may have started by using left-overs of every stripe to put together what looked like a full set, or like full sets. Where necessary he manufactured new pages to complete the work (signatures *A* and *B* in volume I, for instance).

The first Allegheny volume is a mixture of the Riverside and Geneva counterfeits. It seems apparent that there were enough extra leaves from the Geneva counterfeit project to fill in most of the gaps that may have been caused by vermin, moisture, or whatever other reason, in the rescued Bastille pages, which make up the core of that volume. The contract of Panckoucke with the Genevan printers records that beyond the run of two thousand of each page to be printed for sale, another one hundred and fifty of what was amusingly called the *'Chaperone'* were to be run off, to be available to replace damaged or lost pages (Lough, *Essays*, p. 68). It is possible that the large number of Geneva pages that filled the gaps in the Allegheny volume I were from the *Chaperone*. Beside the mixture of Bastille and Geneva pages in this tome there are some left-over pages from the *first* edition of the *Encyclopédie* (5P1, 5P4) and some entirely new counterfeited pages in the early signatures.

Volumes II through XVII of the Allegheny set are made up largely from leaves of the genuine, original edition, which may be some of the remainders Le Breton offered in 1768 to sell at a twenty-five percent discount to Panckoucke and his associates (Lough, *Essays*, p. 61). A few of these tomes had to be patched up with pages of the Riverside counterfeit (signature C in volume II) and the Geneva counterfeit (leaves in volumes VI, p. 541, and VII, pp. i-xii). Two volumes, VI and VIII, were lacking the normal introductory pages. Still this copy with its appended cancelled leaves is a great prize and would have been recognized as such by a purchaser of any discrimination.

An uncomfortable mystery of the Allegheny College set which troubled me for several years was the presence of some

most puzzling leaves in the first volume. Though they were
different from their counterparts in any other set I had
encountered, whether original or spurious, they did resemble in
typography the pages of the 'Riverside type' known to have
been in the Bastille. What was disturbing was that these odd
pages seemed to suggest there might be still *another* edition of
the work that had eluded me but not the magpie who had put
together the Allegheny set. They constituted a most untidy
loose end, and their existence demanded explanation, for they
and similar pages that might turn up in the future would cause
an uneasiness over whether we had really solved the central
riddle of the various editions and variants of the work once and
for all.

Suddenly, while I was doing certain investigations for this
essay, what I am persuaded is the solution to the problem fell
into place. I had been peering through the wrong end of the
telescope. The stars set me right again, for the correlation between
the five and six-pointed asterisks in volume I of the Allegheny
set and copies of the 'Riverside' edition broke down precisely
where the mystery pages appeared in the former (in signatures
where 'Geneva' leaves were not used to fill in gaps). Again in
the manner of M. Poirot we list the physical evidences.

A. *Allegheny volume I*	B. *'Riverside' type, volume I*
Signatures *G,* L-P, and 5Z: (Having unique leaves found in no other known set of the *Encyclopédie*).	Signatures *G,* L-P, and 5Z:
Six-pointed asterisks. Typography: the same as that of the original 'Bastille' counterfeit leaves.	*Five*-pointed asterisks. Typography: characteristic of the pages that had to be re-counterfeited to fill in the gaps in the 'Bastille' volumes.

Solution:

1.   The mysterious pages in the Allegheny volume I listed in column A were part of Panckoucke's *original* illegal printing that ended up in the Bastille.

2.   For some reason there were not as many leaves in the signatures noted as there were in the other signatures of the 'Bastille' printing, perhaps owing to the rigors of imprisonment.

3.   Whoever was engaged in confecting patchwork *Encyclopédies* from the left-overs seems to have put the Allegheny set together early in the process and for the first volume made use of the limited number of 'Bastille' leaves that were available in these critical signatures.

4.   Because these pages apparently were insufficient in number the compositor of subsequent sets of the 'Riverside' type was forced to have new counterfeit ones printed to fill in the gaps. They appear with the characteristic five-pointed asterisks, in the copies at the Riverside campus, the Taylorian and Peabody Libraries, and the Bibliothèque Publique et Universitaire, as indicated in column B.

In summary, our reconstructed genealogy for these sets is as follows.

Stage I.   The Allegheny set came into existence when the anonymous bookseller, perhaps Panckoucke, undertook to use up remainders of pages, partial volumes, and complete volumes bought from the stock of the original publishers, which he was able to fill out with some of his own counterfeit leaves. *Stage II.*   As his supplies of these remannts ran out he went into serious production, using the rescued 'Bastille' counterfeit leaves for the bulk of the first three volumes and confecting still other spurious pages, signatures, and whole volumes (IV-VII) needed to fill in gaps. For volumes VIII through XVII and all the plates he had an ample supply of remainders of the

original tomes. Thus was born the mature 'Riverside' edition
described earlier in this essay. The fact that the Taylorian set
of this edition incorporates most of the very same cancelled
leaves as those in the Allegheny set, including the unmarked
cancel in volume VII, seems a compelling indication that the
two were put together by the same hand and ties the latter all the
more strongly to a common source and lineage with the
'Riverside' edition.

It is entirely possible, indeed I think likely, that through a
systematic census and examination of copies of the *Encyclopédie*
we shall find more specimens of patchwork quilt volumes, like
those of the Allegheny set, belonging to what we postulate is
the first stage of Panckoucke's operation, and some of them
may contain prizes as rewarding as those in the Allegheny copy.
We know with certainty that more examples of the mature
'Riverside' edition will turn up, and no doubt in more than one
state. There is an inevitable instability in this form, and there
might be a considerable refining of our knowledge of it before
a definitive and detailed technical description can be established,
although the essentials of the type are clearly discernable.

The tale of these sets may yet end with an Agatha Christie
twist, and the prime suspect could at the last moment turn out
to be the wrong man. A document may be unearthed that proves
it was, say, Le Breton, the original publisher, and not Panckoucke,
who was responsible for putting them together. He was
certainly the Professor Moriarty of the original *Encyclopédie,*
the 'Ostrogoth', as Grimm called him, who perfidiously altered
articles after Diderot had read the final proofs. There was
nothing to have prevented him from buying up a supply of
Panckoucke's 'Bastille' pages and the needed leaves from the
Geneva edition, which he could have combined with all his
left-over stock to make a patched-up edition. Yet what I have
of detective instincts leads me to think not. Le Breton seemed
in the contractual arrangements to have wanted to divest himself of the *Encyclopédie* business, whereas Panckoucke was a

howling enthusiast for it. At the same time as Panckoucke was arranging to have the Geneva edition printed he had thrown himself with characteristic vigor into the *Supplément* project, and later he engineered the publication of the *Table.* While all of this was going on he was laying plans for the *Encyclopédie méthodique.* An exceedingly strong piece of circumstantial evidence is that Panckoucke did the same sort of patching operation in the 1760's and 1770's with the *Mémoires* of both the Academy of Science and the Academy of Inscriptions that I suspect he did with the various left-over scraps and blocs of the *Encyclopédie.* He bought up the complete stock of these publications when they were a losing proposition, and to complete the sets he had reprinted more than fifty volumes of the mémoires of the two academies. The story of his complex operations involving the purchase and filling in of various forms and versions of these sets is recounted in G.B. Watts, *Panckoucke, Studies on Voltaire,* volume 68, pp. 109-111.

Conclusion

Seen in one way, we have been engaging for some time in a sort of archaeological operation on the physical texts of the *Encyclopédie,* peeling back its layers, digging and sifting through a mass of matter whose location and relationship to other encyclopedic fragments and to documents that have been unearthed makes all the difference. The first stage of these delvings through encyclopedic strata enabled us to establish finally the five physical forms, genuine and counterfeit, of the folio editions bearing the Paris-'Neufchastel' imprint. We must press our advantage on this front, for we know that *all* versions except the first edition are corrupted for scholarly use. Even the second and third editions of volumes I through III by the original publishers are not to be fully trusted. There are variations in signs of attribution in them that ought to give one pause (See our *Inventory,* I, pp. 83-92). The Geneva and

Riverside counterfeits are riddled with corruptions in matters of attribution and typography. Most of the quarto and octavo editions are even worse. They all may be useful for preliminary investigations, but in any finished scholarly study, it is necessary to check carefully against a certified original edition.

One purpose of detection is to prevent further errors and transgressions. The largest possible publicity should be given to certain honest mistakes and certain frauds that have resulted in undependable copies. Booksellers have long been in the habit of putting together volumes from different forms to make complete sets. There were even efforts to revise the classic check points in the Geneva editions so the unsuspecting purchaser would think he had a more valuable prize than he actually possessed. (G.B. Watts, 'Swiss Editions of the *Encyclopédie*', *Harvard Library Bulletin,* 9 (1959), p. 220). Copies being passed as originals are still regularly on sale by booksellers who do not themselves know what they have. There is thus a practical commercial application of these findings, since the variations in the forms of the *Encyclopédie* are not yet widely enough known to affect the book market. I have quite recently seen Geneva counterfeit sets or mixtures of the Geneva and the original on sale at high prices in rare book establishments, passing for the real thing.

Embarrassing errors have been made in reprints. The Frommann-Verlag quarto reproduction of the *Encyclopédie* is marred by the presence of six volumes of the Geneva counterfeits interspersed in the set (in the text: volumes VI, VII, and XII, and in the plates: volumes I, X, and XI). It is well to know also that the first two volumes of the text of the Frommann reprinting are of the inferior second edition. The beautiful and costly reproduction of the plates by the Cercle du livre précieux, printed in Lausanne in 1964-1966, is entirely taken from a Geneva counterfeit. A world census of the copies of the *Encyclopédie* would help prevent a compounding of blunders, commercial and scholarly. At least for sets in public collections it will be possible to make known the edition or mixture of editions each copy is.

Such a census, accompanied by an analysis of as many individual copies as possible, may lead also to some solid new discoveries about the *Encyclopédie*, and this brings us back to the phase of our diggings into the texts upon which we have concentrated in this essay. One thing is certain from the dissection carried out so far on various copies of the *Encyclopédie:* scholars should be alert to possible important variants in texts of the work and should be sensitized to the possibility of finding something new. Somewhere on dusty shelves there may be encyclopedic revelations, 'slouching toward Bethlehem to be born.'

JOHN NOURSE AND THE LONDON EDITION OF *L'ESPRIT DES LOIS*

R. Shackleton

little time only elapsed after their publication before Montesquieu's works became known in English. The *Lettres persanes* appeared in the English translation of John Ozell in 1722, the *Considérations sur les causes de la grandeur des Romains et de leur décadence* appeared in the English of an unknown translator in 1734, and Thomas Nugent's translation of *L'Esprit des lois* was first published in 1750. But the only work of Montesquieu to appear at an early date in England in the original French was *L'Esprit des lois.*

The textually important 1757 edition of *L'Esprit des lois,* with the imprint 'A Londres', must be left out of account, since the imprint is false and the edition was published at Paris by Huart. An early edition of the French text did, however, appear in England during Montesquieu's lifetime and with his blessing. It is the subject of several letters in Montesquieu's correspondance.

The first correspondent to mention this edition was Montesquieu's friend François de Bulkeley. Born in London in 1686, Bulkeley was taken to France by his father, in the train of James II, in 1688. His sister married the Duke of Berwick in 1700 and he spent his life in France on account of Jacobite connections. The first evidence of his acquaintance with

Montesquieu is in 1723 and their friendship lasted until the President's death.

Between 13 and 21 January 1749, Bulkeley received in Paris a letter from an English friend, William Domville, announcing that the London booksellers were planning to publish an English translation of *L'Esprit des lois;* and he asked Bulkeley to seek corrections or modifications from Montesquieu, saying 'by this means he will be at liberty to say many things that his own country will not admit of'. Bulkeley communicated Domville's inquiry to Montesquieu in a letter of 21 January 1749.[1]

William Domville has not hitherto been identified. He belonged to the Irish branch of the family, which normally wrote its name Domvile. His grandfather, Sir William Domvile, was attorney-general of Ireland. His father, likewise Sir William, was member of the Irish parliament for Armagh and Dublin.[2] He himself, educated at Trinity College, Dublin where he graduated in 1703,[3] represented Dublin for a short time in the Irish parliament. But he soon abandoned Ireland for London where he lived in literary and fashionable circles.[4] As a young man he was a close friend of Swift, in whose correspondence and *Journal to Stella* he is not infrequently mentioned. From Montesquieu's correspondence he is seen to have moved in high society, being a close friend of Chesterfield, Carteret, and Bath. In 1749 he had lodgings in Jermyn Street.[5] When he died in

1. Montesquieu, *Œuvres complètes,* Paris (Nagel), 3 vols., 1950-5, III, no. 442. This edition is referred to below as Nagel, followed by the volume number.
2. *Burke's Landed Gentry of Ireland,* 4th ed., London, 1958, s.v. Domville of Loughlinstown.
3. G.D. Burtchaell and T.U. Sadleir, *Alumni Dublinenses,* 2nd ed., 1935, s.v. Domvile.
4. F.E. Ball, *A History of County Dublin,* Part I, Dublin, 1902, pp. 92-3.
5. The address 'Fermyn Street' given in Bulkeley's letter to Montesquieu (Nagel III, p. 1169) is an error in transcription (cf. my 'Montesquieu's

1763, unmarried, he was living in Mayfair. He was a man of
standing and intelligence. He had met Montesquieu in France,
and the two men treated each other as equals, as is shown by a
long letter on government in England which Montesquieu
addressed to the English and of which a draft is preserved in his
Pensées.[6]

In his letter to Montesquieu, Bulkeley mentions only the
projected English translation and does not refer to any English
edition of the French text. It is in a letter of 17 March 1749
that the first mention of a new edition in French appears:
'On travaille fortement à la traduction et à une nouvelle édition
qui ne sera pas si chère'.[7] Meanwhile Montesquieu had supplied
some two or three hundred corrections to Domville and had
similarly supplied them not only to Barrillot for a new Geneva
edition but also to Huart for an edition being prepared in Paris
with *permission tacite*.[8] Writing on 5 May Bulkeley says that
the London edition will be out in fifteen days,[9] and a copy is
actually despatched to Montesquieu by Domville on 4 June 1749
(24 May, O.S.)[10]. He gives the information that the publisher
had produced only 600 copies and that the edition was selling
at 12s. 6d. compared with the 26s. of the Geneva edition.[11]
Montesquieu acknowledges the receipt of his copy on 22 July.[12]

---

5.   Correspondence: additions and corrections', *French Studies*, 1958,
     p. 339). The absence of his name from the ratebooks for the parish
     of St. James (held in the Westminster Public Library) shows that he
     was not a householder.
6.   Nagel II, pp. 592-5.
7.   Nagel III, no. 472.
8.   Nagel III, no. 465.
9.   Nagel III, no. 485.
10. Nagel III, no. 492.
11. The selling price of the Geneva edition in France was 18 *livres*
     (Nagel III, no. 422). At the normal rate of exchange 18 *livres* was
     15s. The mark-up for an imported book is thus seen to be *c*. 75%.
12. Nagel III, no. 499.

Only three days later the celebrated Madame de Tencin, who took the closest interest in the success of *L'Esprit des lois,* conveys to Montesquieu the report by Abraham Trembley, just returned from London, that after Carteret's citation of the work in the House of Lords three or four hundred copies were sold in less than two hours.[13]

The foregoing information is supplied by Montesquieu's correspondence. We are told neither the imprint, nor the forma nor the number of volumes. What is known is limited to t. facts:

1. the edition appeared in May-June 1749 with print number of 600 and was sold for 12s. 6d.;

2. it incorporated corrections supplied by the author;

3. the publisher was the same as that of the English translation, which was to appear in 1750.

Which is the edition in question?

Two serious bibliographical studies of *L'Esprit des lois* exist. The first is by François Gebelin[14] and gives no possible identification of this edition. The second, by A.-A. Chabé,[15] offers a tentative identification in an edition said to bear the imprint 'Londres, 1749' and represented by a single copy listed in the catalogue of the British Museum but destroyed by enemy action. This, on verification from the main entry in the catalogue and from the shelfmark, proves, however to be the well-known quarto edition with the imprint 'A Leyde, chez les libraires associés, 1749.' There is no entry in either the British Museum

13.   Nagel III, no. 495.
14.   F. Gebelin, 'La Publication de *L'Esprit des lois*' (*Revue des Bibliothèques,* 34e année, 1924, pp. 125-58).
15.   A.-A. Chabé, '*L'Esprit des lois*. Montesquieu au travail. Bibliographie des premières éditions' (*Bulletin de la Société des bibliophiles de Guyenne,* 18e année, 1948, pp. 39-64).

catalogue or that of the Bibliothèque Nationale which can refer
to the edition in question.

Some years ago I had the good fortune to acquire personally
a copy of an octavo edition of *L'Esprit des lois,* in two volumes,
without date but with a Geneva imprint. This imprint at the
first glance was unconvincing, and further examination
strengthened my doubts. The device on the titlepage is an
imitation of that of the original edition. Both show a Dorie
column surrounded by foliage and surmounted by a band
bearing the motto *Ex recto decus;* but the new device is
altogether more compact than Barrillot's, measuring 6 cm.
across at the broadest point compared with Barrillot's 7.5 cm.
It tapers towards the base, whereas Barrillot's is broadest
towards the base. It is in all a much less close imitation of
Barrillot's device than that other imitation found in the
contrefaçon signed 'Barrillot'.

This same variant of the *Ex recto decus* device is found also
on the titlepage of the first edition of the English translation,
published in 1750 with the imprint 'London: printed for J.
Nourse, and P. Vaillant, in the *Strand'.* The identity, clear to
the unassisted eye, is confirmed by the Hinman Collator.

The English origin of the octavo edition is further shown
by the presence of a number of press-figures or numerals, found
usually at the foot of versos and intended to identify the work
of individual compositors. These are an exclusive feature of
English printing in the eighteenth century.

The first volume of *The Monthly Review* prints, in the
number for July 1749, a review under the heading:

> *De l'Esprit des Loix. On the Spirit of Laws.*
> *The Octavo Edition, just published at London,*
> *in French, is in two volumes, the 1st of 463,*
> *the 2d of 510 pages.*

This pagination corresponds to that of the edition under consideration, as shown in the description below.

It can therefore be asserted with reasonable confidence that the edition under consideration is the English edition of which the publication was arranged by William Domville, and that the printer's ornaments, as discussed below, make it scarcely less clear that the publishers were John Nourse and his associate Paul Vaillant, of whom Nourse was doubtless the major partner. It may be noted that, though the edition is rare, copies are to be found in the Bodleian Library, where it was recently acquired by gift, in the library of Trinity College, Dublin, and in Harvard University Library, this last being Thomas Gray's copy.

The description of my copy of this edition is as follows:

DE/L'ESPRIT/DES/LOIX./TOME PREMIER (SECOND)./..... *prolem sine matre creatam.* Ovide./NOUVELLE EDITION,/ *Faite sur les* CORRECTIONS DE L'AUTEUR./ [Publisher's device with motto EX RECTO DECUS]/ A GENEVE,/ Chez BARRILLOT & FILS.

8° (20.6 cm.)

Collation:	vol. I A^8b^6 A-B^8 D-$2G^8$
	vol. II π^2a^8 A-$2I^8$ (-2I8)

Pagination:	vol. I xxviii + 463
	vol. II [2] xviii + 510

Contents: vol. I   pp. [i] half-title; [iii] title; [v] − [viii] preface; [ix]−xxviii table for Books I−XIX; [1]−463 text of Books I−XIX
vol. II pp. [1] half-title; [i] title; [iii]−xviii table for Books XX−XXXI; [1]−510 text of Books XX−XXXI

Typography: leaves 1−4 of each gathering are signed; catchwords are on each page; volume number is given on first page of each gathering; footnotes are indicated by asterisks, etc., marginal notes by lower case letters; press figures are frequent in each volume; page numbers are aligned with marginal notes.

Misprints: these are frequent and include:

vol. I

dégalite *for* d'égalité (p. 161)

c'ainsi *for* c'est ainsi (p. 163)

ent-i là *for* eut-il à (p. 178)

résultant *for* résultent (p. 335)

p. xii *misnumbered* xi

p. 405 *misnumbered* 407

vol. II

XIX *for* II (p. 75)

senne *for* sienne (p. 86)

sign. 2I4 *wrongly signed* I4

In 1749 Montesquieu was sending simultaneously corrections to his original text to three separate publishers, to Huart of Paris, to Barrillot of Geneva, and to Nourse of London. Madame de Tencin was at the same time despatching errata to the publishers of counterfeit editions. To Nourse, through Domville, Montesquieu sent two lists, a long one containing two or three hundred corrections on 24 February 1749 and a shorter one on 4 March.[16] The nature and extent of these lists of corrections sent are partially disclosed by Montesquieu's correspondence but can be fully learnt alone by collation of the text. Neither the critical edition of J. Brethe de La Gressaye nor that of Robert Derathé, excellent as they both are, gives a complete listing of variants, the preparation of which would indeed be an immense task. There is no doubt that the Huart edition was the one to which Montesquieu gave most thought and attention. It appeared in the week following Quasimodo (14-19 April). It is not possible from existing documents to say whether the Nourse edition or the second Barrillot edition came first in point of time. Since the latter reproduces the

16.   Nagel III, nos. 462 and 465.

analytical index which Huart commissioned from Toussaint it must have followed the Huart edition, and perhaps by some months, and is therefore likely to have appeared after that of Nourse. An extensive sampling of variants, however, leaves no doubt that Montesquieu was more open-handed in furnishing corrections to Nourse than to Barrillot, from whom he had become rather disaffected, and of all the 1749 editions that of Nourse must rank only after that of Huart in fidelity to the intentions of Montesquieu.[17]

* * *

Typographical conventions of the eighteenth century have been studied in a pioneering article by R.A. Sayce,[18] but printers' ornaments of that period have been studied much less. An inclusive repertory of these ornaments, when the source can be reliably established, would be of great value and would enable scholars to distinguish more readily true and false imprints, and to interpret the false. The ornaments used by Cramer, Marc-Michel Rey, Huart, and Nourse are of particular historical importance.

The publishers of the 1750 English translation of *L'Esprit des Lois* were Nourse and Vaillant. As is stated above, Nourse

17. The coincidence of typographical practices makes it possible to attribute also to Nourse the 1750 octavo edition of the *Défense de l'Esprit des lois* which is to be found in the Bodleian Library with the shelfmark Vet. D 4 e.105. Published with the imprint of Barrillot, this edition has on the titlepage the Nourse variant of the *ex recto decus* device. Its typeface is the same as that of the Nourse edition of *L'Esprit des lois*, it has numerous press figures, and its page numbers stand out from the text in the outer margins, which (since there are no marginal notes) gives an odd appearance to the pages.

18. R.A. Sayce, 'Compositorial Practices and the Localization of Printed Books, 1530-1800', *The Library*, March 1966, pp. 1-45.

was doubtless the major partner, being named first, having a speciality in French books,[19] and having in 1747 published with his sole imprint a translation of Burlamaqui, likewise first published by Barrillot at Geneva. The identity of the printer whom he employed is unknown, and the same printer may have worked for other publishers. The fact imposes a greater degree of caution in forming conclusions than is necessary in the case of publications appearing in France, where the publisher and the printer were often the same person.

Some of the ornaments or *fleurons* used by Nourse's printer have been reproduced in two places, and in each case in relation to the 1759 edition of Voltaire's *Candide*. The first is Ira O. Wade, *Voltaire and 'Candide'* (Princeton, 1959) where, on plate VI, five *fleurons* are reproduced from an edition of *Candide* which Wade attributes to Nourse. The second is Theodore Besterman, *Some eighteenth-century Voltaire editions unknown to Bengesco* (4th edition, *Studies on Voltaire and the Eighteenth Century*, CXI, Banbury, 1973). Here (figs. 39 and 40) eleven *fleurons* are reproduced from an edition referred to as 'C' and not attributed to a publisher. It is not possible to determine from the bibliographical descriptions whether the copies studied by Wade and by Besterman are of the same edition. But all Wade's *fleurons* are reproduced by Besterman, though not all Besterman's by Wade. The coincidences, however, with Nourse's edition of *L'Esprit des lois* are striking.

Nourse's edition contains twelve *fleurons* (omitting one which is clearly an *ad hoc* assembly of small typographic ornaments). They are listed below and are reproduced in facsimile. It is hoped that this may be a small step towards the compilation of the repertory desiderated above.

19. H.R. Plomer, etc., *A Dictionary of the Printers and Booksellers who were at work in England... from 1726 to 1775,* London, The Bibliographical Society, 1932, p. 183.

ORIGINAL EDITION
GENÈVE (BARRILLOT),
[1748]

2. FIRST CONTREFAÇON
GENÈVE (BARILLOT),
[1749]

NOURSE EDITION
GENÈVE (BARRILLOT),
[1749]

1. Flat-topped ornament of leaves;
    I p. viii and two others; also in
    English translation of 1750, I p. 10;
    = Wade *u* and Besterman [*jj*]!

2. Sun above leaves; I p. 10

3. Small vase of fruit amid leaves;
    I p. 26 and another; also in English
    translation of 1750, I p. 259;
    = Besterman *qq*.

4. Bust above mask and between
    branches; I p. 102; also in
    English translation of 1750,
    I p. 41; = Besterman *kk*.

5. Large lozenge-shaped ornament of
    leaves and flowers; I p. 158;
    = Wade *aa* and Besterman *pp*.

6. Vase with leaves in form of half
    wheel; I p. 194 and three others.

8. Linked E's below marquis's coronet, amid foliage; I p. 426; = Wade *p* and Besterman *gg*.

7. Vase between eagles; I p. 214.

9. Vase between two parrots with third below; II p. 21 and two others; also in English translation of 1750, II p. 483.

10. Deep bowl of fruit amid leaves; II p. 151.

11. Uplifted bowl of fruit; II p. 246.

12. Overflowing bowl of fruit; II p. 436.

LA RELIGIEUSE ET SA *PRÉFACE* :
ENCORE UN PARADOXE DE DIDEROT

J. Varloot

ENDANT cent quatre-vingts ans, *La Religieuse* de Diderot s'est présentée au lecteur pourvue d'un appendice caudal, que l'auteur avait appelé *Préface*, jusqu'au moment où l'on songea à le mettre en tête, dans la nouvelle édition des *Œuvres complètes.*[1] La seule existence de ce texte avait tracassé les partisans d'une esthétique de l'illusion, qui la voyaient par lui détruite et auraient souhaité le supprimer, mais dans sa grande édition, Assézat le défendit et le maintint, au nom d'une idéologie de la vérité. Cependant, il lui laissait seulement une valeur d'explication: 'une partie du roman qui explique l'autre, comme le fait une préface, et qui était la seule préface qu'il fallût au livre, *une fois lu'.*[2] Les mots que nous soulignons, où se révèle

1. Diderot, *Œuvres complètes*, Paris, Hermann, 1975 et suiv., publiées par H. Dieckmann, † J. Fabre, J. Proust et J. Varloot, secrétaire général, tome XI, 1975, présenté par Georges May, Herbert Dieckmann, Jane Marsh Dieckmann, Jean Parrish, Jacques Chouillet. On trouvera dans ce volume toutes les données nécessaires à la compréhension du présent article. Toutes nos références sont à cette édition sous le sigle *D.P.V.*
2. Voir dans l'édition Assézat, au tome V, les remarques de Devaines (p. 8) et de Naigeon (p. 206). Nous laissons de côté les problèmes d'esthétique générale, excellemment traités par H. Dieckmann et Robert Mauzi (voir *D.P.V.*, notes 11 et 13 de l'Introduction de G. May).

sans doute le rationaliste un peu étroit, justifiaient à ses yeux le qualificatif 'annexe' qu'il accola au mot *Préface,* sans se rendre compte qu'il commettait un péché au regard de la raison en associant deux termes contradictoires.

Les érudits suivirent la maître-éditeur, et les lecteurs n'osèrent pas faire savoir la perplexité que leur causaient certains détails. Le début du roman proprement dit, abrupt, n'est guère explicite sur ce marquis de Croismare que l'héroïne prétend connaître, mais dont elle dit plus loin qu'elle ignore s'il a des enfants[3], et qui, sauf pout tenir le rôle d'interlocuteur muet, disparaît totalement de la suite jusqu'au moment où elle lui présente une demande d'emploi.

Comme la mort de l'héroïne est suggérée à la fin du roman, le lecteur considère ce roman comme achevé; tout au plus éprouve-t-il quelque besoin d'explication à propos du marquis de Croismare. La *Préface* lui apparaît donc comme une 'seconde partie' (expression d'Assézat) ou 'un second roman' (disait Naigeon) consacré à Croismare. Mais il est étonne d'y trouver des lettres antérieures au récit de la religieuse, qu'il faut alors considérer comme écrit en très peu de temps[4], une annonce a posteriori du premier roman, et, pour comble, l'affirmation qu'il n'existe pas. L'impression finale est décevante, comme d'une remontée dans le temps qui vient trop tard et n'apporte rien à la première œuvre. Et pourtant se recontrent des formules qui situent expressément ce texte 'en annexe', n'était ce titre de *Préface*!

Le problème ainsi posé pendant longtemps l'a été de

---

3. *D.P.V.* tome XI, p. 164. Or, au début, elle a noté qu'il a trois enfants.
4. G. May s'en est étonné (n. 48, p. 59), trouvant qu'elle écrit 'plus vite que la chronologie ne le permet'. Il s'agit plutôt d'une certaine rapidité d'écriture qu'à la fin elle affirme posséder (p. 273), et elle dit, au présent, à la 150ème page de son récit, c'est-a-dire aux trois quarts (p. 231): 'Je commençai donc mon récit comme *je viens* de vous l'écrire' (nous soulignons).

façon complètement différente depuis que les érudits ont pu établir la genèse finale du texte, grâce surtout à la découverte des manuscrits. Le fait principal est que l'on a donné à lire les deux textes dans l'ordre où les a publiés la *Correspondance littéraire* et que les indications qui justifient cet ordre sont venues après coup, simultanément néanmoins avec le choix du titre de *Préface*! Il en résulte qu'il faut remettre en question l'ordre traditionnel, et considérer de plus près les données pour voir, à tout le moins, si l'ordre inverse est possible.

Il est peu de ses œuvres auxquelles Diderot ait plus tenu que *La Religieuse*. La preuve ne s'en trouve pas seulement dans sa correspondance datant des mois où il la composait en 1760, mais surtout peut-être dans les billets à Meister, devenu rédacteur en chef de la *Correspondance littéraire,* et au copiste Girbal, dans les années 1780–1782, pendant que s'exécutaient simultanément une publication dans la revue clandestine fondée par Grimm et la préparation d'une édition de ses Œuvres complètes[5].

Aussi n'est-il pas possible de traiter à la légère ou par un tour de passe-passe le réel problème qu'a posé la coexistence du 'roman' à la première personne qu'est *La Religieuse* et d'une *Préface* qui fut insérée *ensuite* dans la *Correspondance littéraire,* mais qui utilisait en grande partie un texte apparemment dû à Grimm et publié en 1770 dans sa revue, qu'il était alors seul à diriger. Je désire ici m'expliquer plus longuement, sur ce point, que dans la *Correspondance,* où je suivais l'opinion traditionnelle, plaçant la *Préface* en annonce du roman, et dans l'Avant-propos du tome XI des *Œuvres complètes*[6] où nous avons pris Herbert Dieckmann et moi, la décision de placer la *Préface* en tête[7].

5.   Voir ce que nous avons dit dans le tome XV de notre édition de la *Correspondance,* et en particulier sur la simultanéité (nº 944, p. 291).
6.   *Correspondance,* t. XV, p. 288.
7.   *D.P.V.,* t. XI, p. xii, et note 3, p. 38.

* * *

Remarquons d'abord qu'il est actuellement impossible de reconstituer une chronologie génétique. A première lecture, nous ignorons si les lettres qui restent de la mystification épistolaire montée contre le marquis de Croismare sont antérieures ou concomitantes au 'mémoire' que la religieuse rédige à son intention. Le mémoire est sans doute annoncé à un certain moment, mais rien ne prouve qu'il n'était pas écrit auparavant, et l'erreur de date commise en 1782 par Diderot sur la date de la publication des lettres dans la *Correspondance littéraire* (1760 au lieu de 1770) prouve qu'il les situe bien dans la même période que son récit des infortunes de Suzanne. Mais ce prénom même a changé entre 1760 et 1770 (elle s'appelle Angélique comme la soeur et la fille de l'auteur dans le premier manuscrit), alors qu'elle a gardé son premier nom (De la Marre), qui ne se changera en Simonin que plus tard, mais sans que l'auteur s'en souvienne bien lors de la révision de la *Préface*[8],

Il est tout aussi impossible d'affirmer que la *Préface* a été 'retouchée' *après* la révision du roman, ni, bien entendu, composée après lui. Les formules qui pourraient le faire croire s'adressent aux lecteurs de la *Correspondance littéraire* ou même servent d'explication désinvolte: 's'il y eut jamais une préface utile, [...] c'est peut-être la seule dont il fallait renvoyer la lecture à la fin de l'ouvrage'. Cette formule semble laisser entendre que l'ordre suivi aurait été volontaire, mais peut aussi bien être comprise comme une justification a posteriori, dans le style paradoxal de Diderot[9].

---

8. 'Mettez le nom du roman', dit-il en marge aux copistes (variantes H, p. 28, et S, p. 100).
9. Il y a des incohérences dans ces indications. Dans la variante Qc, p. 32, addition de V1a, on trouve: 'qu'on vient de lire' et 'où l'on remarquera'. Ce futur révèle qu'au fond il pense sa préface comme telle; puis il corrige par: 'a dû remarquer', pour être cohérent avec l'ordre suivi dans la revue.

Car qui l'obligeait à choisir ce terme de *Préface,* bel et bien voulu par lui?[10] Il possédait dans son vocabulaire le mot de postface, et bien d'autres termes qui pouvaient introduire un après-texte.

Revenous de plus près sur quelques données internes non négligeables.

1) Le mémoire suppose connu de Croismare toute l'affabulation que révèle seulement la première partie de la *Préface* même si les lettres qui suivent sont 'pour la plupart postérieures au roman' (p. 66), terme au reste peu clair, car il peut faire allusion à l'ordre génétique initial aussi bien qu'à la date de la révision des textes.

2) Le mémoire est 'annoncé' ainsi dans la *Préface.* Madame Madin, qui a recueilli la religieuse, témoigne: 'je la priai de me montrer ce qu'elle avait écrit; j'en fus effrayée: c'est un volume, c'est un gros volume' (p. 59). L'addition: 'c'est un gros volume', faite par Diderot au dernier moment, renvoie aussi bien à un texte à lire qu'à un texte déjà lu. Suzanne, trois lignes plus loin emploie une formule vague 'un peu dans un temps, un peu dans un autre'. D'autre part (p. 63) les 'papiers' que Madame Madin trouve après la mort de Suzanne et qui sont 'l'histoire de sa vie ' ne sont pas datés.

3) Le manuscrit de Suzanne est censé envoyé à Croismare, sinon immédiatement (p. 63) du moins peu de temps après, quand il le réclame dans sa dernière lettre (p. 65). Cette mention peut constituer pour le lecteur l'*annonce* de la lecture de cette 'histoire' , qui s'y enchaîne aisément, si l'on suppose simplement que Croismare a ensuite communiqué le mémoire

---

10.   Variante A, p. 27. Ce titre est dans la *Correspondance littéraire* (manuscrit de Gotha, fol. 71), et se retrouve` dans les extraits constituant le manuscrit de la bibliothèque de l'Arsenal qu'a utilisé H. Dieckmann. Les copistes des fonds Vandeul et de Leningrad ont suivi l'ordre imposé par la *Correspondance littéraire.*

à d'autres (c'est-à-dire à Diderot ou à Grimm). En 1770, Grimm dit ignorer l'existence d'un roman ('Il est bien triste que les Mémoires de sa vie n'aient pas été mis au net', p. 65), mais son expression [11] est au moins la reconnaissance d'une structure générale prévue.

4) En 1781, Diderot se trouve devant deux éléments qu'il s'agit de rabouter pour la *Correspondance littéraire:* le texte de 1770, nous l'avons vu, promet puis donne comme disparue l'histoire de la religieuse; le récit déjà écrit commence par une phrase, note de l'auteur pour lui-même, qui le rattache à la première lettre de Suzanne à Croismare (p. 30, et p. 81, variantes A et B).

Que fait alors Diderot? Il transforme cette phrase pour l'attribuer à Suzanne, ce qui fait croire que *celle-ci* n'a commencé à rédiger son histoire qu'à la date de cette lettre (ce qui provoque l'étonnement de Georges May). Cette utilisation d'une note destinée à lui-même lui permet d'introduire sans préparation le texte à la première personne, sans plus.

Il ne corrige nullement la *Préface* pour prévenir la perplexité du lecteur, dont nous avons parlé plus haut. Les indications qu'on trouve dans les marges, entre les lignes ou sur des feuillets, concernent essentiellement l'ordre de la publication dans la *Correspondance littéraire:* qu'on se reporte aux variantes F (p. 28), Q (p. 65, fin de la variante) et B (p. 67). Quant à l'existence du roman niée par Grimm plusieurs fois (p. 31, p. 32, p. 33, p. 65), il ne rétablit qu'une seule fois la vérité (variante Q, p. 32).

On en a conclu à de la négligence, et qualifié l'œuvre d'inachevée. Sans doute Homère peut somnoler quelquefois, à l'âge atteint alors par Diderot. Mais celui-ci tenait beaucoup à sa *Religieuse,* nous l'avons dit; il sera impatient de recouvrer

---

11. Le terme 'mis au net' signifie, si on le comprend bien, qu'il y a eu un premier jet, des 'lambeaux'.

son manuscrit confié au copiste Girbal: 'Quand ma Religieuse reviendra-t-elle?' [12] Encore moins, selon nous, doit-on parler de 'contradictions'. [13] Il faut recourir à d'autres explications, qui posent en principe la volonté consciente de l'auteur. Même s'il est impossible de prouver ces hypothèses de travail, il faut les prendre en considération pour juger des conséquences qu'elles entraînent sur l'ordre dans lequel doit ou peut être lu l'ensemble *Préface-Religieuse*.

La première qui vient à l'esprit d'un critique moderne, informé des études sur les romanciers du dix-neuvième siècle, c'est que l'auteur aurait voulu publier, avec son texte, son 'avant-texte'. Adoptons, provisoirement, la problématique de ces critiques. [14]

D'un avant-texte, la *Préface* présente beaucoup de traits. Elle contient des matériaux documentaires ou du moins permet d'en reconstituer. C'est ainsi que l'invocation au Dieu de miséricorde (variante J, p. 42) rappelle le couvent de la Miséricorde, que Diderot avait longé souvent rue Mouffetard, et à propos duquel il avait entendu raconter le scandale de 1717, quand Marc Voyer d'Argenson, alors lieutenant-général, amoureux d'une novice, troqua celle-ci contre la restauration du couvent (et d'Argenson venait tout juste de rompre avec Mme de Tencin, à qui Madame Madin fera appel pour sauver sa religieuse). [15] Il est évident que le côté réaliste du roman est

12. Billet n°943 (*Correspondance*, t. XV, p. 289). On pourrait en tirer un sous-titre de la présente étude!
13. Le mot est de Diderot lui-même (p. 66), mais il les qualifie de 'légères', les justifie par la chronologie de la composition, mais en fait présente des excuses polies, après coup, au lecteur.
14. On n'aborde pas ici la discussion en cours sur la notion large ou étroite de l' 'avante-texte'. Nous considérons qu'il est *distinct* du texte, mais ne doit pas en être dissocié.
15. On imagine encore, dans un dossier de coupures, pour le couvent d'Arpajon, cette épigramme paru dans la *Correspondance littéraire* en novembre 1775 (texte inédit extrait du manuscrit de Gotha):

préparé par les indications matérielles dont on trouve les traces dans les lettres de Madame Madin. Mais la *Préface* contient aussi des 'notes de régie' : avertissements au copiste ('Mettez le nom du roman'), réflexions sur l'ignorance de Grimm et, nous l'avons vu, la première phrase du roman était à l'origine une note pour lui-même. Les lettres échangées entre Mme Madin et le marquis de Croismare pourraient être considérées comme des 'fragments préalables', susceptibles de s'organiser en un scénario, mais effacés ensuite, comme on en trouve chez Flaubert. La *Questions aux gens de lettres* (p. 67) nous apprend même qu'il y eut deux dates de ces fragments, et qu'ils ont été 'désécrits', sans d'ailleurs que Diderot lui-même les ait insérés dans un récit 'écrit', puisque Grimm l'a devancé pour ce faire. [16] Le passage d'une structure à une autre, même, est impliqué, en dépit et à cause de l'ignorance de Grimm, nous l'avous vu, dans la *Préface*.

L'hypothèse d'un 'avant-texte' serait donc séduisante, si Diderot avait pu songer à publier tout son dossier, c'est-à-dire

15. Là dans le sein de la magnificence
     L'oisiveté par des vœux imposteurs
     Se vante encor d'embrasser l'indigence;
     La chasteté s'y garde comme ailleurs.
     C'est un serail de sultanes jalouses
     Et qui parfois pour charmer leur ennui,
     D'un même Dieu se disant les épouses,
     Font des enfans qui ne sont pas de Lui.

16. L'affirmation de Diderot, car la *Question* est de sa main bien qu'il feigne de l'attribuer au journaliste (variante C, p. 67) est-elle contredite par le fait qu'il a transposé (pp. 286—287) dans le roman un fragment de la *Préface* (variante L'et note 13, p. 36)? On constate au contraire qu'il a remanié le texte de la *Préface* comme s'il avait voulu reconstituer le style initial de son fragment (il faudrait les publier sur deux colonnes). On peut ajouter que le bref portrait de Croismare inséré en tête du roman, sans contredire le long portrait inséré par Grimm dans la *Correspondance littéraire* (p. 69), le récuse littérairement.

préparé une édition critique de ses manuscrits! La coutume n'était alors qu'aux 'mises au net'. Reste cependant qu'il n'a pas vraiment modifié le texte de la *Correspondance littéraire* et qu'il le publie bien comme une explication 'utile' (p. 66) qui, comme l'indique le terme de 'préface' qu'il emploie expressément, peut, si elle ne le doit pas, être lue avant le roman.

Si la *Préface* n'est pas vraiment le carnet de route du créateur, que peut-elle être? Et n'en avons-nous pas diminué la valeur en lui attribuant la nature d'un 'avant-texte'? Pourquoi ne pas considérer l'ensemble Préface-roman comme intrinsèque, et constituant non pas deux romans nu deux parties d'un même roman, mais une œuvre double? [17] Cette formule mérite développement, mais écartons une première objection. On peut dire, en effet, que si Diderot avait considéré les deux textes comme entièrement de lui, il aurait réécrit la *Préface*. S'il y a songé une fois dans la correction marginale (p. 32, variante Q) où il parle en son nom personnel pour affirmer contre Grimm l'existence de son roman, il a ensuite attribué la rectification à Meister, et il n'est pas intervenu ailleurs contre les 'moi' de Grimm (p. 50, par exemple). On pourrait répondre que l'objection n'est valable qu'à l'égard du tissu conjonctif dont Grimm enrobe les membres épistolaires de la *Préface,* mais on peut plus valablement considérer celle-ci comme une espèce de dialogue, qui en rappelle d'autres. En effet, dans sa revue, plus ou moins secrètement, Grimm annotait le texte de son ami (par example ses *Salons*), instaurant ainsi un dialogue un peu particulier, où le meneur de jeu n'est pas entendu de l'acteur. Mais Diderot n'est pas allé jusqu'au bout de cette formule, ne serait-ce qu'en faisant parler un autre à sa place, et en maintenant plusieurs niveaux de fiction dramatique : les

---

17. Nous avons parlé de 'double ouvrage' (D.P.V., t. XI, p. XII, en accord avec la formule éclairante de Robert Mauzi (éd. de Cluny, p. XI).

lettres elles-mêmes, le récit de Grimm, les remarques attribuées
à Meister, et la voix muette de l'auteur. Il en résulte que les
deux textes diffèrent totalement : l'un fondé sur une illusion
identifiant l'auteur et le héros, l'autre fonctionnant dans une
distanciation totale. L'un est comme l'italique de l'autre, sans
qu'on puisse imaginer que l'un est issu génétiquement de l'autre,
même par une désorganisation suivie d'une refonte totale. Nous
voyons plutôt dans leur existence parallèle et, dans une certaine
mesure, inverse, une duplicité de la création, du reste bien
connu de la part de Diderot.

On peut cependant émettre une autre objection à cette
façon de voir, en s'étonnant que l'auteur ait cependant désiré
que chacun de ses textes pût être lu séparément : une simple
preuve en est l'adjonction du court portrait de Croismare au
début du 'roman'. Mais c'est justement qu'il ne voulait pas, selon
nous, que l'un fût considéré comme le simple appendice de
l'autre. La mystification qui est au point de départ de l'ensemble
est réassumée en tant que trame structurelle d'ensemble. Et
l'ordre de la lecture place bien la *Préface* en tête, comme le
montre une comparaison avec le début de *Mystification* et le
préambule de *Jacques le fataliste*.

Le Diderot qui associe la *Préface* à son roman est *déjà*
l'auteur de *Jacques le fataliste* et l'on peut constater quelques
analogies entre les deux procédés de composition romanesque.
La modification de la première phrase du 'mémoire' de la
religieuse a suffi à insérer le roman dans le processus de l'échange
épistolaire, et malgré l'absence de passages répétés d'un texte
à l'autre le principe semble bien être le même : rompre la
linéarité narrative du processus classique par une formule
binaire. Dans *Jacques,* il y a alternance systématique des
niveaux passé et présent, et, pour emprunter le langage
technique du cinéma, surimpression par retour en arrière (flash-
back) ; enfin, report à la fin du roman du récit annoncé au
début. Dans *La Religieuse,* la surimpression est en quelque

sorte globale et cette juxtaposition fait songer plutôt à un système dramatique où la pièce est jouée simultanément sur deux scènes. Sur l'une des deux, les acteurs seront, à la façon pirandellienne, en quête d'auteur; sur l'autre, il joue lui-même le héros ou l'héroïne. Ici donc, nulle interposition visible de l'auteur, nul clin d'œil du narrateur au lecteur. S'il y a discours de l'auteur, il est tacite: dans l'année 1760, nous avons voulu mystifier le charmant marquis, et je m'y suis prêté avec d'autres, en composant des lettres et des billets, mais parallèlement je me suis identifié au personnage, et j'ai imaginé le détail de sa vie.

Nous sommes donc, de toute façon, comme dans *Jacques,* dans le monde de la fiction, mais dans un monde double créé dans deux décors simultanés. *La Religieuse* se révèle alors, dans l'histoire du roman, comme œuvre 'moderne' elle aussi. Et l'on est en droit de se demander si Diderot n'en était pas un peu conscient. Il s'agit en tout cas d'une inspiration brusque, comme peut en donner le retour à une œuvre vieille de vingt ans. Mais sans doute aussi la résurgence de l'esprit diabolique qui avait inspiré la mystification initiale. Grimm avait qualifié les comploteurs d' 'enfants de Bélial' c'est-à-dire de Satan (p. 33) [18] mais il disait 'nous autres' (variante T). Or voici que Diderot corrige et s'attribue la paternité de la machination infernale : 'Cet enfant de Bélial', c'est lui seul. [19] Et nous sommes tentés d'imaginer qu'il ne faisait pas seulement allusion à la farce montée à Croismare, mais à l'ensemble romanesque 'duplex' qu'il lançait à la mer de la postérité.

18.   Voir aussi p. 50. Dans sa note 10 (p. 33) G. May s'est contenté d'une citation de saint Paul, mais sans l'*Ancien Testament* Bélial est le chef des démons.
19.   Et il insiste sur son rôle. Voir les variantes, E, p. 34, et Ia, p. 31.

THE HOUSE OF THEBES IN THE LATE EIGHTEENTH CENTURY

P. Yarrow

T will be recalled that the story of Œdipus and his children consists of four main episodes:—

(1) Œdipus, despite the efforts of his parents and himself, commits parricide and incest in fulfilment of a prophecy (Sophocles' *Œdipus the King*);

(2) after a period of exile, his life comes to an end at the temple of the Eumenides at Colonus (Sophocles' *Œdipus at Colonus*);

(3) his two sons, Eteocles and Polynices, quarrel over the throne of Thebes, and end by fighting and killing each other (Aeschylus' *Seven against Thebes* and Euripides' *Phoenician Women*); and

(4) his brother-in-law, Creon, now King of Thebes, forbids the burial of Polynices, but Antigone, one of Œdipus' daughters, secretly disobeys his order, is discovered, and is put to death (Sophocles' *Antigone*).

Ducis's *Œdipe chez Admète*, performed on 4 December, 1778, a version of the second episode, is the first treatment of any part of the story of the house of Thebes since the four plays of La Tournelle published in 1730 and 1731. It is a free adaptation of Sophocles' *Œdipus at Colonus,* combined with Euripides' *Alcestis.* The prediction that Œdipus' corpse will be a boon for the country in which he dies, becomes a simple statement by the High Priest that

> Mars le dieu des combats
> Attache à ton cercueil les lauriers et la gloire;
> Il doit être à jamais l'autel de la victoire;
> Le monde y portera son encens et ses vœux.

(III, 5)

Creon's attempt to force Œdipe back to Thebes is therefore pointless and is suppressed; though Polynice tries to enlist the help of Admète and to persuade his father and Antigone (Ismène disappears) to accompany him and his army against Thebes. Since Ducis combines the story of Œdipus with that of Alcestis and Admetus, the scene is laid, not at Colonus, but at Pherae; the Eumenides demand the life of Admète; and Œdipe gives his life to save that of his host, and dies absolved by the gods.

Ducis's tragedy is admirably qualified to appeal to an audience endowed with sensibility. Virtue reigns in heaven and earth. The gods, says Œdipe, have given him more happiness than unhappiness.

> Leurs secrètes faveurs, tes généreux bienfaits,
> Ont surpassé souvent tous les maux qu'ils m'ont faits;
> Vous me voyez gémir sous la main qui m'immole;
> Mais vous n'entendez pas la voix qui me console.

(III, 2)

Œdipe's conscience is clear:

> Sur mon front cependant, dis-moi, reconnais-tu
> L'inaltérable paix qui reste à la vertu?
> Je marche sans remords vers mon dernier asile:
> Œdipe est malheureux, mais Œdipe est tranquille.

(V, 2)

His life has shown that

> ... il n'est point de malheur où survit la vertu,

(V, 7)

and his virtue reconciles him with the gods. Admète is a good king, beloved of his people, in contrast with his father whose war-like exploits have ruined his subjects, been condemned by the Eumenides, and must be atoned for by the death of Admète:

Quel bien leur a produit la splendeur de tes armes?
Chacun de tes exploits fut payé par des larmes.
Porte ailleurs tes drapeaux, tes chants victorieux;
Les soupirs de ton peuple ont monté jusqu'aux cieux...

(I, 1)

Admète wants his son brought up to be a good king:

Formez-le pour son peuple, et non pas pour sa cour.

(IV, 2)

Ducis seems to have read his *Télémaque*. Antigone is, as her father tells her, the model of filial devotion:

Oui, tu seras un jour, chez la race nouvelle,
De l'amour filial le plus parfait modèle.

(III, 2)

Even Polynice has been transformed. He still hates his brother, and resents his wrongs; but his main emotion in Ducis's play is remorse for having banished his father from Thebes:

Pour dire un fils ingrat, on dira Polynice.

(IV, 1)

One of his reasons for hating his brother, indeed, is that it was Etéocle who incited him to this unfilial step. Although Polynice is doomed to march against Thebes and kill, and be killed by, his brother in mortal combat, his remorse wins his father's foregiveness.

The pathos of the situation of Œdipe, the blind outcast, attended by his fair and devoted young daughter, the spectacle of Polynice at his father's feet, imploring his father's foregiveness, but being cursed before winning it; that of Polynice, Alceste, and Œdipe, all bent on sacrificing their lives to save Admète; and the dramatic ending, the scene in the temple, in which Œdipe, before the whole Theban people, dies at the altar, reconciled with the Eumenides, who proclaim their forgiveness by a clap of thunder — all these things no doubt contributed to the success of Ducis's play.

The same appeal to sensibility is evident in the opera,

Œdipe à Colone, in three acts, with words by N.F. Guillard and music by Sacchini, performed at Versailles on 4 January, 1786, in the presence of Louis XVI and Marie-Antionette, to whom it is dedicated. In Act I, Thésée has promised Polinice not only to help against his brother —

> Le droit de Polinice est la cause des Rois

(I, 1)

— but his daughter, Eriphile. As they approach the temple of the Eumenides to seal their alliance, Polinice's remorse at his treatment of his father awakens, and the goddesses express their wrath. In Act II, we first see Polinice in a 'Désert épouvantable' near the temple, filled with remorse:

> Je ne voulois que le voir & l'entendre,
> Mes pleurs auroient coulé sur son sein attendri:
> De mes remords, il n'eût pu se défendre;
> Un père est toujours père, & je l'aurois fléchi.

(II, 1)

In the next scene, Œdipe and Antigone arrive: Œdipe's remorse, too, not only at his father's death, but at his treatment of Polinice, is revived by the vicinity of the temple:

> Laisse-moi, malheureux Polinice,
> Je t'ai maudit.

(II, 2)

Thésée's subjects now try to drive him away, but Thésée gives him shelter. In the last act, Polinice tells Antigone that he is willing to renounce everything in order to help her to look after their father:

> Oui, je renonce en ce moment
> A mes droits, à mon sceptre, à la main d'Eriphile.

(III, 1)

Such favourable dispositions in father and son naturally lead — though not before Œdipe has cursed his sons — to a reconciliation:

> Viens dans mes bras, je suis encor ton père,
> *(Ant. & Pol. se jettent à ses pieds.)*
> J'embrasse mes enfants,

The opera ends happily with the Eumenides forgiving Polinice, and sanctioning his marriage with Eriphile, with Œdipe (looking forward to a happy life in Athens) giving his blessing, and with everyone singing in a final chorus:

> Le calme succède aux tempêtes;
> La paix & le bonheur renaissent dans ces lieux:
> Le Ciel ne verse plus ses fléaux sur nos têtes;
> Œdipe, en pardonnant, a désarmé les Dieux.

(III, 4)

Little need be said of the *Œdipe à Colone* of Ducis, successfully performed at the Théâtre de la République on 17 Priarial, An V (6 June, 1797), with Monvel in the title rôle, or of that of Marie-Joseph Chénier. Ducis's play is essentially *Œdipe chez Admète,* reduced to three acts and with fewer references to kings. The scene reverts to Athens; Thésée replaces Admète; and Alceste disappears. Thésée, condemned (like Admète) to atone for his father's misgovernment, is saved by Œdipe.[1] Chénier's play - probably a revised version, dating from the Consulate, of an *Œdipe mourant* accepted by the Comédie Française in 1785[2] — is a fairly faithful version of Sophocles' tragedy. He retains the chorus and the choric odes, but shortens and modifies his original, taking greater liberties with it than he does in his *Œdipe, Roi* (see below). Like Ducis, he omits Ismene, and allows Polynice's remorse to win the forgiveness of Œdipe, though not that of the Eumenides.

* * * *

1. 1, 3 — 4 correspond to I, 1 — 2 of the earlier play; 1, 5, to II, 3 — 4; II, 1 — 5, to III, 1 — 5; III, 2 — 3, to IV, 1 — 2 (III, 3 also contains a passage from II, 1); III, 4 — 8, to V, 1 — 5; and III, 9, to V, 7.
2. A. Lieby, *Etude sur le théâtre de Marie-Joseph Chénier,* Paris, 1901, pp. 17, 436.

The fascination of the first episode for so many writers of the seventeenth and eighteenth centuries up to 1731 (including Corneille, Voltaire, and Houdar de la Motte) is not easy to understand. The lack of a love interest and the paucity of the material compelled them to invent episodes; they were out of sympathy with the conception of ineluctable fate; and they were repelled by the improbabilities and improprieties with which it bristles. Laius drives out with a small escort in quite unkingly fashion; Œdipus destroys the sphinx, arrives in Thebes, and marries Jocasta before the surviving attendant returns; instead of saying that Œdipus has killed Laius, the attendant puts it about that Laius was killed by a band of robbers; the death of Laius remains unavenged without ill effects for several years, until the gods suddenly take it into their heads to afflict Thebes with a plague; the Corinthian shepherd arrives opportunely on the very day that Œdipus has decided to investigate the death of Laius, and conveniently happens to be there at the very moment when the Theban shepherd, whom Œdipus has sent for, comes — and they recognize each other after an interval of three or four decades. All the dramatists who treated the subject, from Corneille to La Tournelle, strive to explain or remove these defects, and usually make matters worse in doing so. So does Louis-Léon-Félicité, duc de Brancas and comte de Lauraguais, whose *Jocaste* was published — it was never performed — half a century after La Tournelle's adaptations, in 1781.

Jocaste is preceded by a long *Dissertation sur les Œdipes de Sophocle, de Corneille, de Voltaire, de la Mote, & sur Jocaste.* The writer criticizes the plays of his predecessors, attributes their faults to their having chosen to adapt Sophocles' tragedy; insists that they are inherent in the subject, which is not the death of Laius, but the punishment of his death twenty years later; and says that he himself has preferred to treat the death of Laius. The subject of Œdipus, he says in a revealing passage, is unsuited to the modern theatre, since it depends on fatality and is therefore undramatic.

> Si l'on me demande pourquoi j'ai traité le sujet le plus intraitable, je dirai qu'il était encore plus aisé de s'écarter du plan de Sophocle, que d'imiter Corneille & Racine dans leurs genres. Et j'ai préféré ce sujet à ceux que j'ai dans la tête, parcequ'il m'éloignait absolument de l'arche du temps présent, qu'un simple Israëlite comme moi ne pourrait toucher sans être frappé de mort. Puisqu'on veut la savoir, voilà le secret de mon choix, qui n'est pas, comme on voit, celui de mon goût.

Layus, when Brancas's play opens, has just gone to consult the oracle about the sphinx. In order not to waste time, he has taken only one attendant, Euphémon, with him. The Grand Prêtre du Destin, Phorbas, reports the sphinx's words:

> Je vins pour prévenir Layus sur son destin:
> Il me dédaigna trop. Il voit déjà sa fin.
> Je vois la mienne aussi. Mon vainqueur va paraître.
> Jocaste est sa conquête. Il sera votre maître.
> Mais des maux que j'annonce, & que vous souffrirez,
> Par Jocaste & par lui vous serez délivrés.
>
> (I, 5)

This alarms Jocaste. In Act II, we learn that Layus and Euphémon have been found dead, that the sphinx has been destroyed, but that its dying breath infected the air and started a plague. Anaxes (who is Layus's brother and the Grand Prêtre de l'Hymen), Phorbas, and the people urge Jocaste — behind the scenes — to marry the victor, in accordance with the sphinx's words. She obeys, and appears in Act III with her new husband, Eudox. He tells her that his feelings towards her are a mixture of 'tendresse' and 'horreur',

> Les sentiments du crime & ceux de la vertu.
>
> (III, 4)

He relates that he is the son of humble parents; that, though he has often been away for two days on hunting expeditions, this is the first time he has been absent for as much as three days; that his father, also called Eudox, has warned him never to leave Cithaeron:

> Vous n'en pouvez sortir sans descendre aux enfers;
>
> (III, 4)

and that he has been punished for his disobedience on this occasion by having killed two men. Jocaste is horrified to find that she has married the murderer of Layus.

In Act IV, we learn from a conversation between Jocaste's two sisters, Iphise and Naxos (one a pessimist, the other an optimist), that Layus, learning that his son, Œdipe, was destined to kill his father, caused him to be entrusted to Eudox on Cithaeron, and that he is still alive. Jocaste tells her sisters that, when she agreed to marry Eudox, it was — like Andromaque — with the intention of killing herself; but that she could not.

> J'allais saisir le fer... mais alors... ô faiblesse!
> (Grands Dieux! pourquoi mêler l'horreur & la tendresse!
> Eudox retient ma main... je me trouve en ses bras.
> Dans l'instant un instinct que je ne conçois pas,
> Mais tendre, quoique fort; mais doux, quoiqu'invincible,
> M'inspira pour Eudox, & me rendit sensible.
>
> (IV, 4)

She never loved Layus, she says, and is now in love for the first time in her life. She relates how the ghost of Layus separated her and Eudox as they embraced each other. In the last act, a conversation between Jocaste and her sister, Iphise, reveals that Layus told them different things. He told Iphise that Œdipe was destined to kill him; he told Jocaste that Œdipe was destined to love her incestuously. Jocaste is sure that Eudox is Œdipe. The appearance of Layus's ghost has made Eudox suspect that he is the murderer of Layus; Jocaste greets him as her son. Layus's body is brought back, and Eudox recognizes it as that of the man he killed. Jocaste dies, Œdipe stabs himself, and the plague ends.

Lauraguais deserves credit for having avoided an extraneous love affair and episodes; but his play is feeble, and merely substitutes one set of improbabilities for another. The plague is no longer sent as a belated reminder by the gods; but it is caused by the breath of the sphinx. The sphinx's words seem an inadequate reason for compelling Jocaste to marry Eudox. A serious weakness is that we do not know why she agreed to marry him or what her feelings are; she appears in the third act only when she is on her way to the temple to marry Eudox. Nor is it clear why Layus told his sisters of only one part of the prophecy about his son, and Jocaste only of the other.

After taking to opera with Marc-Antoine Désaugier's parody, *Le Petit Œdipe* (1779) and the *Œdipe à Thèbes ou Œdipe et Jocaste* of comte Duprat with music by Méreaux (1791), Œdipus returned to tragedy with two faithful adaptations of Sophocles, both published posthumously, and neither performed — the *Œdipe Roi ou La Fatalité* in three acts of Léonard, published in 1797, and the *Œdipe, Roi* of Marie-Joseph Chénier, probably written during the Consulate[3] and published in 1818. Chénier, though abridging or expanding his original in places, and making one or two minor changes in the interests of *vraisemblance* or *bienséance,* follows it pretty closely, even keeping the chorus and the choric odes. It is interesting to observe that there is no death penalty in Chénier's Thebes, and that Œdipe is a constitutional monarch:

> Citoyen comme vous, et dans le rang suprême
> Aux décrets du pouvoir obéissant moi-même...

(I, 2)

---

3.   Lieby, pp. 212, 228, 436. For Léonard's play, see W.M. Kerby, *The Life, Diplomatic Career and Literary Activities of Nicholas Germain Léonard,* Paris, 1925, pp. 372—84.
      M. Horn-Monval also lists:— Buffardin d'Aix, *Œdipe à Thèbes ou Le Fatalisme* (published 1784); Bernard d'Héry, *Œdipe Roi,* tragédie lyrique en 5 actes (published 1786); and an *Œdipe Roi* by Doigny du Ponceau, published, like his *Antigone,* in his works in 1826 (*Répertoire bibliographique des traductions et adaptations françaises du théâtre étranger du XVIe siècle à nos jours,* vol. I, *Théâtre grec antique,* Paris, 1958, p. 98).

* * * *

The third episode, the quarrel between the brothers, was
treated only once in our period, though Polynice also appears in
adaptations of *Œdipus at Colonus*. G. Legouvé's *Etéocle* was
first performed at the Théâtre de la République on 27 Vendé-
miaire, An VIII (18 October, 1799). It is influenced by Ducis's
plays, introducing Œdipe, depicting Polinice as remorseful,
and making Œdipe forgive his sons. This is, in fact, the only
episode, since there is no love interest, no Creon, and no reference
to Menoeceus; the play is a simple one. The first act shows
Jocaste and Antigone discussing the situation, and pleading
with Etéocle. In the second act, Polinice sees his mother and
sister. The third act contains the interview between the brothers.
In the fourth act, the battle has begun. Etéocle proposes the
single combat; Polinice agrees, but only on condition that
Œdipe is set free. Œdipe enters, and curses his sons. In the last
act, Œdipe begins to relent. We hear that Polinice has mortally
wounded his brother. The brothers return; Œdipe forgives
them both; Etéocle seizes his sword and kills Polinice, an ending
borrowed from Alfieri's *Polinice* (1783).

Legouvé carries to its furthest point the tendancy, evident
to Racine's *Thébaïde* and Alfieri's *Polinice,* to make Polynices
good and Eteocles bad. Etéocle has unjustly turned out his
brother, imprisoned his father, and refused to let Jocaste and
Antigone see him. He is a bad king, whose ascendancy over
the Thebans is due entirely to his tyranny. He enjoys power:

> La puissance! combien mon ame en a joui!
> Qui peut voir à ses pieds, sans en être ébloui,
> Des milliers de sujets, prodiguant leurs services,
> Deviner ses désirs, adorer ses caprices,
> D'un encens éternel enivrer son orgueil,
> Et briguer en tremblant la faveur d'un coup-d'œil?
> Voilà ce qu'un rival à m'enlever aspire;
> Plutôt mourir cent fois que de quitter l'empire.

(III, 2)

He hates his brother:

> Oui, si je le reçois, c'est qu'en cette entrevue
> Ma haine jouira d'éclater à sa vue!

(III, 2)

He is eager to fight Polinice, and proposes the single combat partly to satisfy his hatred, and partly because he feels that the Thebans are beginning to waver in their obedience to him. He kills his brother treacherously.

Polinice, on the other hand, is the favourite brother of Antigone, who has no doubt that he has been unjustly treated by his brother. Nor indeed has Jocaste:

> Etéocle sans doute est le plus criminel.

(I, 1)

Even Œdipus prefers him. Antigone has no doubt either that Polinice will be a good king:

> Ah! de Thèbe, au contraire, affermissant les droits
> Polinice vainqueur ferait aimer ses lois,
> Et, par l'humanité gouvernant ses provinces,
> Serait l'honneur du trône et l'exemple des princes.

Again Jocaste agrees:

> Il est vrai; s'il montra cette altière chaleur
> Que donne la jeunesse et sur-tout la valeur,
> Toujours plus généreux, plus humain que son frère,
> La bonté tempéra son fougueux caractère.

(I, 1)

Polinice returns his sister's affection. When she tells him how much she has missed him, he tells her that

> Si la fille d'Adraste a charmé son époux,
> Ce fut en m'ecoutant l'entretenir de vous.

(II, 2)

He is overcome with remorse for having agreed to the imprisonment of Œdipe; voluntarily allowed Etéocle to reign first; is unwilling to fight his brother; offers to compromise:

> Je devais régner seul; eh! bien, régnons ensemble;

(III, 3)

and agrees to the single combat only on condition that his father is set free.

The description of Polinice's sufferings in exile is modified in a way calculated, no doubt, to remind the audience of the exiled royal family:

> Je partis; et fuyant sans secours, sans asile,
> Seul avec mon courroux, j'errai de ville en ville,
> Et souffris de vingt rois les refus, les mépris,
> Que souvent les heureux prodiguent aux proscrits,
> Jusqu'au jour, où j'obtins cet affreux avantage
> De venir par le fer disputer mon partage.

(II, 1)

* * * *

The burial of Polynice by Antigone appears twice on the French stage in this period. Doigny du Ponceau's *Antigone ou la piété fraternelle* was first performed on 31 July, 1787 — a century after Pader d'Assézan's *Antigone,* the last treatment of the subject, performed in 1686 and published the following year. Like Pader d'Assézan, Doigny de Ponceau begins his play while the brothers are still fighting, though he restores Euripides' version of the single combat, according to which it is Etéocle who inflicts a mortal wound on his brother, only to be stabbed to death as he bends over him. Like Rotrou, Doigny du Ponceau introduces the character of Adraste, Polynice's father-in-law. As regards the story of Antigone herself, he follows Sophocles fairly faithfully. His Antigone however, is motivated by 'les devoirs sacrés de la religion', and the play opens with her kneeling before an altar; and he introduces an original episode, an attempt on the part of Adraste to rescue her. The play was performed twice, and not published until it appeared, reduced to three acts, in the author's collected works.[4]

Marmontel's *Antigone, tragédie lyrique en trois actes,* with music by Zingarelli, was first performed at the Académie royale de musique on 30 April, 1790. Créon's order that Polynice shall not be buried arouses general disapproval:

> CHOEUR *du peuple (bas).*
> O rigueur effroyable!
> CHOEUR *de la suite de Créon.*
> C'est ainsi qu'on est roi.
> CHOEUR *de femmes.*
> Est-ce ainsi qu'on est roi?
> HÉMON
> Ah! mon père!
> EURIDICE ET ISMENE
>   Ah! Seigneur!
> ANTIGONE, *à part*
>   Ah! barbare!
> CRÉON
>   Est-ce moi
> Qui suis impitoyable?
> C'est le ciel, c'est la loi.
>
>   (Act I)

In the last act, Hémon admits that he was Antigone's accomplice. Antigone is taken off to her cave; Hémon joins her, and is about to stab her and himself, when Créon and his wife, Euridice, arrive. Créon is moved:

> Il est trop cruel d'être roi,
> Quand il faut cesser d'être père.

At this moment, the goddess of Clemency appears, and all ends happily:

> Créon, tu sais te vaincre, et tu sais pardonner.
>   C'est ici le jour de ta gloire.
> Que ce temple à jamais consacre la mémoire
> De l'exemple éclatant que tu viens de donner.

4. The play is known to me only from the accounts of H. Carrington Lancaster *(French Tragedy in the Reign of Louis XVI and the Early Years of the French Revolution,* Baltimore, 1953, pp. 95–7) and Simone Fraisse *(Le Mythe d'Antigone,* Paris, 1974, pp. 30–1).

* * * *

Two prose narratives of the whole Theban cycle should be
mentioned. Barthélemy devotes two or three pages in the first
part of the Introduction to his *Voyage de jeune Anacharsis en
Grèce* (1788) to a summary of the story of Œdipus and his
sons – the chief point of interest being that the sphinx becomes
Sphinge, the natural daughter of Laius. Chapter XI contains an
account of a performance of Sophocles' *Antigone*.

Of greater interest is Pierre-Simon Ballanche's prose epic
in six books, *Antigone*, published in 1814, five years after
Chateaubriand's *Martyrs*, and by no means the least readable of
the versions. The story of Œdipus occupies the first two books;
the war between the brothers the next three; and the burial of
Polynice and the death of Antigone, the last one. Besides adding
many supplementary details and episodes, Ballanche makes a
number of changes in the traditional story. The discovery of
Œdipe's guilt is simplified; prompted by Tirésie, he sends for
Phorbas, who tells the whole story. The revelation kills
Jocaste, who neither commits suicide, nor survives to mediate
between her sons. Œdipe dies, or rather vanishes, on Cithaeron,
not at Colonus. There is little to choose between the brothers,
though Polynice suffers from remorse, and enjoys his sister's
preference, while Etéocle is a tyrant who has alienated the
affection of his subjects. Ménécée is killed by a javelin thrown
by his own side. The brothers meet and begin fighting by
chance, but do not stop when they recognize each other.
Etéocle mortally wounds Polynice, but is killed by him as he
rushes at him 'pour lui porter un dernier coup'.[5] Créon is
ambitious, foments the quarrel between the brothers, and
exults when their death makes him king of Thebes. His wife,
Eurydice, does not appear, having died on giving birth to Hémon.
Antigone tells the guards who she is, performs the funeral rites
in their presence, and is immediately taken to Créon – there is

5.   Ballanche, *Antigone*, in *Œuvres*, vol. I, Paris, 1833, p. 264.

nothing defiant or underhand about Ballanche's submissive and self-sacrificing heroine. Like Jocaste, Antigone and Hémon are innocent of suicide: Antigone dies as Hémon reaches her — but not of starvation ('elle s'était flétrie, semblable à un beau rosier dont l'orage aurait brisé la tige'[6]); and the effort of rising from his sickbed to go to Antigone's cave and of carrying her body out, reopens the wounds Hémon had received in the previous day's battle.

In his preface, Ballanche claims to have Christianized the story (though he has not altogether eliminated fatality); and in the epilogue he says that his epic symbolizes human destiny. Œdipe representing suffering humanity, and Antigone — who owes something no doubt both to Bertille d'Avèze and to Mme Récamier[7] — the consoler and expiatory victim vouchsafed to mankind by God. 'L'homme, ce roi détrôné, traverse son exil, toujours accompagné de l'Antigone que le ciel lui envoya.'[8].

* * * *

The works described above were written between 1778 and 1814, after nearly half a century during which the Theban legends had been neglected. Why so much activity, relatively speaking, should have been concentrated in this quarter of a century, can only be conjectured. The revival of interest in Greece in the closing years of the century, and Ducis's successful discovery that the story of Œdipus at Colonus was admirably suited to the sensibility of his contemporaries, probably have

6. p. 306.
7. A.J.George, *Pierre-Simon Ballanche*, Syracuse, New York, 1945, pp. 43, 45.
8. p. 329.

something to do with it.

No literary historian of the previous period could avoid mentioning Garnier's *Antigone,* Rotrou's *Antigone,* Corneille's *Œdipe,* Racine's *Thébaïde,* or Voltaire's *Œdipe,* all of which are probably still quite widely read; and in our own day Cocteau's *Machine infernale* and Anouilh's *Antigone* show no signs of being forgotten. It would be idle to suppose that many people have heard of, let alone read, Ducis's *Œdipe chez Admète* or Ballanche's *Antigone.* The period with which we have been dealing is one of the peaks neither of French literature nor of the history of the Theban legends. It is not, however, devoid of interest. It illustrates the remarkable attachment of the eighteenth century, so bold in other ways, to tradition in literature. It also shows how superficial that attachment was. Subjects were taken from Greek drama; but they were treated with great freedom, and adapted to contemporary taste and preoccupation. Contemporary taste is reflected in the revival of interest in Œdipus at Colonus and Antigone, and in the operatic treatment of the legend; and the story of the house of Thebes showed a remarkable ability to adapt itself to the monarchical, republican, and humanitarian creeds of the period.

Robert Anderson, University of Durham
E.R. Anderson, University of Edinburgh.
L.J. Austin, Jesus College, Cambridge.
G.N. Bromiley, University of Durham.
William S. Brooks, University of Bath.
Andrew Brown, Voltaire Foundation, Oxford.
Harcourt Brown, Brown University, Providence, R.I.
J.H. Brumfitt, University of St. Andrews.
Edmund J. Campion, University of Tennessee, U.S.A.
S.F. Davies, Queen's University, Belfast.
F.K. Dawson, University of Nottingham.
A.H. Diverres, University College of Swansea.
Daniel Dupecher, Georgetown University, Washington, D.C., U.S.A.
Alison Fairlie, Girton College, Cambridge.
John Falvey, University of Southampton.
Patrick L.H. Fein, University of Rhodesia.
M.H. Fitzpatrick, University College of Aberystwyth.
Charles Fleischauer, Carleton University, Canada.
D.J. Fletcher, University College of Aberystwyth.
John Fortier, Louisbourg, Canada.
L.H. Ginn, University of Sheffield.
Basil Guy, University of California, Berkeley, U.S.A.
Gaston H. Hall, Richmond House, Kenilworth.
F.G. Healey, University of Surrey.
James Jackson, University of Leeds.
Eva Jacobs, Bedford College, London.
Walter Kirsop, Monash University, Australia.
Joanna Kitchin, University of Edinburgh.
R.C. Knight, Greenfield Terrace, Swansea.
I.D. McFarlane, Wadham College, Oxford.
J.H. Marshall, Westfield College, London.
H.T. Mason, University of East Anglia.
Sheila M. Mason, University of Birmingham.
Georges May, Yale University.
Peter Moes, University of Toronto, Canada.
Janet Morgan, Trinity College, Dublin.
Deryk Mossop, University of Durham.
Elizabeth Ratcliff, University of Newcastle upon Tyne.

John Renwick, New University of Ulster.
Walter Rex, University of California, Berkeley, U.S.A.
Pat Rogers, University of Bristol.
Alison M. Saunders, University of Aberdeen.
Marjorie Shaw, University of Sheffield.
C.N. Smith, University of East Anglia.
J.S. Spink, Woodside Park Road, London.
Martin S. Staum, University of Calgary, Canada.
Norman Suckling, Haydon Bridge, Hexham.
O.R. Taylor, Queen Mary College, London.
P.J.S. Whitmore, City of London School.
P.J. Whyte, University of Durham.
D.S. Wilson, Springwell Road, Durham.

Annette Allen, East Ardsley, Yorkshire.
C.G. Baudiffier, 11 rue Duhesme, Paris.
A.M. Chouillet, 7 route de la Reine, Boulogne-Billancourt, Paris.
Suzanne Delorme, Centre International de Synthèse, Paris.
Jean Deprun, University of Provence, Aix-en Provence.
Roland Desné, University of Rheims.
Jean Pierre Despin, 9 rue Racine, 78220, France.
L. Desvignes, University of Saint-Etienne.
Gilbert Dorval, 9 rue Albert de Lapparent, Paris.
Edouard Guitton, 2 Villa de Bourg-l'Evêque, Rennes.
H. Lagrave, rue de la Poterie, Gradignan, France.
J. Marchand, 77 rue Blomet, Paris.
Marc Meurisse, Institution Notre Dame des Dunes, Dunkirk.
Takujo Obase, 7-3-18, Koyama, Shinagawa-ku, Tokyo.
Werner Oechslin, Stapferstrasse, Zurich.
John Renwick, Church Street, Portstewart, N. Ireland.
Michel Roland, 39 Avenue Jean Jaurès, Argenteuil, France.
Hermann Sauter, Zeisiweg 25, Mainz.
F. Schalk, Raschdorffstrasse 23, Cologne.
Hidéo Watanabe, University of Kagawa, Japan.

LIBRARIES
Aberdeen University.
Bath University.
Birmingham University.
Bonn University, Romanisches Seminar.
Bristol University.
British Columbia University, Vancouver.
Cambridge University:
    Christ's College.
    Jesus College.
    Modern and Medieval Languages Libraries.
    St. Catharine's College.
Delaware University, U.S.A.
Dundee University.
Durham University.
East Anglia University.
Edinburgh University.
Exeter University.
Freiburg University, Romanisches Seminar.
Göteborg University, Sweden.
Groningen University, Holland.
Harvard College, U.S.A.
Kent University.
Köln University, Romanisches Seminar.
Leeds University.
Dept. of French, Leeds.
Leicester University.
Leiden University, Holland.
Liverpool University.
London University:
    Bedford College.
    Birkbeck College.
    King's College.
    Queen Mary College.
    Royal Holloway College.
    University Library.
    Westfield College.

Manchester University.
McGill University, Montreal, Canada.
Montpellier University.
Newcastle upon Tyne University.
Newfoundland, Memorial University.
North London Polytechnic.
Nottingham University.
Oxford University:
    Christ Church.
    Lady Margaret Hall.
    St. Anne's College.
    St. Hilda's College.
    Taylor Institution.
Queensland University, Australia.
St. Andrew's University.
Sheffield University.
Stirling University.
Strathclyde University.
Sussex University.
Tulane University, U.S.A.
Victoria University, Toronto, Canada.
Wales, University Colleges of:
    Aberystwyth
    Bangor
    Lampeter, St. David's.
Warwick University.
Wellington University, New Zealand.
Western Australia, University of.
Yale University, U.S.A.

Amiens University.
Amsterdam Free University.
Antwerp, St. Ignatius University.
Caen University.
Centre National de la Recherche Scientifique, Paris.

Clermont-Ferrand (II) University.
Erlangen-Nürnberg University, Institut für Romanistik.
Geneva, Biobliothèque Publique et Universitaire.
Mainz University, Romanisches Seminar.
Neuchâtel, Bibliothèque Publique.
Paris (IV)-Sorbonne University.
Saarbrücken University.
Saint Etienne University.